Praise for *Money for Nothing*

"Many recent books have pointed accusatory fingers at the problems of specific firms like Bear Stearns, Lehman Brothers, and Fannie Mae. . . . But *Money for Nothing* casts a much wider net. . . . The authors write in a nonpedantic, readable style, and they don't mince words . . . they also offer a valuable new perspective by focusing on the tragicomic miscues of the people who were ostensibly meant to 'govern' out-of-control managements."

—Harry Hurt III, *The New York Times*

"Illustrate[s] the stresses and conflicts facing many boards in corporate America . . . Gillespie and Zweig suggest some two dozen reforms that could go a long way toward creating effective boards."

—Laurent Belsie, *The Christian Science Monitor*

"Lays out a compelling case for how CEOs and their minions have subverted the purpose of boards to oversee management and made them their lapdogs. The book outlines numerous solutions to fix this problem. If they weren't so sensible, they might have a chance of being implemented. . . . The stories of poor governance that fill the book would make you laugh, if they didn't cause you to be outraged."

—Eric Jackson, TheStreet.com

"Messrs. Gillespie and Zweig are wrestling with an important question: how to steer corporate directors to act on behalf of the shareholders they don't know instead of simply supporting the management they know and may even feel beholden to."

—James Freeman, *The Wall Street Journal*

"A readable primer on the nature of corporate finances."

—Robert J. Hughes, Smartmoney.com

"This brilliant book properly shines the light of day on the true enablers of the systematic looting of the American shareholder and the financial crisis that brought our economy to its knees. I predict *Money for Nothing* will prove a world changer for humiliated investors and those corporate directors who betrayed them."

—Frederick E. (Shad) Rowe, founder and president of Investors for Director Accountability and former chair of the Texas Pension Review Board

"Rarely have I opened a book and enjoyed every minute of the next several hours of reading. There are so many aspects of the elusive nature of the modern U.S. director that are sketched with real life insight, precise observation and literary grace that *Money for Nothing* will be a classic for many years to come."

—Robert A.G. Monks, author, shareholder advocate, and cofounder of Institutional Shareholder Services

"Both thoughtful and lively, this is a fascinating discussion of a little-seen force in corporate America."

—*Publishers Weekly*

"A fabulous new book about the role that corporate boards played in the financial crisis and are playing in America today."

—William Cohan, author of *House of Cards: A Tale of Hubris and Wretched Excess on Wall Street;* Bloggingheads.tv

"The authors look behind the headlines to reveal and document the systematic failure of corporate boards who are supposed to look out for shareowner interests but are still too often picked by the very ones they are supposed to advise and monitor . . . the CEOs. . . . They tell us how the game is fixed and how the rules can be changed to play fair."

—James McRitchie, publisher, CorpGov.net

*f***P**

MONEY FOR NOTHING

How CEOs and Boards Are Bankrupting America

JOHN GILLESPIE and

DAVID ZWEIG

FREE PRESS
New York London Toronto Sydney

fP
Free Press
A Division of Simon & Schuster, Inc.
1230 Avenue of the Americas
New York, NY 10020

First Free Press trade paperback edition January 2011

Designed by Katy Riegel

Manufactured in the United States of America

1 3 5 7 9 10 8 6 4 2

The Library of Congress has cataloged the hardcover edition as follows:

Gillespie, John.
Money for nothing : how the failure of corporate boards is ruining American business and costing us trillions / John Gillespie and David Zweig.
p. cm.
1. Corporate governance—United States. 2. Chief executive officers—United States. 3. Boards of directors—United States. 4. Corporations—Corrupt practices—United States.
I. Zweig, David. II. Title.
HD2741.G534 2010
338.60973—dc22 2009032328

ISBN 978-1-4165-5993-1
ISBN 978-1-4165-9770-4 (pbk)
ISBN 978-1-4165-9776-6 (ebook)

This book was previously published with the subtitle
How the Failure of Corporate Boards Is Ruining American Business and Costing Us Trillions.

To my wife, Susan Orlean, la migliore fabbra

—JWG

To my mother, Jeanne,
and the memory of my father,
Felix, and my son, Ben

—DBZ

Contents

Preface

WE DON'T COME to the subject of corporate boards as antagonists; in fact, both of us were trained and employed at the hub of the American business world, starting with the MBA program at Harvard Business School and then, over the next twenty-odd years, at Lehman Brothers, Morgan Stanley, Bear Stearns, Time Inc., and Dow Jones. We believe that well-run, responsible, and responsive corporations can exist and be profitable, and that many already do and are. We've had the chance to see boards of directors working—or not working—up close, and we've been directly affected by them as employees, shareholders, and citizens. We have also witnessed a number of the companies where we've worked underperform and collapse in large part because of negligent or nonexistent leadership in the boardroom.

Yet even with our experience in the business world and our MBA educations, we couldn't understand how boards came to operate the way they do, and how they've come apart; we *could* easily see how remote and impenetrable they would appear to most of the millions of shareholders who depend on them—in spite of the fact that boards are elected by shareholders and are legally required to represent their interests.

Certainly, most individual shareholders are passive. They

don't read annual reports, they don't vote in board elections, and they don't question or challenge corporate leadership. Why? Because, until recently, they trusted American business and investment. Shareholders were confident that if they put their money into companies, their investments would grow and the directors would make decisions with the shareholders' best interests in mind. Not only has the current economic wreck broken people's bank accounts and retirement funds, it has shattered something even more essential: the trust that executives and boards work openly and responsibly, and that they serve someone beyond themselves—shareholders, taxpayers, employees, customers, suppliers, creditors, or communities.

We wanted to know more about how boards have contributed to this problem and to find out how the relationships among shareholders, directors, and CEOs have gone awry. Our initial inquiry into why so many boards seem to have failed led us quickly to this realization: there is little consensus or comprehension about how boards work, let alone about how to repair their failings. It is as if the American economy has been driving a race car without having the slightest idea of how a steering wheel works—not to mention the brakes.

We spoke with scores of board members, CEOs, consultants, accountants, lawyers, recruiters, shareholder activists, government officials, investors, and academics. We pored over the history and literature of corporate leadership and traveled the country to see the impact boards have had. To understand what directors think, we read surveys and attended conferences where board members spoke among themselves. We were surprised at how many directors and CEOs were willing to talk with us frankly, both on and off the record, about their experiences. Over time, we came to realize that they, like all of us, want to be understood—especially now, when they are under attack. To better appreciate the dynamics of what goes on behind boardroom doors, we studied the cultural anthropology, behavioral economics, and neuroscience of corporate leaders and business decision making. To understand the institutional investors that now control 70 percent of the shares in American companies, we explored why they so often seem apathetic and routinely vote with management. We also focused on the sometimes conflicted and always costly governance gatekeepers—the professional services providers who have taken over many of the responsibilities of corporate boards, shielded directors from accountability, and helped forestall or circumvent reforms, almost always with shareholders' own money.

We have tried to present examples and commentary that highlight representative issues and portray corporate leadership in all its complexity, instead of a simplistic morality tale of good versus evil. The common themes that emerge from these stories go well beyond the usual bromides about power corrupting, pride preceding a fall, and history repeating itself when its lessons go unheeded. Rather than focusing only on the failures, we have looked as well at companies and boards that have succeeded in representing their shareholders and providing models for others. Finally, we have presented a comprehensive set of measures that we believe could bring lasting reform to our dysfunctional culture of corporate leadership.

Boards have come a long way in the nearly forty years since Harvard Business School professor Myles Mace dismissed them as "nothing more or less than ornaments on the corporate Christmas tree." Unfortunately, most boards haven't come far enough to make a real difference in guarding and growing our investments—and far too many remain negligent and ineffective. Most have never reached anywhere near their potential to provide the monitoring, advice, and connections that they, in theory, are paid to provide on behalf of shareholders—or even, at the very least, to be a constraint on the excessive risk and compensation that have recently plagued American businesses. The past efforts to fix corporate governance failures were well intentioned and some have been helpful in relieving specific symptoms of whatever caused the most recent collapse. But they have proven insufficient to prevent the recurring scandals and crises that have cost us trillions of dollars and now threaten our economy and quite possibly our very way of life. Our aim is to expose the seriousness of the situation and to encourage reforms before the next destructive cycle of boom and bust leads to an economic disaster even greater than the one we have recently endured.

When you mix power with vast amounts of money, dominant personalities, the adrenaline of high-stakes challenges, the complexity and whip-fast speed of modern enterprise, a global arena, and the very human vulnerabilities of avarice and ambition, you have the explosive force that powers the present-day corporate world. In the best cases, that energy is channeled and governed and the results can drive economies to great heights. At its worst, this force is allowed to run out of control and imperils the wealth and welfare of entire nations. The best device for channeling and governing it should be—and needs to be—the board of directors.

MONEY FOR NOTHING

1

Out of Control

THIS IS WHAT HAPPENS when a corporate giant collapses and dies.

All eyes are on the CEO, who has gone without sleep for several days while desperately scrambling to pull a rabbit out of an empty hat. Staffers, lawyers, advisors, accountants, and consultants scurry around the company headquarters with news and rumors: the stock price fell 20 percent in the last hour, another of the private equity firms considering a bid has pulled out, stock traders are passing on obscene jokes about the company's impending death, the sovereign wealth fund that agreed to put in $1 billion last fall is screaming at the CFO, hedge fund shorts are whispering that the commercial paper dealers won't renew the debt tomorrow, the Treasury and the Fed aren't returning the CEO's calls about bailout money, six satellite trucks—no, seven now—are parked in front of the building, and reporters with camera crews are ambushing any passing employee for sound bites about the prospects of losing their jobs.

Chaos.

In the midst of this, the board of directors—the supposedly well-informed, responsible, experienced, accountable group of leaders elected by the shareholders, who are legally and ethically required to protect the thousands of people who own the company—are . . . where? You would expect to them to be at the center of the action, but they are merely spectators with great seats. Some huddle together over a computer screen in a corner of the boardroom, watching cable news feeds and stock market reports that amplify the company's death rattles around the world; others sit beside a speakerphone, giving updates to board colleagues who couldn't make it in person. Meetings are scheduled, canceled, and rescheduled as the directors wait, hoping for good news but anticipating the worst.

The atmosphere is a little like that of a family waiting room outside an intensive care unit—a quiet, intense churning of dread and resignation. There will be some reminiscing about how well things seemed to be going not so long ago, some private recriminations about questions never asked or risks poorly understood, a general feeling of helplessness, a touch of anger at the senior executives for letting it come to this, and anticipation of the embarrassment they'll feel when people whisper about them at the club. Surprisingly, though, there's not a lot of fear. Few of the directors are likely to have a significant part of their wealth tied up in the company; legal precedents and insurance policies insulate them from personal liability. Between 1980 and 2006, there were only thirteen cases in which outside directors—almost all, other than Enron and WorldCom, for tiny companies—had to settle shareholder lawsuits with their own money. (Ten of the Enron outside directors who settled—without admitting wrongdoing—paid only 10 percent of their prior net gains from selling Enron stock; eight other directors paid nothing. A number of them have remained on other boards.) More significant, the CEO who overshadowed the board will hardly hurt at all, and will probably leave with the tens or even hundreds of millions of dollars that the directors guaranteed in an employment contract.

So they sit and wait—the board of directors of this giant company, who were charged with steering it along the road to profit and prosperity. In the middle of the biggest crisis in the life of the company, they are essentially backseat passengers. The controls, which they never truly used, are of no help as the company hurtles over a cliff, taking with it the directors' reputations and the shareholders' money. What they are waiting for is the dull thud signaling the end: a final meeting with the lawyers and investment bankers, and at last, the formality of signing the corporate death certificate—a bankruptcy filing, a forced sale for cents on the dollar, or a government takeover that wipes out the shareholders. The CEO and the lawyers, as usual, will tell the directors what they must do.

THIS IS NOT JUST A GLOOMY, hypothetical fable about how an American business might possibly fail, with investors unprotected, company value squandered, and the governance of enormous and important companies breaking down. This is, unfortunately, a real scenario that has been repeated time and again during the recent economic meltdown, as companies have exploded like a string of one-inch firecrackers. When the spark runs up the spine of the tangled, interconnected fuses, they blow up one by one.

Something is wrong here. As Warren Buffett observed in his 2008 letter to Berkshire Hathaway shareholders, "You only learn who has been swimming naked when the tide goes out—and what we are witnessing at some of our largest financial institutions is an ugly sight."

Just look at some of the uglier sights. Merrill Lynch, General Motors, and Lehman Brothers, three stalwart American companies, are only a few examples of corporate collapses in which shareholders were burned. The sleepy complicity and carelessness of their boards have been especially devastating. Yet almost all the public attention has focused on the greed or recklessness or incompetence of the CEOs rather than the negligence of the directors who were supposed to protect the shareholders and who ought to be held equally, if not more, accountable because the CEOs theoretically work for them.

Why have boards of directors escaped blame? Probably because boards are opaque entities to most people, even to many corporate executives and institutional investors. Individual shareholders, who might have small positions in a number of companies, know very little about who these board members are and what they are supposed to be doing. Their names appear on the generic, straight-to-the-wastebasket proxy forms that shareholders receive; beyond that, they're ciphers. Directors rarely talk in public, maintaining a code of silence and confidentiality; communications with shareholders and journalists are invariably delegated to corporate PR or investor relations departments. They are protected by a vast array of lawyers, auditors, investment bankers, and other professional services gatekeepers who keep them out of trouble for a price. At most, shareholders might catch a glimpse of the nonexecutive board members if they bother to attend the annual meeting. Boards work behind closed doors, leave few footprints, and maintain an aura of power and prestige symbolized by the grand and imposing boardrooms found in most large companies. Much of this lack of transparency is deliberate because it reduces accountability and permits a kind of Wizard of Oz "pay no attention to the man behind the curtain" effect. (It is very likely to be a man. Only 15.2 percent of the directors of our five hundred largest companies are women.) The opacity also serves to hide a key problem: despite many directors being intelligent, experienced, well-qualified, and decent people who are tough in other aspects of their professional lives, too many of them become meek, collegial cheerleaders when they enter the boardroom. They fail to represent shareholders' interests because they are beholden to the CEOs who brought them aboard. It's a dangerous arrangement.

On behalf of the shareholders who actually own the company and are risking their money in anticipation of a commensurate return on their investments, boards are elected to monitor, advise, and direct the managers hired to run the company. They have a fiduciary duty to protect the interests of shareholders. Yet, too often, boards have become enabling lapdogs rather than trustworthy watchdogs and guides.

There are, unfortunately, dozens of cases to choose from to illustrate the seriousness of the situation. Merrill, GM, and Lehman are instructive because they were companies no one could imagine failing, although, in truth, they fostered such dysfunctional and conflicted corporate leadership that their collapses should have been foretold. As you read their obituaries, viewer discretion is advised. You should think of the money paid to the executives and directors, as well as the losses in stock value, not as the company's money, as it is so often portrayed in news accounts, but as *your* money—because it is, in fact, coming from your mutual funds, your 401(k)s, your insurance premiums, your savings account interest, your mortgage rates, your paychecks, and your costs for goods and services. Also, think of the impact on ordinary people losing their retirement savings, their jobs, their homes, or even just the bank or factory or car dealership in their towns. Then add the trillions of taxpayers' dollars spent to prop up some of the companies' remains and, finally, consider the legacy of debt we're leaving for the next generation.

DURING MOST OF HIS nearly six years at the top of Merrill Lynch, Stanley O'Neal simultaneously held the titles of chairman, CEO, and president. He required such a high degree of loyalty that insiders referred to his senior staff as the Taliban. O'Neal had hand-picked eight of the firm's ten outside board members. One of them, John Finnegan, had been a friend of O'Neal's for more than twenty years and had worked with him in the General Motors treasury department; he headed Merrill's compensation committee, which set O'Neal's pay. Another director on the committee was Alberto Cribiore, a private equity executive who had once tried to hire O'Neal.

Executives who worked closely with O'Neal say that he was ruthless in silencing opposition within Merrill and singleminded in seeking to beat Goldman Sachs in its profitability and Lehman Brothers in the risky business of packaging and selling mortgage-backed securities. "The board had absolutely no idea how much of this risky stuff was actually on the books; it multiplied so fast," one O'Neal colleague said. The colleague also noted that the directors, despite having impressive résumés, were chosen in part because they had little financial services experience and were kept under tight control. O'Neal "clearly didn't want anybody asking questions."

For a while, the arrangement seemed to work. In a triumphal letter to shareholders in the annual report issued in February 2007, titled "The Real Measure of Success." O'Neal proclaimed 2006 "the most successful year in [the company's] history—financially, operationally and strategically," while pointing out that "a lot of this comes down to leadership." The cocky message ended on a note of pure hubris: "[W]e can and will continue to grow our business, lead this incredible force of global capitalism and validate the tremendous confidence that you, our shareholders, have placed in this organization and each of us."

The board paid O'Neal $48 million in salary and bonuses for 2006—one of the highest compensation packages in corporate America. But only ten months later, after suffering a third-quarter loss of $2.3 billion and an $8.4 billion writedown on failed investments—the largest loss in the company's ninety-three-year history, exceeding the net earnings for all of 2006—the board began to understand the real measure of failure. The directors discovered, seemingly for the first time, just how much risk Merrill had undertaken in becoming the industry leader in subprime mortgage bonds and how overleveraged it had become to achieve its targets. They also caught O'Neal initiating merger talks without their knowledge with Wachovia Bank, a deal that would have resulted in a personal payout of as much as $274 million for O'Neal if he had left after its completion—part of his board-approved employment agreement. During August and September 2007, as Merrill was losing more than $100 million a day, O'Neal managed to play at least twenty rounds of golf and lowered his handicap from 10.2 to 9.1.

Apparently due to sheer embarrassment as the company's failures made headlines, the board finally ousted O'Neal in October but allowed him to "retire" with an exit package worth $161.5 million on top of the $70 million he'd received during his time as CEO and chairman. The board then began a frantic search for a new CEO, because, as one insider confirmed to us, it "had done absolutely no succession planning" and O'Neal had gotten rid of anyone among the 64,000 employees who might have been a credible candidate. For the first time since the company's founding, the board had to look outside for a CEO. In spite of having shown a disregard for shareholders and a distaste for balanced governance, O'Neal was back in a boardroom within three months, this time as a director of Alcoa, serving on the audit committee and charged with overseeing the aluminum company's risk management and financial disclosure.

At the Merrill Lynch annual meeting in April 2008, Ann Reese, the head of the board's audit committee, fielded a question from a shareholder about how the board could have missed the massive risks Merrill was undertaking in the subprime mortgage-backed securities and collateralized debt obligations (CDOs) that had ballooned from $1 billion to $40 billion in exposure for the firm in just eighteen months. Amazingly, since it is almost unheard of for a director of a company to answer questions in public, Reese was willing to talk. This was refreshing and might have provided some insight for shareholders, except that what she said was curiously detached and unabashed. "The CDO position did not come to the board's attention until late in the process," she said, adding that initially the board hadn't been aware that the most troublesome securities were, in fact, backed by mortgages.

Merrill's new CEO and chairman, John Thain, jumped in after Reese, saying that the board shouldn't be criticized based on "20/20 hindsight" even though he had earlier admitted in an interview with the *Wall Street Journal* that "Merrill had a risk committee. It just didn't function." As it happens, Reese, over a cup of English tea, had helped recruit Thain, who lived near her in Rye, New York. Thain had received a $15 million signing bonus upon joining Merrill and by the time of the shareholders' meeting was just completing the $1.2 million refurnishing of his office suite that was revealed after the company was sold.

Lynn Turner, who served as the SEC's chief accountant from 1998 to 2001 and later as a board member for several large public companies, recalled that he spoke about this period to a friend who was a director at Merrill Lynch in August 2008. "This is a very well-known, intelligent person," Turner said, "and they tell me, 'You know, Lynn, I've gone back through all this stuff and I can't think of one thing I'd have done differently.' My God, I can guarantee you that person wasn't qualified to be a director! They don't press on the issues. They get into the boardroom—and I've been in these boardrooms—and they're all too chummy and no one likes to create confrontation. So they get together five times a year or so, break bread, all have a good conversation for a day and a half, and then go home. How in the hell could you be a director at Merrill Lynch and not know that you had a gargantuan portfolio of toxic assets? If people on the outside could see the problem, then why couldn't the directors?"

The board was so disconnected from the company that when Merrill shareholders met in December 2008 to approve the company's sale to Bank of America after five straight quarterly losses totaling $24 billion and a near-brush with bankruptcy, not a single one of the nine nonexecutive directors even attended the meeting. Finance committee chair and former IRS commissioner Charles Rossotti, reached at home in Virginia by a reporter, wouldn't say why he wasn't there: "I'm just a director, and I think any questions you want to have, you should direct to the company." The board missed an emotional statement by Winthrop Smith, Jr., a former Merrill banker and the son of a company founder. In a speech that used the word *shame* some fourteen times, he said, "Today is not the result of the subprime mess or synthetic CDOs. They are the symptoms. This is the story of failed leadership and the failure of a board of directors to understand what was happening to this great company, and its failure to take action soon enough . . . Shame on them for not resigning."

When Merrill Lynch first opened its doors in 1914, Charles E. Merrill announced its credo: "I have no fear of failure, provided I use my heart and head, hands and feet—and work like hell." The firm died as an independent company five days short of its ninety-fifth birthday. The Merrill Lynch shareholders, represented by the board, lost more than $60 billion.

AT A JUNE 6, 2000, stockholders annual meeting, General Motors wheeled out its newly appointed CEO, Richard Wagoner, who kicked off the proceedings with an upbeat speech. "I'm pleased to report that the state of the business at General Motors Corporation is strong," he proclaimed. "And as suggested by the baby on the cover of our 1999 annual report, we believe our company's future opportunities are virtually unlimited." Nine years later, the GM baby wasn't feeling so well, as the disastrous labor and health care costs and SUV-heavy product strategy caught up with the company in the midst of skyrocketing gasoline prices and a recession. GM's stock price fell some 95 percent during Wagoner's tenure; the company last earned a profit in 2004 and lost more than $85 billion while he was CEO. Nevertheless, the GM board consistently praised and rewarded Wagoner's performance. In 2003, it elected him to also chair the board, and in 2007—a year the company had lost $38.7 billion—it increased his compensation by 64 percent to $15.7 million.

GM's lead independent director was George M. C. Fisher, who himself presided over major strategic miscues as CEO and chairman at Motorola, where the Iridium satellite phone project he initiated was subsequently written off with a $2.6 billion loss, and later at Kodak, where he was blamed for botching the shift to digital photography. Fisher clearly had little use for shareholders. He once told an interviewer regarding criticism of his tenure at Kodak that "I wish I could get investors to sit down and ask good questions, but some people are just too stupid." More than half the GM board was composed of current or retired CEOs, including Stan O'Neal, who left in 2006, citing time constraints and concerns over potential conflicts with his role at Merrill that had somehow not been an issue during the previous five years.

Upon GM's announcement in August 2008 of another staggering quarterly loss—this time of $15.5 billion—Fisher told a reporter that "Rick has the unified support of the entire board to a person. We are absolutely convinced we have the right team under Rick Wagoner's leadership to get us through these difficult times and to a brighter future." Earlier that year, Fisher had repeatedly endorsed Wagoner's strategy and said that GM's stock price was not a major concern of the board. Given that all thirteen of GM's outside directors together owned less than six one-hundredths of one percent of the company's stock, that perhaps shouldn't have been much of a surprise.

Wagoner relished his carte blanche relationship with GM's directors: "I get good support from the board," he told a reporter. "We say, 'Here's what we're going to do and here's the time frame,' and they say, 'Let us know how it comes out.' They're not making the calls about what to do next. If they do that, they don't need me." What GM's leaders were doing with the shareholders' dwindling money was doubling their bet on gas-guzzling SUVs because they provided GM's highest profit margins at the time. As GM vice chairman Robert Lutz told the *New York Times* in 2005: "Everybody thinks high gas prices hurt sport utility sales. In fact they don't . . . Rich people don't care."

But what seemed good for GM no longer was good for the country—or for GM's shareholders.

Ironically, GM had been widely praised in the early 1990s for creating a model set of corporate governance reforms in the wake of major strategic blunders and failed leadership that had resulted in unprecedented earnings losses. In 1992, the board fired the CEO, appointed a nonexecutive chairman, and issued twenty-eight structural guidelines for insuring board independence from management and increasing oversight of long-term strategy. *BusinessWeek* hailed the GM document as a "Magna Carta for Directors" and the company's financial performance improved for a time. The reform initiatives, however, lasted about as long as the tailfin designs on a Cadillac. Within a few years, despite checking most of the good governance structural boxes, the CEO was once again also the board chairman, the directors had backslid fully to a subservient "let us know how it comes out" role, and the executives were back behind the wheel.

In November 2005, when GM's stock price was still in the mid-20s, Ric Marshall, the chief analyst of the Corporate Library, a governance rating service that focuses on board culture and CEO-board dynamics, wrote: "Despite its compliance with most of the best practices believed to comprise 'good governance,' the current General Motors board epitomizes the sad truth that compliance alone has very little to do with actual board effectiveness. The GM board has failed repeatedly to address the key strategic questions facing this onetime industrial giant, exposing the firm not only to a number of legal and regulatory worries but the very real threat of outright business failure. Is GM, like Chrysler some years ago, simply too big to fail? We're not sure, but it seems increasingly likely that GM shareholders will soon find out."

By the time Wagoner was fired in March 2009, at the instigation of the federal officials overseeing the massive bailout of the company, the stock had dropped to the $2 range and GM had already run through $13.4 billion in taxpayers' money. In spite of this, some directors still couldn't wean themselves from Wagoner, and were reportedly furious that his dismissal occurred without their consent. Others were mortified by what had happened to the company. One prominent director, who had diligently tried to help the company change course before it was too late, had eventually quit the board out of frustration with the "ridiculous bureaucracy and a thumb-sucking board that led to GM making cars that no one wanted to buy." Another director who left the board recalled asking Wagoner and his executive team in 2006 for a five-year plan and projections. "They said they didn't have that. And most of the guys in the room didn't seem to care."

The GM shareholders, represented by the board, lost more than $52 billion.

IN A COMPANY as large and complex as Lehman Brothers, you would expect the board to be seasoned, astute, dynamic, and up-to-date on risks it was undertaking with the shareholders' money. Yet the only nonexecutive director, out of ten, with any recent banking experience was Jerry Grundhofer, the retired head of U.S. Bancorp, who had joined the board exactly five months before Lehman's spectacular collapse into bankruptcy. Nine of the independent directors were retired, including five who were in their seventies and eighties. Their backgrounds hardly seemed suited to overseeing a sophisticated and complicated financial entity: the members included a theatrical producer, the former CEO of a Spanish-language television company, a retired art-auction company executive, a retired CEO of Halliburton, a former rear admiral who had headed the Girl Scouts and served on the board of Weight Watchers International, and, until two years before Lehman's downfall, the eighty-three-year-old actress and socialite Dina Merrill, who sat on the board for eighteen years and served on the compensation committee, which approved CEO Richard Fuld's $484 million in salary, stock, options, and bonuses from 2000 to 2007. Whatever their qualifications, the directors were well compensated, too. In 2007, each was paid between

$325,038 and $397,538 for attending a total of eight full board meetings.

The average age of the Lehman board's risk committee was just under seventy. The committee was chaired by the eighty-one-year-old economist Henry Kaufman, who had last worked at a Wall Street investment bank some twenty years in the past and then started a consulting firm. He is exactly the type of director found on many boards—a person whose prestigious credentials are meant to reassure shareholders and regulators that the company is being well monitored and advised. Then they are ignored.

Kaufman had been on the Lehman board for thirteen years. Even in 2006 and 2007, as Lehman's borrowing skyrocketed and the firm was vastly increasing its holdings of very risky securities and commercial real estate, the risk committee met only twice each year. Kaufman was known as "Dr. Doom" back in the 1980s because of his consistently pessimistic forecasts as Salomon Brothers' chief economist, but he seems not to have been very persuasive with Lehman's executives in getting them to limit the massive borrowing and risks they were taking on as the mortgage bubble continued to overinflate.

In an April 2008 interview, Kaufman offered an insight that might have been more timely and helpful a few years earlier in both the Lehman boardroom and Washington, D.C.: "If we don't improve the supervision and oversight over financial institutions, in another seven, eight, nine, or ten years, we may have a crisis that's bigger than the one we have today. . . . Usually what's happened is that financial markets move to the competitive edge of risk-taking unless there is some constraint." With little to no internal supervision, oversight, or constraint having been provided by its board, the bigger crisis for Lehman came sooner rather than later, and it collapsed just four and a half months later.

After Lehman's demise, Kaufman has continued to offer advice to others. Without a trace of irony or guilt, he said to another interviewer in July 2009, "If you want to take risks, you've got to have the capital to do it. But, you can't do it with other people's money where the other people are not well informed about the risk taking of that institution." In his recent book on financial system reform (which largely blames the Federal Reserve for the financial meltdown and has an entire section listing his own "prophetic" warnings about the economy), Kaufman neglects to mention either his role at Lehman or his missing the warning signs when he personally invested and lost millions in Bernie Madoff's Ponzi scheme. He does, however, note that "The shabby events of the recent past demonstrate that people in finance cannot and should not escape public scrutiny."

Dr. Doom did heed his own economic advice, while providing an instructive case of exquisite timing—as well as of having your cake, eating it too, and then patting yourself on the back for warning others of the caloric dangers of cake. Lehman securities filings show that about ten months before Lehman stock went to zero, Kaufman cashed in more than half of the remaining stock options that had been given to him for protecting shareholders' interests. He made nearly $2 million in profits.

"The Lehman board was a joke and a disgrace," said a former senior investment banker who now serves as a director for several S&P 500 companies. "Asleep at the switch doesn't begin to describe it." The autocratic Richard Fuld, whose nickname at the firm was "the Gorilla," had joined Lehman in 1969 when his air force career ended after he had a fistfight with a commanding officer. He served since 1994 as both CEO and chairman of the board, an inherent conflict in roles that still occurs at 61 percent of the largest U.S. companies.

A lawsuit filed in early 2009 by the New Jersey Department of Investment alleges that $118 million in losses to the state pension fund resulted from fraud and misrepresentation by Lehman's executives and the board. The role of the board is described in scathing terms:

> The supine Board that defendant Fuld handpicked provided no backstop to Lehman's executives' zealous approach to the Company's risk profile, real estate portfolio, and their own compensation. The Director Defendants were considered inattentive, elderly, and woefully short on relevant structured finance background. The composition of the Board according to a recent filing in the Lehman bankruptcy allowed defendant "Fuld to marginalize the Directors, who tolerated an absence of checks and balances at Lehman." Due to his long tenure and ubiquity at Lehman, defendant Fuld has been able to consolidate his power to a remarkable degree. Defendant Fuld was both the Chairman of the Board and the CEO . . . The Director Defendants acted as a rubber stamp for the actions of Lehman's senior management. There was little turnover on the Board. By the date of Lehman's collapse, more than half of the Director Defendants had served for twelve or more years."

John Helyar is one of the authors of *Barbarians at the Gate,* which documents the fall of RJR Nabisco in the 1980s. He also cowrote a five-part series for Bloomberg.com on Lehman Brothers' collapse. Helyar was a keen observer of those companies' boards when they folded. "The few people on the Lehman board who actually had relevant experience were kind of like an all-star team from the 1980s back for an old-timers' game in which they weren't even up on the new rules and equipment," Helyar told us. "Fuld selected them because he didn't want to be challenged by anyone.

Most of the top executives didn't understand the risks they were taking, so can you imagine a septuagenarian sitting in the boardroom getting a PowerPoint presentation on synthetic CDOs and credit default swaps?"

In a conference call announcing the firm's 2008 third-quarter loss of $3.9 billion, Fuld told analysts, "I must say the board's been wonderfully supportive." Four days later the 159-year-old company declared the largest bankruptcy in U.S. history. The Lehman shareholders, represented by the board, lost more than $45 billion.

THE DISASTERS at Merrill Lynch, GM, and Lehman were not isolated instances of hubris, incompetence, and negligence. Similar stories of boards and CEOs failing to do their jobs on behalf of the companies' owners can be told about Countrywide, Citigroup, AIG, Fannie Mae, Bank of America, Washington Mutual, Wachovia, Sovereign Bank, Bear Stearns, and most of the other companies directly involved in the recent financial meltdown, as well as many nonfinancial businesses whose governance-related troubles came to light in the resulting recession. In the short term, the result has been the loss of hundreds of billions of dollars for shareholders, and economic devastation for employees and others caught in the wake. In the long term, a growing crisis of confidence among investors could cripple our economy, as capital is diverted away from American corporate debt and equity markets and companies suffocate from lack of funding.

Investor mistrust takes hold fast and punishes instantly in the modern economy. Enron, once America's seventh-largest corporation, crashed in a mere three weeks once the scope of its failures and corruption was exposed and its investors and creditors began to withdraw their funds. Today's collapses can happen even faster.

Because the companies are larger, their operations more interconnected, and their financing so complex and subject to hair-trigger reactions from institutional investors with enormous trading positions, the impacts are greatly magnified and reverberate globally. Bear Stearns went from its CEO claiming on CNBC that "our liquidity position has not changed at all" to being insolvent two days later.

Of the world's two hundred largest economies, more than half are corporations. They have more influence on our lives than any other institution—not just profound economic clout, but also enormous political, environmental, and civic power. As they have grown in influence, they have also become more concentrated: In 1950, the 100 largest industrial companies owned approximately 40 percent of total U.S. industrial assets; by the 1990s, they controlled 75 percent. Global corporations have assumed the authority and impact that formerly belonged to governments and churches. Boards of directors are supposed to be the most important element of corporate leadership—the ultimate power in this economic universe—and while some companies have made progress during the past decade in improving corporate governance, the recurring waves of scandals and the blatant victimization of shareholders that appear in the wake of economic crashes prove that our approach to leading corporations is badly in need of fundamental reform.

Ideally, a board of directors is informed, active, and advisory, and maintains an open but challenging relationship with the company's CEO. In reality, this rarely happens. In most cases, board members are beholden to CEOs for their very presence on the board, for their renominations, their compensation, their perquisites, their committee assignments, their agendas, and virtually all their information. Even well-intentioned directors find themselves hopelessly compromised, badly conflicted, and essentially powerless. Not that all blame can be put on bullying, manipulative CEOs; many boards simply fail to do their jobs. They allow themselves to be fooled by fraudulent accounting; they look away during the squandering of company resources; they miss obvious strategic shifts in the marketplace; they are blind to massive risks their firms assume; they approve excessive executive pay; they neglect to prepare for crises; they ignore blatant conflicts of interest; they condone a lax ethical tone. The head of one of the world's largest and most successful private equity firms told us that he considers the current model of corporate boards "fundamentally broken."

Boards are prone to give away the shareholders' store. A 2004 study of CEO employment agreements in large companies showed that 96 percent of the CEOs with such contracts could not be fired "for cause" for incompetence, and 49 percent even if they breached their fiduciary duties. Michael Jensen, a former Harvard Business School professor and corporate governance expert, says, "Understand that if I fire you for something other than 'for cause' as specified in your contract, I have to pay you the total compensation associated with your contract for its entire life, including bonuses, etc. CEO Bob Nardelli received more than $200 million in severance pay when he was dismissed from Home Depot 'without cause,' and Michael Ovitz received $130 million after being fired in 1996 for incompetence but 'without cause' after 14 months on the job as president of the Walt Disney Company. He received more pay for being fired than he would have received had he remained employed for his entire contract."

IS BAD CORPORATE GOVERNANCE a recent phenomenon? Definitely not. Disastrous cycles of crises and failed reforms of business leadership date back to the dawn of corporate history.

Two of the all-time worst fiascos involved large-scale companies in the eighteenth century—the South Sea Company in England and the Society for Establishing Useful Manufactures in the United States.

As businesses reached a certain size, it became impractical for the owners to control all aspects of the operations themselves. So they borrowed the concept of representative governance from the organizational structures found in town councils, craft guilds, and the church hierarchy. Things were somewhat simpler and more cost-effective back then. The term *board* comes from the use of a wooden plank across two sawhorses to create a table where the directors held their meetings. The board members sat on stools and their leader had a chair. He was thus the "chairman."

Boards of directors were chosen to oversee joint stock companies such as the British and the Dutch East India companies, which had been granted authority under royal charters to trade in specific goods, services, or geographic regions. But trouble developed almost immediately in the form of conflicts of interest, negligence, incompetence, and cronyism. The South Sea Bubble of 1720, sometimes now referred to as the Enron of England, so harmed the reputation of corporate governance that new companies were largely banned for much of the next century. Formed in 1711 to assume a portion of England's national debt, the South Sea Company was secured by future government interest payments and a monopoly on trade with South America. Nine years later, amid rumors of endless riches flowing from gold mines—and fueled by massive accounting fraud, stock manipulation, and the bribery of public officials by the company's directors—the company's stock price skyrocketed, appreciating by nearly 1,000 percent during an eight-month period.

As recounted in Charles Mackay's *Extraordinary Popular Delusions & the Madness of Crowds*, investors went wild bidding up stocks with little regard for risks. At the height of the bubble, hundreds of new companies were being formed overnight to soak up speculative demand, including one titled *"A company for carrying on an undertaking of great advantage, but nobody to know what it is,"* which promised a 100 percent annual return. (The founding chairman, after raising a substantial sum of deposits in a single afternoon, disappeared.) Although one South Sea Company director was widely quoted as being able to feed his horses on gold, the company made almost no profits from the South American trade, other than modest returns from transporting African slaves. Punctured by news that the chairman and many of the other thirty-two directors were dumping their stock, the bubble suddenly burst and the company's stock plunged 87 percent, causing economic ruin throughout the country.

A subsequent parliamentary inquiry exposed widespread corruption by the directors and resulted in fines for most of them amounting to seven-eighths of their wealth. As one historian noted, "Sadly, the plea of ignorance asserted by many of the company's directors during the investigation and prosecution following the company's collapse in 1720 is eerily reminiscent of the response of directors to scandals ever since."

New "bubble laws" that prohibited the issuance of stock and restricted the formation of new companies were enacted in reaction to the crash, but also because the remains of the South Sea Company wanted to stifle competition. The laws, which kept companies and their boards under very strict control, were not repealed until 1825.

In 1776, Adam Smith had already identified one of the key problems of corporations. Writing about the governance of joint-stock companies in his classic study *The Wealth of Nations,* he observed: "The directors of such companies . . . being the managers rather of other people's money than of their own, it cannot well be expected, that they should watch over it with the same anxious vigilance with which the partners in a private copartnery frequently watch over their own . . . Negligence and profusion, therefore, must always prevail, more or less, in the management of the affairs of such a company."

A separate problem resulting from the nature of corporate governance was identified almost 180 years ago by Alexis de Tocqueville, the perceptive French visitor to the United States who, in a chapter titled "How Aristocracy May Emerge from Industry" in the second volume of *Democracy in America,* explored the tendency of industrialists to become a narrow, self-sustaining, and isolated group within American society. He warned that "the manufacturing aristocracy that we see rising before our eyes is one of the hardest that have appeared on earth"—and declared it a situation which threatened to create a "permanent inequality of conditions and aristocracy."

This dim view of the corporate leadership class was apparently held by many in America, and businesses were constrained through state charters that granted them only limited functions. The largest such enterprise by far was the Society for Establishing Useful Manufactures, or SUM—a project founded by Alexander Hamilton. In 1791, SUM received the first manufacturing charter granted by the New Jersey legislature and planned to produce cloth, shoes, and other goods in a sort of early-day industrial park. Hamilton envisioned it growing rapidly into a huge manufacturing hub that would establish America as a global trading power.

It is remarkable how closely board and CEO malfeasance at SUM and the company's resulting financial collapse parallel those of modern-day, scandal-ridden corporations. SUM's board of thirteen directors was supposedly elected by the shareholders but actually was chosen by Hamilton, who also named New York financier William Duer as governor (chairman) and the French city planner, Major Pierre Charles L'Enfant, who had just laid out the city of Washington, D.C., as superintendent (CEO).

Even considering the less stringent standards of that era, some of the conflicts of interest are breathtaking. Hamilton, while serving as the U.S. treasury secretary, used his political influence to obtain tax exemptions, monopolies on specified products, and a direct state investment of $10,000 for SUM. He promoted the company using his Treasury stationery, personally helped sell the initial stock offering, and later arranged a below-market-rate bailout loan for the failing company from the head of a bank that held federal funds, while making confidential assurances that he would see that the bank did not suffer a loss. Hamilton proved to be a micromanager. He wrote detailed rules for the directors on what workers were to do with broken tools and, as the company ran into trouble, spent days at a time at board meetings dictating strategy. He personally recruited industrial spies who had stolen secrets from British companies on their latest textile machinery. He hired one such spy as SUM's foreman, while subsidizing his living expenses from the U.S. Treasury.

Like many an imperial CEO, L'Enfant quickly spun out of control and had to be replaced after a year spent wasting much of the company's capital not on building a factory, but on an extravagant scheme to replicate his plan for Washington, D.C., on the New Jersey SUM site. Two-hundred-foot-wide avenues at right angles were envisioned, despite the near-wilderness setting of hills and streams. When L'Enfant left, he stole the plans.

Hamilton's choices for directors turned out to be an even bigger disaster than his selection of L'Enfant. Composed almost entirely of local financiers instead of people with manufacturing experience, the board proved practically useless. Its deputy governor, Archibald Mercer, wrote Hamilton about the firm's dire financial straits and admitted "For my part, I confess myself perfectly ignorant of every duty relating to the Manufactoring business."

The board governor, William Duer, who was also the largest shareholder, was a compulsive gambler and speculator who, in a conspiracy with several other SUM directors and investors, led an attempt to corner the market for certain bank stocks and government bonds. Duer's market manipulation triggered a massive speculative bubble and the resulting Panic of 1792, the young nation's first market crash. Securities dropped 25 percent in value within a two-week period, forcing Hamilton to stabilize markets much as the modern-day Federal Reserve and Treasury did in the 2008 financial meltdown. Duer, who had borrowed massive amounts to fund his scheme, was wiped out, taking thousands of investors with him. In the aftermath, the board discovered that Duer had embezzled much of the company's accounts. Duer refused to resign as the SUM governor and spent the rest of his life in debtors' prison, where he was protected from an angry mob of hundreds of investors who gathered one night, shouting for his head and throwing rocks at the prison walls.

A committee of investigation found that another SUM director, John Dewhurst, had stolen $50,000 he was supposed to use for buying materials in England. Disgusted investors withdrew their pledged funds, and SUM, mortally wounded, struggled in vain to recover. By early 1796, the company had shut down its operations, leaving only a bunch of abandoned buildings amid the weeds. The lesson Hamilton drew from the embarrassing experience is summed up in a letter he wrote to a friend when Duer's duplicity was revealed—and it is a key point for those seeking to reform corporate governance today: "Public infamy must restrain what the laws cannot."

Despite this rough start, the Industrial Revolution and the need for growth capital caused many restrictions to lapse, and publicly held corporations governed by boards quickly became the norm. So, too, did successive waves of speculative booms and busts—and scandals involving boards—with canals, railroads, oil, steel, the Robber Baron–era monopolistic trusts, the gold and silver price manipulations, the 1929 stock market crash, the conglomerate mania, the defense contractor bribery scandals, the junk bond buyout movement, the savings and loan crisis, the Long-Term Capital Management collapse, and so on through to the Enron and WorldCom–era scandals, the dot-com and real estate financial bubbles and massive neo-Ponzi schemes of our time. Two consistent themes have emerged. First, as companies have grown larger, more interconnected, and more powerful, the crashes are occurring more frequently and are increasingly destructive, with repercussions on a global scale. Second, the governance reforms that have been attempted in their wake focus narrowly on the perceived cause of the most recent crash. Nothing really changes because these reforms impose ineffective, costly, or counterproductive legal and structural requirements rather than deal with the cultural problems of CEO-board collusive relationships and the lack of shareholder power. With the assistance of lawyers, accountants, and bankers, the boards and executives quickly find creative ways around the new rules. Even worse, people are lulled into a false sense of security that the problem has been addressed, investors return to the markets, and the cycle continues.

Post-Enron reforms such as the Sarbanes-Oxley Act and new stock exchange requirements calling for more independent directors and periodic board sessions without the CEO have not done enough to prevent recurring governance disasters. In fact, some changes have had unintended negative consequences; others have high costs that outweigh the benefits for shareholders and society. As a result, too many boards are now focused on cover-your-ass legal processes and box-checking exercises rather than on formulating company strategy, identifying risks, and evaluating executive performance. Real reforms will come only from improvements in the composition and culture of boards, and not just from additional regulatory controls or structural requirements.

Even the companies that have avoided major governance scandals are suffering from new burdens. A recent survey showed that directors now spend nearly twice the time on board work than they did twenty years ago. Fifty-nine percent of directors have declined a board seat due to the risks associated with the role, and 55 percent believe it is more difficult to recruit high-quality directors. The increasing time commitment required of board members, the complexity of contemporary business problems, the threat of reputational liability, the inherent conflicts between monitoring and advisory responsibilities, and the frustration of serving in a role under intense scrutiny in a brutal economic environment have made the job of a director unattractive to many capable people and difficult for anyone to discharge effectively. That means fewer strong, informed, committed board members, and as a result, too many boards stocked with weak, acquiescent, uninvolved directors.

When speaking among themselves, some directors voice increasing concerns about how some of their colleagues have discharged their duties. For each of the past seven years, a large annual survey of directors has shown that almost a third of board members answer yes when asked if they believe a fellow director should be replaced, usually because he or she lacks sufficient skills, is unengaged, has served too long, or is unprepared for meetings. William George, the highly regarded former CEO and chairman of Medtronic, Harvard Business School professor, and board member at several S&P 500 companies, told a forum of directors in 2008 that "Serving on a board is about one thing: it's about responsibility for the preservation and growth of the enterprise. If you can't pass that test, you can't blame it on the CEO, you can't blame it on your fellow directors. You have to look at yourself in the mirror. We are in a major crisis of corporate leadership." For better or worse, leadership is the hinge on which our current economy swings. In the last round of scandals from earlier this decade—Enron, Tyco, Adelphia, WorldCom, and others—most of the governance failures revolved around improper accounting and financial malfeasance. This time they have centered on excessive borrowing and risk taking in an overheated market, and on boards approving executive compensation systems that not only encouraged such risks but virtually guaranteed they would lead to disaster.

The depth of the problems stemming from such failures by CEOs and directors often comes to light only after an economic bubble has burst. In the meantime, as Citigroup's CEO and chairman Charles Prince told the *Financial Times* in mid-2007 just before the bank's risky portfolio began to implode, "As long as the music is playing, you've got to get up and dance. We're still dancing." When the music stopped abruptly, as it did just a few months later, some of the dancers such as Prince were fired, but most were not. Those who had been in charge blamed others, claimed to be victims, or suggested that it was all out of their control despite their having suggested otherwise when justifying their compensation packages. The CEOs and directors of failed financial services firms continually referred to the "financial tsunami" and other outside forces during their media appearances and congressional testimony. AIG's former CEOs Martin Sullivan and Robert Willumstad, for example, both told Congressman Henry Waxman's oversight committee that financial disclosure laws requiring the firm's securities to be valued at current market levels were to blame for AIG's troubles. Lynn Turner, the former chief accountant at the SEC, responded: "That's like blaming the thermometer, folks, for a fever."

H. Rodgin Cohen, a banking lawyer who heads Sullivan & Cromwell and was in the boardrooms advising shell-shocked directors and CEOs at Lehman Brothers, Bear Stearns, AIG, Wachovia, Fannie Mae, and twelve other major financial companies during their 2008 crises, recalled what it was like in the trenches: "Think about it. You're sitting around on a Friday night and you're being told the bank probably cannot open for business on Monday—or, if it does, it's going to be shut down very quickly." He observed that "any modern financial system is built on confidence and when that confidence evaporates in individual institutions, the lifespan of that institution is measured in days. When it declines in the system as a whole, you have credit gridlock." Cohen partly blames poor regulatory supervision, especially in the Federal Reserve's failure to oversee nonbank mortgage lenders like Countrywide who were issuing Option Adjustable Rate Mortgages that allowed subprime borrowers to get in over their heads by deferring principal and interest payments. Cohen also told us that too many bank leaders were driven by competitive psychology in trying to beat Goldman Sachs's profitability and "failed to recognize risks," in part because of the mistaken assumption that having an accounting expert on the board's audit committee—a Sarbanes-Oxley reform measure enacted in 2002—already addressed such concerns. "Boards should have a risk committee and a risk expert," he says.

AN ESTIMATED 57 million American households own stock in public companies, sometimes directly, but more often through mutual funds, pension plans, and 401(k) accounts. Boards have legal duties to represent the best interests of the shareholders. Directors are typically required by state law to avoid self-dealing and conflicts of interest, and to exercise care, loyalty, and good faith in protecting shareholders. In modern economic thinking, boards should also monitor the interests of employees, customers, suppliers, creditors, and the communities and the environment in which a firm operates, because these interests can be critical to increasing the long-term value of the shareholders' investment.

On behalf of shareholders, boards' specific duties are to choose and when necessary replace the chief executive officer of the business; evaluate the performance of senior managers; set executive compensation; approve key strategic and financial decisions; nominate candidates for shareholders to elect as directors; and insure the company's integrity, sustainability, and compliance with laws and regulations as it tries to grow. Directors are expected to contribute wisdom and long-term vision to a company, steering it away from peril and toward success. In effect, boards are the executive, legislative, and judicial branches of business government, as well as the bankers, the police, and the tribal elders. They are the final check and balance on behalf of the owners, standing in for them by overseeing management.

In reality, many boards fail miserably in these duties. Under the corporate laws of most states, board members avoid liability even if their actions or, more likely, their inaction lead to catastrophic losses for shareholders. This is especially true in Delaware, where the vast majority of large companies choose to incorporate precisely because of that state's management-friendly laws and courts. Shareholders have little to no influence over which state is selected for incorporation, thus setting off the notorious "race to the bottom" by corporate leaders to those jurisdictions where there is little deterrence for mis-, mal-, and nonfeasance by boards.

Delaware's "business judgment rule" excuses almost any bad

board behavior under the assumption that directors have acted in good faith, even if they didn't act, and even if they have shown devastating negligence. To be held liable, they must have "knowingly and completely failed to undertake their responsibilities" or had "an actual intent to do harm"—a standard that has let thousands of failed boards off the hook over the years. If shareholders are foolish enough to engage in a lawsuit, they run into process and cost nightmares like that with the AIG civil case which took from 2004 until 2009 just to get to the stage of not having the case summarily dismissed. The first five pages of the judge's opinion is a list of just some of the lawyers involved: 114 attorneys from 43 different firms, including 22 based in Wilmington, Delaware. The tens of millions in legal fees for the parties on all sides are largely being paid by AIG's shareholders—80 percent of whom are now, of course, us—the U.S. taxpayer. As one director remarked to us, "As long as you can show you've conducted a minimal amount of process and haven't committed an outright crime, you just can't be sued successfully." Consequently, boards fear reputational damage more than legal or financial liability. The one effective constraint is the threat of embarrassment in the rare instances when the consequences of their failures come to public attention.

Board members are selected from the same gene pool. They are a relatively narrow, elite group with homogeneous backgrounds, values, and worldviews. The joke among diversity advocates is that boards are overwhelmingly "male, pale, and stale"—and, indeed, women and minorities are still shockingly underrepresented in American boardrooms. Despite substantial progress during the last half of the twentieth century (until 1964, there had not been a single African American director of a Fortune 500 company), the growth in diversity has stagnated in recent years and actually declined in a number of categories. Boards lack diversity not just in terms of gender, ethnic origin, and age, but, more important, in their members' range of relevant experiences, in their personalities, and in how they perceive and deal with business issues.

Very few board members have a significant percentage of their own personal wealth invested in the company. Of course, they often get lots of stock from grants or options, which are supposed to align their interests with those of the investors. But it is feared that too much alignment will lead them to manipulate stock prices. Too little and they have no particular reason to care about them. As corporate governance expert Nell Minow said, "At the end of the day, 99 percent of board decisions are based on the fact that it's not their money."

Being on a board is a part-time job. Frequently, board members lack the time to be sufficiently committed to their duties, especially if their own company or the one on whose board they sit develops a crisis. Members who are retired and do have the time may lack the energy or current business experience required to be active, effective, and assertive contributors in the boardroom. The very role of the board is increasingly contradictory. Directors are asked to provide a long-term strategic view while they are caught up in details and processes that leave insufficient time for vision. They are supposed to independently monitor executives while also providing them with knowledgeable advice, counsel, and connections.

The go-along-to-get-along culture of boards is usually very ingrained, and all the check-the-box reform efforts do little to change it. Collegiality and passivity are the norm; directors who ask tough questions or vote against management proposals are often ignored, passed over, and cut out. And, of course, as human beings, directors are no less prone than the rest of us to the biases, emotions, and behavioral psychology that affect people under stress making decisions in groups.

Representative democracy for a company's actual owners is

still largely a myth. Despite recent improvements that have somewhat increased shareholders' voices in governance, levelheaded observers such as former SEC commissioner William Donaldson have compared our system to "the old Soviet-style elections" in which shareholders basically have no choice other than to vote for those nominated, abstain from voting, or sell their stock. Except in a tiny handful of cases, board elections are a closed and self-perpetuating exercise without a real choice. Well over 99 percent of the nominees put forward by boards win election. Mounting a proxy fight to elect alternative directors is prohibitively expensive and intentionally blocked by bureaucratic processes that make even getting a list of shareholders nearly impossible. Ballots are secret to the voters, but not to management. Thus, the CEO knows in advance how the vote is going and who has voted for or against the company's recommendations. In close elections, companies can use this information to arm-twist institutional investors to ensure the outcome.

The bylaws of most corporations allow boards to ignore shareholder proposals, even if they receive an overwhelming majority, because such votes are merely advisory. Since their votes seem meaningless and the process itself is so cumbersome and confusing, most individual shareholders practice rational apathy. Only a third of them bother to vote in corporate elections. However, these shareholders still hold strong opinions about boards and were angry about a number of issues even before the recent financial meltdown. In mid-2007, a national survey of investors holding $100,000 or more of stocks or mutual funds showed 78 percent think boards are giving CEOs too much in compensation; 89 percent think jail time should be mandatory for corporate officers or board members convicted of practices harmful to employees, investors, and the public; and 79 percent say prosecutors should try very aggressively to recover company losses from that executive or board member's *personal* assets.

Large institutional investors have a fiduciary duty to vote on behalf of those who actually provide the money for the stock they control, but some of these institutions have conflicts with their constituents' interests. Mutual funds, pension funds, endowments, insurance companies, and other large institutional investors now collectively control more than 70 percent of the shares of U.S. public companies. In most cases, with the exception of some activist public and union pension funds and hedge funds, they simply vote their shares according to a company's recommendations, or they farm out the decisions and paperwork to a proxy advisory service. Mutual funds, in particular, have an inherent conflict in such votes because many of them want to manage the 401(k) and other investment funds for companies. There's not much upside, but a great deal of downside to voting against the management of their current or potential customers.

Companies spend enormous sums of shareholders' own money to fight proposed reforms directly or through organizations such as the Business Roundtable and the U.S. Chamber of Commerce. The SEC's proposal in the post-Enron era to allow shareholders to nominate a limited number of directors was dropped after a massive lobbying campaign led by the Roundtable, an association of CEOs whose companies account for a third of the total value of the U.S. stock markets. In mid-2009, in the wake of renewed efforts to reform the director nomination process, the U.S. Chamber of Commerce announced a $100 million "sweeping national advocacy campaign encompassing advertising, education, political activities, new media, and grassroots organizing to defend and advance America's free enterprise values in the face of rapid government growth and attacks by anti-business activists." A Chamber executive's op-ed piece on corporate governance titled "If It Isn't Broke, Don't Fix It!" argues that "the existing system has been working well and reforms have occurred in a steady and diverse way . . . We shouldn't throw out the baby with the bathwater."

Too many investors are focused only on short-term stock price movements rather than on creating long-term value. The resulting pressure on CEOs and boards to meet quarterly expectations has distorted financial accounting, encouraged creative "earnings management," triggered unproductive stock buybacks instead of investment in new businesses, and created bonus systems that reward go-for-broke risk taking.

The gatekeepers in this system have assumed too much power and responsibility from boards. Beleaguered directors increasingly rely on this vast army of lawyers, auditors, investment bankers, recruiters, rating agencies, consultants, and others who provide support services for corporate governance. Each gatekeeper serves a purpose, but some are fundamentally conflicted, and collectively they cost hundreds of billions of shareholders' dollars, often to provide reputational camouflage to directors or shield them from accountability. As Columbia Law School professor John Coffee writes in his book *The Gatekeepers*: "The watchdogs hired by those they have to watch typically turn into pets, not guardians."

Perhaps most disconcerting for directors themselves, the primary purpose of corporate governance has become a matter for debate: should the focus be solely on increasing shareholder value or on insuring the firm's long-term sustainability or on balancing the interests of various stakeholders? There is not even agreement on exactly what constitutes the best practices, how to resolve the monitoring-versus-assistance roles, or whether the quality of corporate governance can predict how a company performs.

As a result of all of these factors, corporate boards remain the weakest link in our free enterprise system. To work well, this system depends on a delicate balance of power among three key actors: CEOs as managers, governments as regulators, and directors as representatives of owners. For the past decade, CEOs have largely been in control while regulators and boards have failed to do their jobs. Deregulation eliminated much corporate oversight, while lax or nonexistent enforcement of securities laws and the negligence of boards encouraged the excessive risk taking and the self-dealing executive compensation schemes that have intensified our current troubles. Now, in the wake of the economic disaster and the massive taxpayer bailout of failing companies, government may possibly be reasserting its power.

But past attempts simply to legislate reforms have backfired. In 1993, for example, in response to executive compensation that seemed outrageously high, Congress changed the tax laws to ban the deductibility of CEO salaries more than $1 million unless performance targets were met—with the targets largely undefined in the loophole-filled legislation. The average salary for large company CEOs at the time was approximately $750,000. Boards immediately raised their CEOs' salaries to at least the $1 million level and approved bonus plans with targets often set by the executives themselves. *BusinessWeek* called the law "the biggest inside joke in the long history of efforts to rein in executive pay" and pointed to the board of power plant operator AES, which had included maintaining a "fun" workplace as one of its CEO's performance goals. Boards also began the gigantic grants of stock options that became, by far, the largest component of CEO pay, with their stunning transfer of market profits to just a few individuals and all the new abuses that options have entailed. Data from the Economic Policy Institute show that compensation for the five top executives in U.S. companies soon rose to become about 10 percent of all corporate profits—twice what it was in the mid-1990s. The average CEO in 2007 was paid $275 for every dollar paid for a typical worker, up from a ratio of 24 to 1 in 1973. Over the past twenty years, CEO pay has grown more than 16 times as fast as the average worker's, and American CEOs now earn 2.25 times the average of CEOs in other wealthy countries.

New legislation and greater enforcement of existing regulations are certainly necessary, but if implemented in a continuing vacuum of corporate leadership, they will surely miss the mark. At a 2009 House hearing, for example, a member of Congress actually asked "Why not just require of all the members of the board of directors a fiduciary duty to the shareholders?"—a duty that, of course, has been in existence for hundreds of years. The trick is to require those fiduciary duties to be exercised and to take enforcement action if they aren't. The emergency actions taken during the recent financial crisis by the Federal Reserve, the U.S. Treasury, the SEC, the FDIC, and other regulators have shown that most of the necessary laws are already on the books. As Eliot Spitzer commented to us, "the problem over the past decade wasn't that regulators and boards lacked the power—it's that they lacked the willpower to do their jobs."

IS IT FAIR to single out the failures of corporate boards as a major cause of the recent credit crisis and economic meltdown? To be sure, there is plenty of interconnected blame to go around for a mess this big. One could construct an elaborate Rube Goldberg device illustrating the chain reaction from just a top-10 list of the contributing malefactors, which might include these: the Federal Reserve holding interest rates at unnecessarily low levels for too long, American consumers' debt-fueled spending binge, governments encouraging home ownership by inappropriate borrowers, financial institutions ignoring risks to reap profits from complex mortgage securities, investors obsessed with short-term gains, credit-rating agencies selling inaccurate AAA ratings, coopted professional services providers failing to raise the alarm, business schools churning out executives focused on money instead of values, financial media cheerleading rather than investigating, and business organizations marshalling massive campaign contributions and lobbying efforts to deregulate the financial services industry. Two more elements should be added at the front and the end of the chain leading to the economic bomb that exploded: the predominant "Chicago School" economic philosophy that championed unfettered free markets and deregulation, and, finally, the failsafe device that didn't work—the SEC. When the SEC reduced its enforcement division staff by 146 people and gutted the Office of Risk Assessment to just one person early in 2007, a catastrophe was virtually ensured to occur. As Robert Monks, the dean of shareholder activists, told us, "The SEC wasn't just asleep at the switch, the switch was deliberately turned off."

Certainly all of these played a role, but it is curious that among the perpetrators of the ongoing tragedy, the many boards of directors who failed to do their jobs have received by far the least attention. The boards were supposed to monitor risks, provide judgment, and supervise the managers on behalf of shareholders. Boards, at the very least, should have acted in the classic sense like a governor on an engine that measures and regulates the machine's speed and, if necessary, turns it down to keep it from blowing up. Ideally, they should have done what Plato envisioned when first using the word *govern* metaphorically from the Greek term meaning *to steer.*

Suppose that, instead of going along for the ride, boards had steered us in the right direction by asking tough questions, second-guessing shortsighted strategies, and exercising leadership. What if they had been true stewards of other people's money and invited management to follow them in this calling? Surely, they would have reduced the incalculable financial devastation and human suffering that has followed. Society wondered whether it stood on the precipice of economic disintegration in mid-September 2008 as stock markets throughout the world plummeted, credit froze, and confidence in the financial system disappeared in the wake of the Lehman Brothers bankruptcy and the near collapses of Fannie Mae, AIG, and Citigroup. We still don't truly know how far we have moved from that disaster and whether it may soon be repeated on a more catastrophic scale. If we are ever to make it to safety, it is well past time for boards—the governors and stewards of the largest economies on earth—to step up and do their jobs.

2

Ripple Effects

THE REACH OF GLOBAL BUSINESSES is vast, and the interconnections among them are staggeringly complex. When the system works well, it's a powerful mechanism for good; when it doesn't, the toxic effects surge outward quickly and harmfully. What starts with bad decisions or poor oversight in a company's boardroom can wreak havoc in myriad ways. When it comes to corporate governance, the butterfly effect—popularized by a 1972 scientific presentation on chaos theory by Edward Lorenz titled "Does the Flap of a Butterfly's Wings in Brazil Set off a Tornado in Texas?"—definitely applies.

Look at the ripple effects that resulted from former Illinois governor James Thompson's inattentiveness as the chairman of the audit committee for Hollinger International. The Chicago-based media company once owned more than five hundred newspapers, including the *Chicago Sun-Times, Daily Telegraph* (London), and *Jerusalem Post*. Hollinger declared bankruptcy in 2007 after its CEO, Conrad Black, and other executives were convicted for looting the company of tens of millions in illegal payments. Despite having little business experience during a distinguished career as a prosecutor and politician, Thompson had become much in demand as a corporate director once he left the governor's office in 1991. He sat on as many as ten boards, while also serving as the chairman of a large Chicago law firm and as a lobbyist.

In 1994, Thompson joined the Hollinger board as an independent director and for a number of years ran the audit committee, which was supposed to be the financial watchdog on behalf of shareholders. In addition to Thompson, Black had packed the board with other former government officials—including secretary of state Henry Kissinger, defense policy advisor Richard Perle, and the U.S. ambassadors to the UK and Germany. Their prestige was supposed to burnish the company's reputation, and their connections were meant to open doors or help keep them closed. They brought little to the table, however, in advising on the business or monitoring the managers who were clearly running amok.

The independent board members paid little attention to the exorbitant self-dealing payments to the executives. They were repeatedly approved until Hollinger's largest shareholder, Tweedy, Browne, a money management firm that owned nearly 18 percent of the company's shares, called on the directors in 2003 to create a special committee to examine the payments and seek the return of the money. Only then did Hollinger, and later the SEC, launch the investigations that eventually led to Black and others being charged with siphoning off some $400 million—almost all the company's profits for seven years—through schemes such as selling newspaper companies for below their value (including one for $1) to a separate company they owned and paying themselves grossly inflated management fees. They were also accused of taking millions in bogus noncompete fees, in some cases essentially for agreeing not to compete with themselves.

At the end of August 2004, the special committee, which

was composed largely of new, independent board members and assisted by former SEC commissioner Richard Breeden, issued a 513-page report that condemned what it called "a corporate kleptocracy" run by Hollinger's executives. It was especially harsh in reviewing the many failures of the audit committee and concluded that the "Committee's 'review' of the annual management fee did not pass a threshold level sufficient to characterize what it did as a 'review' (let alone a 'negotiation'), and that any 'approval' given was not based on any serious analysis. Indeed, in many cases approvals were not based on any analysis at all." The report also detailed the lavish spending by Black and his wife, Barbara, that was subsidized by shareholders. This included "summer drinks" for $24,950, a "Happy Birthday Barbara" dinner party at New York's La Grenouille restaurant for $42,870 (the report says Black deemed it a company function "because many of the attendees were Hollinger directors"), three dinners for Kissinger and his wife for $28,480, refurbishing a Rolls-Royce for $90,000, staff for their personal residences for $1.4 million, and a collection of Franklin Roosevelt memorabilia for $8.9 million, as well as corporate donations totaling $6.5 million that helped maintain the Blacks' social standing and were made in their names rather than the company's.

The report says that Black and his management colleagues had deliberately misled the directors, but concludes that "on balance, however, the Audit Committee's ineffectiveness is primarily a consequence of its inexplicable and nearly complete lack of initiative, diligence, or independent thought. The Audit Committee simply did not make the effort to put itself in a sufficient position to recognize untruthful or misleading information, or even to make informed decisions on the issues before it . . . Delaware law (and Hollinger's Articles of Incorporation) exculpates board members from personal liability for discharging their duties in a negligent, or carelessly inattentive manner . . . However, at some point a director's failure to question even the most basic elements of a significant related-party transaction calls into question whether any decision made by that director was a decision at all but rather only a rubber stamping of a non–arm's length transaction."

At Black's criminal trial, which focused largely on the outrageous noncompete fees, Thompson spent an uncomfortable three days on the witness stand trying to explain how he had missed eleven references in various documents—several of which bore his signature—relating to $15.6 million in noncompete payments to Hollinger executives. Thompson testified that he had usually just "skimmed" the documents Hollinger sent him. The defense attorney grilled him mercilessly: "So skimming doesn't mean you read quickly . . . It means some things you don't see at all . . . From the chairman of the board to the everyday shareholder, these people relied on you." Thompson conceded that he'd signed some financial statements he hadn't read and that his signature probably convinced other directors to approve them as well. In a radio interview after the convictions, Thompson tried to explain away his ineffectiveness: "I wasn't on trial, so I don't have to feel vindicated," he said. "You can't go on a corporate board with the assumption management is going to be dishonest." Thompson left the Hollinger board before the company's bankruptcy; as of the fall of 2009, he was still serving on three other public company boards.

The story doesn't end with Black's conviction, unfortunately. The damage went far beyond the initial losses to shareholders. As of late 2007, Hollinger—renamed the Sun-Times Media Group—had spent nearly $200 million just on the legal aftermath. This included more than $107 million for defending Black and the executives from the criminal and various civil charges (their contracts required shareholders to indemnify them for legal costs, including appeals all the way to the Supreme Court), $62.5 million for the special committee's investigation, and over $28 million for litigation attempting, largely without success, to recover money from Black and others. The amounts shareholders got from insurance (including $20 million paid to settle negligence claims against the directors) and other sources amounted to about $70 million less than these costs alone even before accounting for what had been stolen by the executives. "There was some value in these companies, but it's been destroyed through professional fees right from the beginning," explained one observer. "As soon as allegations of fraud are raised, the professionals step in; and once you get into that game, the fees keep adding up; and because they get paid first, in the end, they are always the ones who benefit; and shareholders are left out to dry."

While the squabbling over the company's carcass continued, its stock dropped from a 2004 high of $20.35 to $1. By mid-2009, the company, which owed the IRS more than $600 million in back taxes related to the prior financial malfeasance, had declared bankruptcy again, and its stock was trading at 1 cent. As the company burned through $5 million in cash a month, its premier remaining newspaper, the *Chicago Sun-Times*, which had once been a sturdy big-city daily, began an accelerated slide toward bankruptcy, layoffs, and skipping payments to its employee pension fund.

Investors may feel a company's lurches and wobbles first and most directly, but everyone from senior managers to a laid-off employee's hairdresser or auto mechanic, who may themselves lose their jobs as the laid-off employee tries to economize, will suffer when a company goes down. In the case of Hollinger, these victims include, among hundreds of others, taxpayers who foot the bill for the prosecution; readers of the *Sun-Times* who count on it as a source of information; unsecured creditors such as a Seattle newsprint vendor who was owed $1.5 million; and the entire city of

Chicago's economy and civic culture, which lost a major employer and may be on the verge of becoming a one-newspaper town.

The breadth of the impact when companies collapse is frightening, and the culpability of corporate boards in contributing to their demise is shameful. The mind boggles at the losses represented by the $7 trillion of American shareholders' investments that vaporized during 2008 in the stock market crash and the additional $3.3 trillion lost in the value of homes. The estimated global costs in total financial market losses amounted to a staggering $50 trillion for the year, including $25 trillion in stock values. And despite signs of economic recovery, there's likely more to come, because so many of the world's financial institutions have yet to fully account for the losses from bad investments still on their balance sheets. In April 2009, the International Monetary Fund (IMF) estimated that financial institutions globally would have to write off a total of $4.1 trillion through 2010. It further warned that the damage would take years to fix and would likely lead to a credit famine in Britain, the United States, and Europe.

According to the stock market commentator Douglas A. McIntyre, who was one of the early critics of financial services boards and himself a former board member of four public companies, "Other than cases of outright fraud like Enron or WorldCom, the most egregious failures of corporate boards have been those of the financial services directors who somehow missed all the red flags that were flapping in their faces. Why didn't they bother to ask what risks were being undertaken as their portfolios within just a few years went from single-digit percentages of esoteric derivatives to a majority, or their earnings went from 8 percent to 25 percent, or their borrowing from 15 times their equity to over 30 times? What were they thinking? It will probably take at least a decade for the global economy to recover from their negligence."

THE SHAREHOLDERS and employees of Bear Stearns may well take more than a decade to recover from the financial and emotional shock they experienced as the firm, its stock value, and thousands of jobs vaporized in a matter of days. It was all on display at what, in effect, served as Bear Stearns's funeral—the special shareholders' meeting to approve the sale of what had once been the nation's fifth largest and most consistently profitable investment bank. It took place in New York on the sunny spring morning of May 29, 2008, and one of us, who used to work at Bear Stearns, attended the services.

There was a circus atmosphere on the streets outside the forty-five-story Bear Stearns building on Madison and West Forty-seventh Street—a grand, elegant tower built just a few years earlier, when times were flush and seemed like they would always be so. The entry plaza was a gridlock of rubbernecking bystanders, financial network vans, and reporters seeking interviews. ("I'd be happy to talk about it after I'm laid off next week," said one weary-looking female banker.) An artist, Geoffrey Raymond, was set up on the corner with an oversized painting of Bear Stearns chairman and former CEO Jimmy Cayne on which employees and shareholders could write comments—in red ink for employees, purple for shareholders, black for anyone else. The employee and shareholder comments ranged from "Hubris, thy name is Jimmy" and "I just got my letter!" to "Pass the bong," a reference to a *Wall Street Journal* article suggesting that the seventy-four-year-old Cayne had smoked marijuana while playing at bridge tournaments during his frequent absences from the company. Cayne was later named to *Portfolio* magazine's list of the "20 Worst American CEOs of All Time" (at No. 4 after Enron's Kenneth

Lay, Countrywide's Angelo Mozilo, and Lehman's Richard Fuld) based on selections by a panel of business school professors who were asked to consider each CEO's record of destroying value and lack of management skills.

Security was tight at the building's entrance; shareholders had to run a gauntlet of ID checks, metal detectors, and guards. Reportedly, Cayne himself had been accompanied by an armed bodyguard when he came to the building in the weeks after Bear Stearns's sale had been arranged. The auditorium on the second floor indeed had the ambience of a funeral, all solemn faces and hushed voices, even though the eighty-five-year-old company had effectively died ten weeks before. In mid-March, after a week in financial freefall and futile negotiations to raise capital or sell the company, Bear Stearns was on the brink of a bankruptcy that could have triggered a disaster for global markets. At the last minute, with no real alternatives, the board approved a Federal Reserve–assisted sale to JPMorgan Chase at $2 a share, later raised to $10—less than one-seventeenth of the stock's value only fifteen months earlier. Bear Stearns shareholders lost approximately $20 billion.

Among the three hundred or so people waiting for the meeting to begin, there were many senior executives of Bear Stearns, but not a single outside board member was in sight. About a third of the firm's stock was held by employees, so those in the room had suffered some of the biggest individual losses. Most of them had nothing to do with the mortgage-backed securities that triggered the company's fall, yet many had lost their life savings and would be out of their jobs in a matter of days.

In truth, even though it created a commotion, the shareholders' meeting was largely a formality. JPMorgan already controlled more than 49 percent of the stock, and the board had pledged to vote its holdings for the sale. Ironically, Cayne had already sold all of his 5.61 million Bear Stearns shares for about $61 million the day after JPMorgan's final bid and was thus unable to vote at the meeting. Cayne, looking drained and somber, sat at a table on the stage next to the new CEO Alan Schwartz, his successor as CEO after Cayne had been eased out of the role in January. The body language of the two was awkward, with both leaning in opposite directions and mostly looking down or off to the side.

The meeting lasted all of ten minutes, including the emotional and rambling remarks that Cayne made during the vote tally, at first echoing Schwartz's thanks to employees, then noting "It's a sad day, but we'll get through it . . . That which doesn't kill you makes you stronger and at this point we all look like Hercules. Life goes on." He suggested others were to blame, perhaps those betting on the firm's downfall by shorting the stock: "We don't know now, but we'll eventually know whether there was a conspiracy." Or perhaps, as he suggested, it was simply an act of God. "We built a great company . . . but then we ran into a hurricane." He ended with a bit of contrition: "I personally apologize. Words can't describe the pain I feel and I'm not alone. Management feels an enormous amount of pain. Fourteen thousand workers and their families are feeling it, too. I'm sorry . . ." He was struggling to say more but was interrupted by the news that the votes had been counted and Bear Stearns was gone.

The domed, octagonal Bear Stearns boardroom was ten floors above the auditorium where the death knell of the company was being sounded. The boardroom was almost a parody of an efficient nerve center of ultimate power, sort of a cross between the UN Security Council meeting room and the war room set from *Dr. Strangelove*. Thirty-two leather-covered swivel chairs surrounded a ring-shaped maple table with microphones at each seat. While the rest of the building was adorned with the firm's impressive, 1,500-piece contemporary art collection, the boardroom itself was deliberately spartan, its walls holding only large flat-screen monitors set into the mahogany paneling. The room had a cloistered, hushed atmosphere—a world away from the buzzing commotion of the trading floors and the investment banking office suites where the toxic securities that helped bring down the company were packaged and sold.

It was here that the board ran through its motions over the years, although, in an inadvertant touch of symbolism, it hadn't been used for the endgame flurry of meetings leading to the firm's sale because most of the building's larger meeting rooms, as well as Cayne's private office, were occupied by teams of lawyers, advisors, and potential buyers. The boardroom was also where the directors approved paying Cayne a total of $156 million—including salary, bonuses, stock options, and restricted stock grants—for the five years from 2002 to 2006. It was well known within the company that the independent directors—a group of nine that had not a single female member and only one person of color—had been largely selected by Cayne and did little, usually deferring to the three insiders who also served on the board, including former CEO and chairman Alan "Ace" Greenberg and the current CEO, Alan Schwartz, as well as Cayne, who remained as chairman. It was an insular, chummy group: six of the independent board members had served together for more than thirteen years and the three executives had been together for more than twenty years. As William Cohan, the author of *House of Cards,* which chronicled Bear Stearns's collapse, told us, "It was essentially a management-dominated, insider board that paid little attention to the risks the company was taking and did the right thing only at the end." Cohan had interviewed Paul Friedman, a senior managing director and chief operating officer of the firm's fixed income division, about the board. Friedman said, "We didn't have a board. We had this group of cronies and Jimmy. I guess if you had a real board that had real outsiders with real expertise, you would actually get them involved and they might have some role to play, but not here."

In fact, it would be somewhat surprising if they had been able to play any significant role at all, given that many of the directors were stretched incredibly thin. Bear Stearns was one of only two publicly traded U.S. companies that had three directors—including two on the important finance and risk committee—who sat on at least five public company boards. It was hard not to imagine that this situation played a role in the board missing so many obvious vulnerabilities—the overconcentration on mortgage-related risks, the huge increases in the firm's borrowing, an absentee CEO who had stayed on too long and then was made chairman, and a bonus structure that rewarded return on equity, which led to keeping the amount of outstanding stock as low as possible and thus to an insufficient capital cushion for a rainy day. Warren Batts, who teaches corporate governance at the University of Chicago and received the 2006 Director of the Year award from the National Association of Corporate Directors, commented to *Financial Week* that "any company with directors sitting on five or six boards raises the question: How in the heck are they doing the work? I wouldn't be able to schedule that many meetings. For Bear's board, it either all happened too quickly or it was like the Keystone Kops fire drill there . . ."

In any case, the reality was that the company was run by the senior managers on the firm's executive committee, which met 115 times in 2006 according to SEC filings, while the board of directors, during that same time, held only six meetings. J. Richard Finlay, a governance consultant and commentator, called it "one of the most incurious and acquiescent boards in history" and asked whether the firm should even be considered to have had a real board at all. He fixed much of the blame on Cayne, who disappeared to go golfing on most Fridays and was hard to reach while at ten-day-long bridge tournaments in Nashville and Detroit during much of the firm's two biggest crises: the collapse of two Bear Stearns mortgage-backed hedge funds in 2007 when he was still the CEO, and the insolvency crisis in March 2008 when he was chairman of the board. "It has often been asserted, in the aftermath of boardroom debacles, that directors were asleep at the wheel," Finlay wrote. "In Mr. Cayne's case, there is compelling evidence that he was not even on the ship."

When the board met on a phone call on Thursday evening, March 13, 2008, to be briefed for the first time on the rapidly developing crisis, Cayne joined the meeting late from the Detroit hotel where his bridge tournament was being held. According to *House of Cards,* as the directors discussed the firm's options, including declaring bankruptcy, Cayne reportedly was asked a question and the board discovered that he had dropped off the call to return to the bridge table with some of the team members whom he hired for around $500,000 a year to play with him. Cayne's wife apparently had to get him to come back to discuss a possible vote.

As it became clear on Friday evening that the Federal Reserve was going to pull out of a guarantee that Bear Stearns executives had thought gave them twenty-eight days to resolve the liquidity crisis, the company faced the choice between declaring bankruptcy on Monday morning and being acquired at a fire sale price over the weekend. A bankruptcy would likely have wiped out the shareholders and many of the firm's debt holders as well. The stock had dropped 47 percent on that day alone, customers were withdrawing funds in a panic, and lending to the company had dried up.

The board members began to gather at the headquarters, but there was actually little they could do. As described in the special stockholders' meeting documents, the board met several times and finally "continuously" over the weekend for a series of updates, reviews, and discussions with management and advisors on what few options remained. Cayne was among the last to arrive, finally appearing in New York on Saturday evening after taking a private jet from Detroit. His major contribution was to advocate that the board threaten to play what he called "the nuclear card"—suggesting it would take the bankruptcy route in hopes of forcing the federal government to bail out the firm to avoid an immediate global credit meltdown. Cayne's closest friend on the board was the lead outside director, Vincent Tese, a wealthy communications businessman. Over breakfast Sunday morning, Tese talked Cayne out of the rash idea. The board unanimously approved the JPMorgan deal that night before the Asian markets opened.

Besides approving the sale, among the board's few votes that weekend was one that reduced the directors' own risks by amending the company's bylaws on Sunday so that funds would be advanced for defending the board against lawsuits. In other words, Bear Stearns shareholders and creditors would pay to further insulate the directors from charges of negligence. By the end of the weekend, standard language was added to the merger agreement to indemnify all Bear Stearns present and former directors and officers, so that JPMorgan shareholders would pay for any legal, insurance, and liability costs for six years after the merger. Because a bankruptcy would put the board in an uncertain position among the other creditors and possibly jeopardize the indemnification payments, critics suggest that this situation can put directors into a conflict with shareholders because it makes a board more likely to favor a merger even at a suboptimal price.

As it turned out, after the $2 per share deal was announced, a glitch in the hastily written merger documents came to light that might have allowed Bear Stearns shareholders to turn down the merger for a year while the firm shopped itself elsewhere.

With the Federal Reserve threatening to pull its guarantees that made the deal work and JPMorgan becoming uneasy, the merger/bankruptcy drama continued for another week. It was finally worked out with JPMorgan increasing the payment to $10 a share in exchange for near certainty that the approval was locked in. During these endgame negotiations, two of the independent board members—Tese and Frederic Salerno, a retired Verizon chief financial officer—played a valuable and constructive role (as Tese had the previous week on Cayne's "nuclear card") even though they were the among the directors who served on five or more other boards. It suggests, ironically, that if they had only been so actively engaged earlier, things might possibly not have come to such a sorry pass for the firm, its shareholders, and its employees.

The Bear Stearns story also exemplifies the myriad problems that develop when boards fail in managing CEO succession. Despite the firm having become a public company in 1985, it still operated like the authoritarian regimes that the old Wall Street partnerships had been.

Cayne had deposed Ace Greenberg, the former CEO, in a boardroom coup in 1993. But "Jimmy stayed on too long," said a senior managing director of the company—a banker who had been with Bear Stearns for nearly two decades and was now about to be unemployed. "He lost energy and a sense of how big and complex the operation had become, so our risks just got out of control." The banker mentioned a recent meeting he'd had with Cayne that betrayed another problem at the firm the board should have controlled—the excessive executive compensation that, at one point, had made Cayne the richest investment banking CEO: "Jimmy was shaking his head over how much money he'd lost and I said to him 'Well, there aren't that many people who've achieved enough to be able to lose a billion dollars.' And he just looked at me and said, '1.2 billion.'"

Ace Greenberg, with his relentless focus on reducing costs and containing risks, his requirement that senior bankers donate a minimum of 4 percent of their pay to charity, and his magic shows for employees' children that were broadcast at Christmas via video conference to Bear Stearns offices throughout the world, symbolized what the firm's culture had once been. Greenberg, who was now eighty, embodied frugality and old-school values. He made a point of drumming those values into new employees through his legendary memos about recycling paper clips and only licking one-half of an envelope flap so that it could be used again. Everyone had a personal story. A banker clearing out his office recalled his "welcome to Bear Stearns" lunch with Ace in the executive dining room many years before. It had lasted about eight minutes and featured Ace growling at the waiter for serving him two hot dogs when he'd only ordered one. "Ace and Jimmy had a real falling-out," the banker said. "They really hate each other now. Did you notice that Ace came into the shareholders' meeting late and walked slowly down to the front while Jimmy was talking?"

The banker then told a story that underscored how much the firm's risk-averse culture and the level of oversight by the CEO and chairman had changed. When he'd landed the firm's first deal with a major airline some years before, he had been blindsided by the client asking at the last minute to waive a standard clause in the contract giving Bear Stearns an out if the airline's credit rating was downgraded before the deal closed, and saying that another investment bank was willing to do that. "Just as we were signing the deal," he said, "the phone rings and it's Ace saying, 'I heard about what you're doing. I don't like it one bit.' I told him that we had considered the risks, modified the contract to shorten the closing to five days, and I thought we'd be okay. Ace paused and replied: 'Oh, really? Would you bet your career on that?' I said, "I guess so," and before hanging up Ace said, "Call me when it closes." Five days later, when he phoned Ace from the lawyer's offices to report that everything had gone smoothly, Greenberg replied, 'I already know.'"

The morning Bear Stearns died, the same banker brought a former colleague to pay a last visit to a sacred spot on one of the six 42,000 square-foot trading floors in the building. This was where Ace Greenberg's desk sat right in the middle of hundreds of others in the room, an arrangement he'd maintained throughout his career. The two bankers walked up behind Greenberg and looked out over the vast, empty room where a handful of people were quietly clearing out their drawers, illuminated by the three flat screens at each seat flashing market data to no one. Then they glanced back at Greenberg sitting there all alone at his desk, on the phone with his customers, still at work.

THE TOXIC MORTGAGE SECURITIES that helped ruin Bear Stearns were already tainted by ethical corruption at firms like Countrywide Financial, which pushed the fraudulent loans the securities were made from. Countrywide, the mortgage lender acquired by Bank of America in July 2008, was among the worst offenders in abusive sales practices for subprime home loans. No failure of corporate governance was as acutely painful as that of Countrywide; nothing hit closer to home, literally or figuratively, and led to more palpable misery.

In June 2009, Angelo Mozilo, Countrywide's cofounder, CEO, and chairman, was charged by the SEC with fraudulently selling stock for $140 million in gains while he allegedly knew the company was in trouble, yet promoted the stock to the public and used shareholders' money to repurchase his own shares. Over much of his thirty-nine years with Countrywide, Mozilo had been a good salesman and operations manager. He seemed well paired with his cofounder, David Loeb, who served for the first thirty-one years as the CEO and chairman. Loeb acted as the inside strategist and risk monitor, providing a balance to the mercurial Mozilo. After Loeb retired in 2000, however, Mozilo became the very picture of an imperial CEO, thoroughly dominating the board and intimidating employees by personally keeping an eye on who showed up late for work. Countrywide's board provided no check on Mozilo's megalomania, his pay, or his risk taking, especially after the company's stock had appreciated an astounding 23,000 percent from 1982 to 2003—a performance that Mozilo apparently attributed largely to himself. The directors seemed happy just to be along for the ride.

Mozilo often referred to the company as "my baby" and was obsessed with becoming the nation's largest mortgage lender. Against the advice of Countrywide's longtime strategy consultant, Mozilo in mid-2003 publicly set a goal to "dominate" the mortgage market by tripling Countrywide's market share in five years, thus triggering a frenzied plunge into the subprime loans and ethical corruption that blew up the company. The riskiest mortgages paid the highest fees, so Countrywide spun out of control just as it seemed to be minting money. At the company's extravagant offices in the mountains northwest of Los Angeles, the senior executives' suite was decorated with Hudson River School paintings. Mozilo, who drove both a gold Rolls-Royce and a yellow Lamborghini, presided most days at the head of a private dining room table that seated twenty. His low regard for employees was betrayed in an interview with a *New York Times* reporter in 2005, a year after Mozilo had made more than $70 million from salary, bonuses, and gains from exercising stock options and had amassed a net worth of about a half billion dollars. Pointing to the small cubicles with low partitions so that workers could be better observed, Mozilo said, "Whether it's smaller or larger, they adapt, like fish to a fish tank." Countrywide had earlier agreed to settle for $30 million a lawsuit on behalf of employees who said they hadn't been paid for overtime, and then began to expand operations in states like Texas where employment laws were more management-friendly.

A 2006 internal email from Mozilo to Countrywide executives referred to the company's 80-20 loan program, which allowed two separate subprime mortgages to pay the entire cost of a home, as "the most dangerous product in existence and there can be nothing more toxic." Another Mozilo email made the news in 2008 when he accidentally hit "reply" instead of "forward" and sent a message back to Dan Bailey, a desperate North Carolina home owner who was pleading for a hardship loan modification to avoid foreclosure on the 900-square-foot home he had lived in for sixteen years. Mozilo's email, which was meant for internal eyes only, read: "This is unbelievable. Most of these letters now have the same wording. Obviously they are being counseled by some other person or by the Internet. Disgusting."

With the help of millions of shareholders' dollars in lobbying fees, Countrywide remained largely unregulated and grew rapidly to become the nation's largest mortgage lender. One key to its success was ensuring that the government-sponsored mortgage purchaser Fannie Mae continued to buy and assume the default risks on much of the massive volume of loans Countrywide was generating. A confidential VIP program known internally as "Friends of Angelo" provided substantial discounts on fees and interest rates for some U.S. senators, congressional staffers, a state judge, and senior executives at other companies that did businesses with Countrywide, including Fannie Mae's former chairman, its CEO, and other senior executives. By 2006, Countrywide financed nearly one in five residential mortgages in the United States.

Mark Zachary, who had been a regional vice president in Houston, said he was fired after writing to his superiors that the practice of using inflated home appraisals so that buyers could borrow the closing costs, flipping unqualified customers into higher cost loans requiring no documentation, and coaching borrowers to vastly overstate their incomes was "setting people up for further failure in life by putting them in loans and houses they do not belong in." Zachary told a reporter that the unethical practices were condoned by Countrywide's highest leaders: "It comes down, I think from the very top that you get a loan done at any cost."

A lawsuit by the State of California in 2008 charged that "Countrywide was, in essence, a mass-production loan factory, producing ever-increasing streams of debt without regard for borrowers . . . Countrywide Financial used deceptive tactics to push home owners into complicated, risky, and expensive loans so that the company could sell as many loans as possible to third-party investors." The suit was joined by ten other states and later settled for up to $8.68 billion in reduced principal and interest rates on troubled mortgages. Because the suit was settled after Countrywide's sale, most of the costs would come from the pockets of Bank of America's shareholders.

Countrywide paid each of its directors from $344,988 to $538,824 in 2006, more than twice the average for the five hundred largest U.S. corporations, while Mozilo himself made $48 million, not including gains on stock options. The board as a whole met only five times in person that year and held ten meetings via telephone. The seventy-five-year-old lead director, Harley W. Snyder, had been on the board for fifteen years and also chaired the compensation committee, which included former basketball star Oscar Robertson. Two union-affiliated pension groups blew the whistle on them in late 2007. The American Federation of State, County and Municipal Employees (AFSCME), which represents pension funds that held 3.5 percent of Countrywide's stock, called on the compensation committee members to resign. The

CtW Investment Group cited conflicts of interest and excessive directors' pay, while noting that the independent board members had cashed out more than $24 million in stock gains during the two years prior to the housing market crash. This included more than three-quarters of the shares Snyder held, which he sold for $7.2 million. "Directors who are making as much as CEOs make at other companies may lose the perspective of shareholder advocate, and instead blur their self-interest with that of the executive," the Federation's president, Gerald W. McEntee, told the *Los Angeles Times*. CtW's executive director, William Patterson, was even more blunt. In a letter to Snyder on the failure to monitor the CEO, he wrote, "Your excessive compensation, together with your aggressive divestment of your own Countrywide stock at the peak of the housing bubble, militates powerfully against any inclination you might have to lead your fellow independent directors or hold Mr. Mozilo accountable."

In mid-2008, at a conference for corporate directors, one of us spoke briefly with Martin Melone, the former chair of Countrywide's audit and ethics committee, and asked how the company could have justified pushing loans of such doubtful quality as the market was deteriorating. He looked down and quietly replied, "Everyone had to move product." Then, noticing the name tag signifying that he was speaking with a writer, Melone quickly turned away and disappeared into the crowd. Later, another former Countrywide director, who has served on numerous other boards, wrote in an email that he didn't expect significant changes in the corporate governance system to occur until there is real access for shareholders to nominate board candidates.

COUNTRYWIDE SHAREHOLDERS, represented by the board, lost more than $22 billion. The loss was enormous, but the devastation also crushed communities throughout the country in ways almost impossible to fathom.

Princessa Drive is a street of eighteen houses in Palmdale, California, about an hour north of downtown Los Angeles in the high desert near Edwards Air Force Base. It is part of the Bella Vista development, a joint venture financed by Countrywide Financial and KB Homes. Like Countrywide, KB Homes had serious governance problems. KB's CEO and chairman, Bruce Karatz, who was paid $232 million from 2003 to 2005, resigned from the company under fire in 2006, and was indicted for fraud in 2009 for failing to disclose that he had taken millions in shareholders' money by cherrypicking the best times in the past to date the stock options he had been awarded by KB's board. The Bella Vista development had been plopped down in the Antelope Valley's lunar landscape between 2006 and 2007 amid tumbleweeds and cactuses, chock-a-block with other housing tracts with wishfully grand names like Royal View Estates, Wildflower at the Reserve, and The Collections. When Palmdale changed overnight from being one of America's fastest growing cities—its population had grown twelvefold between 1983 and 2006—to one of the hardest hit by the mortgage meltdown, many of the projects stopped dead. They became partially completed houses surrounded by chain-link fencing or were still just dirt graded into quarter-acre lots. The only growth business was the nearby five thousand–inmate maximum security state prison. In 2008, adjacent zip codes in Palmdale and Lancaster, Palmdale's immediate neighbor to the north, had the nation's highest concentration of foreclosures in one small area.

From the "street view" image on Google Maps, Princessa Drive has the look of an intact and perhaps even a flourishing neighborhood—and, by all accounts, that's what it was for most of its first year of existence when the pictures were taken. By late 2008, though, ten of the eighteen houses on the street were in foreclosure or had simply been abandoned after the owners sent "jingle mail" by mailing the keys back to the bank in the mortgage payment envelope. Two others had never been occupied because the owners had bought them without intending to live in them at all—they had acquired them as speculators, expecting to flip them for a quick profit. When one of us visited Princessa Drive four days before Christmas that year, there was a bleak, ghost-town atmosphere to the neighborhood, with few people in view, almost as if a neutron bomb had gone off nearby, wiping out human life and leaving just the buildings. A basketball stand lay on its side in one driveway; lockboxes for keys and plastic bags holding foreclosure notices hung from dozens of doorknobs.

The four- and five-bedroom houses had cost $450,000 to $700,000, and many had been financed entirely with debt, using the now notorious 80-20 Countrywide product with two separate subprime mortgages. They were now worth less than half those amounts, according to Joe Mayol, a local real estate broker whose main business had become coaxing people out of bank-owned houses by offering "cash for keys"—usually a $2,000 payment if the occupant left within twenty-four hours.

Mayol described the "green pool" problem. Swimming pools at abandoned houses had become choked with rotting algae and turned into mosquito breeding pits that public health officials, fearing the spread of West Nile virus, tried to spot from helicopters. An aerial survey in mid-2007 had identified a thousand suspected green pools in the Antelope Valley. Other abandoned houses in the surrounding neighborhoods had been boarded up after methamphetamine labs were discovered in them or to keep out squatters and vandals, who stole the appliances, hardware, outdoor air-conditioning units, and even the flooring. Jimmy Boults, an affable, middle-aged audio-visual technician who was one of the few remaining home owners on Princessa Drive, reminisced about being the first resident to move in. He hosted neighborhood barbecues to welcome new residents and projected movies on a screen in his backyard on summer evenings. But those days ended within a year as the owners disappeared and anonymous tenants who kept to themselves moved in. The houses on either side of Boults's two-story, center-hall colonial were now bank-owned and had been empty for several months. Another with a charred roof on the street behind him was plastered with public-health warning stickers. "The guy who owned it's in jail," he said. "Tried to set it on fire for the insurance when he couldn't sell it."

Two doors down, Linda Gray, an energetic sixty-four-year-old former city worker who had recently retired with her seventy-six-year-old husband, Theodore, opened the door only after determining that it wasn't a bank representative knocking. She had packed their things in boxes in anticipation of being evicted before Christmas. "We'll get three days' notice to be out," she said. The Grays had paid $540,000 for the house after they had been talked into a number of upgrades. She said they could put only $8,000 down and were switched at the closing into an option adjustable-rate mortgage with very low initial payments that they could defer, even though that meant the principal would increase. They didn't discover until the monthly payments had skyrocketed a year later that the mortgage documents had put their income as $140,000 when it was actually $60,000. She also said that KB and Countrywide, as part of the high-pressure sales pitch, claimed they would refinance the house in six months when it would have appreciated significantly. "They said we'd get money back as soon as we refinanced," Gray said. "Instead, the value just started dropping and dropping right away."

In hopes of staying in their home, Gray and her husband were working with a forensic mortgage auditor to find mistakes in the sales documents and evidence of a fraudulently inflated appraisal. "The managers and boards of these mortgage companies are to blame, as well as the regulators," the auditor said. "They just did not do their jobs—period. I mean, that's what you're paying the fees for. When you have people living off $40,000 or so a year who get defrauded and then have their life savings disappear almost overnight, someone needs to be held accountable."

Gray pointed at a house down the street and said that a renter in it had been hauled away by the police a few weeks earlier. "He got caught renting out abandoned houses he didn't own to folks he'd found on Craigslist and by putting up 'Cheap rent!' flyers in laundromats. He'd collect the first and last months' rent, a security deposit, and tell them they'd have to use the broken garage entrance until he could get new front door keys made." She shook her head and looked up and down Princessa Drive. "They said this was going to be the next Beverly Hills. It sounded like our dream come true, but it's turned into a nightmare—and it's not over yet."

IT IS ASTONISHING how far you can be from the boardrooms of companies that triggered the economic meltdown and still find victims who suffered devastating losses. While two-thirds of the estimated $4.1 trillion in bad loans and securities originated in the United States, many of the investors who bought them, placing their trust in the good faith of our financial institutions' leaders, are overseas. The losses these investors have sustained may be surpassed only by the resulting damage to America's reputation in the global markets and by the investors' fears of being burned again. Here, for example, is the story of dozens of small towns, churches, and charities in the Australian outback that are unlikely to be making the same mistake anytime soon.

Grange Securities was an Australian investment bank that served as a financial advisor to many of the country's small municipalities and nonprofits whose guidelines required conservative investments. In January 2007, Lehman Brothers, seeking new global markets for the billions in exotic securities it was creating, bought Grange for $95 million. Jesse Bhattal, Lehman's Asia chief executive, sounded more like a military commander than a business leader at a news conference in Sydney announcing Lehman's strategy: "This acquisition is about setting up a beachhead, and we will play in the next five years or so a dominant role . . . which will be both aggressive and at the same time very focused."

Part of that aggression was focused on selling risky securities to town councils and charities while playing highly conflicted roles as a promoter, advisor, and investment manager. Lehman sales representatives were "laughed out of offices across Sydney when making their pitch to institutional investors, but the councils say they were unaware of the risks," financial experts told the *Sydney Morning Herald*.

The small, rural community of Parkes, for example, was facing $9.2 million in exposure to Grange CDOs that its council had been assured were safe and liquid. The CDOs had lost 90 percent of their value by the fall of 2008. A report in *Euromoney* magazine said that Parkes was "among some of the 150-odd Australian councils, churches, universities, charities, hospitals, and community groups nursing a $2 billion black eye after buying now-toxic collateralized debt obligations from Grange. Some observers believe the exposure could go much higher, wasting years of rural thrift at the worst possible time in Australian agricultural history as the country copes with a crippling decade-long drought." Some thirty

Australian communities and individuals were suing Lehman's bankruptcy estate but were in the back of the line with other "contingent creditors" who were being offered 5.6 cents on the dollar by the bankruptcy administrators. In the meantime, the communities worried about how they would pay for essential services like roads, garbage collection, and water projects.

"The whole process was cynical and corrupt from top to bottom," Michael West, the Australian business columnist who broke much of the story on the Lehman CDOs, told us. "Lehman was manipulating these unsophisticated clients as a supposed advisor while making millions in profits dumping toxic securities on them. They even set up a secondary market to trade the dodgy CDOs among the councils, churning some of their accounts twice over. I think the Lehman bankers knew exactly how big the risks were on what they were flogging and didn't care because they were dazzled by the fees. Lehman's board should have known and stopped it, but they clearly had no idea what was going on."

SO WHO PAYS for bad corporate governance? The answer, of course, is that we all do. Except perhaps for two categories of people: the CEOs, who leave with millions of dollars in their accumulated salaries and bonuses, deferred compensation, stock options and retirement packages—and often with board seats awaiting them at other companies; and the directors themselves, who escape liability and even blame because so little is expected of them within their companies—the legal system absolves them, and the shareholders, as well as all the rest of us affected so profoundly by their failures, often don't even know who they are.

3

Networks of Power

ACCORDING TO AN air force fact sheet, the F-22A Raptor fighter jet provides "an exponential leap in war-fighting capabilities that cannot be matched by any known or projected fighter aircraft." Retired general Richard Myers could be thought of in virtually the same way—as a new class of board member with the ability to stealthily navigate the corridors of government at high speed. He can deliver maximum impact on strategic and tactical missions, projecting Northrop Grumman power in the public, private, and military sectors of society. He also projects United Technologies power. And Aon Corporation power. And Deere & Co. power. He sits on all four boards.

Until 2005, Myers served as chairman of the Joint Chiefs of Staff, retiring after forty years' service near the pinnacle of an enterprise, the Defense Department (DOD), that then employed 3 million workers at 5,000 locations and commanded a $400 billion budget. A DOD website explicitly compares the department to a private company: "If the President is our CEO, and the Congress is our Board of Directors, then our stockholders are the

American people. We exist to protect these citizen stockholders, for without their support we would be out of business." Myers's shift into the private sector was not unusual. All five joint chiefs who exited between 2002 and 2007 joined corporate boards, mostly in the defense industry. It is a lucrative move. At his peak as a general, Myers earned only $215,000; in 2008, he collected $915,000 in directors' fees.

Richard Myers is a notable member of what Wharton Business School professor Michael Useem describes as an "Inner Circle," an elite at the top of multinational corporations that extends far beyond Wall Street financial services. As business becomes less regional and ever more centralized, nationally and internationally, it is characterized by a larger and more powerful web of interconnected personal relationships among people with common interests. The corporate elite apply their time and energy inside and outside the corporate sphere, Useem explains, "whether it be support for political candidates, consultation with the highest levels of national administration, public defense of the 'free enterprise system,' or the governance of foundations and universities."

The small universe of board members constitutes a de facto club with self-perpetuating power, largely invisible even to the people on whom they have enormous impact. Most are already wealthy and as directors are well compensated, in fees and stock options, for their time. The average S&P 500 director received $212,750 in 2009. Directors say they aren't in it for the money—they are attracted by the chance to learn about other businesses, to make connections, or to remain actively involved after retirement. The majority are senior executives of other companies, current or former officers of the company itself (usually limited to the CEO and, less often, the chief financial officer), academics—often college presidents or business school professors—and former government officials. More than two-thirds of them are older white men.

There has been some improvement in gender and ethnic diversity, but even so, fewer than one in seven of the directors of large American companies are female, and nearly a quarter of boards do not have a single member of an ethnic minority. The women and minority members who do get selected are often "overboarded." That is, the same people serve on so many boards that it becomes difficult for them to be truly effective. A classic example is Vernon Jordan, the prominent African American lawyer, who while helping Monica Lewinsky to find a job, was simultaneously on ten corporate boards, while his wife, Ann, was on five. The *Washington Post* calculated that Jordan, who was also a full-time partner at the Akin Gump law firm (which happened to represent eight of the ten firms on whose boards he sat) was obligated to attend eighty-four board meetings and fifty-seven committee meetings a year, in addition to duties at his own firm and elsewhere. Former Green Bay Packers star Willie Davis, who after his football days got an MBA and founded a company that owns twenty-one radio stations, has served on as many as eleven boards at the same time, including those of Kmart, Johnson Controls, Dow Chemical, L.A. Gear, Alliance Bank, Metro-Goldwyn-Mayer, and Manpower.

Or consider Wendy Gramm, the former chair of the Commodity Futures Trading Commission and wife of former senator Phil Gramm. Ms. Gramm left government in 1993 and immediately joined Enron's board—just six weeks after she had shepherded a ruling through the commission exempting Enron's energy futures trading from government regulation. As a member of Enron's audit and compliance committee, she had a particular responsibility to examine financial risks and prevent conflicts of interest. Gramm attended the Enron board meeting of June 28, 1999, via a pay phone on the side of a road in northern Virginia, with a handful of faxed background papers rustling in the wind. Her sworn statement to investigators noted that she was having trouble hearing the discussion as she and the rest of the board hastily approved a waiver of conflict-of-interest rules so that CFO Andrew Fastow could run the first of the off-balance-sheet partnerships that led to Enron's spectacular collapse. Shareholders ultimately lost $90 billion. In late 2000, Gramm's husband pushed through a bill without committee hearings that led to further deregulation of energy markets. As a result, Enron was able to manipulate electricity prices, and within six months of the bill's enactment Enron helped trigger thirty-eight artificially created blackouts in California and Washington State that cost ratepayers nearly $11 billion. While serving as an Enron director, where she was estimated to have been paid between $915,000 and $1,853,000 from 1993 to 2001, Gramm wrote an op-ed piece for the *Wall Street Journal* entitled "The Good That Derivatives Do," saying, "If another major default or market shock occurs, we must all resist the urge to find scapegoats, or to overregulate what we just do not understand."

Wendy Gramm had also been a director of State Farm Insurance Co., IBP, Inc., the Chicago Mercantile Exchange, and INVESCO Funds Group, Inc., although she left all of her boards in the wake of the Enron scandal and remained the chairman of regulatory studies for the Mercatus Center, a conservative think tank at George Mason University that received $60,000 in donations from Enron and its CEO Ken Lay, including $45,000 while she served as a director. She apparently did not see the irony in a letter she sent to the SEC in 2003 opposing a proposal that would have allowed shareholders greater say in nominating board members: "Boards who consistently operate at variance with shareholder interests (i.e., who do not maximize share values) will see the values of their firm's shares fall, other things equal," she wrote. "As the shares become cheaper, the firm becomes a more attractive target for takeover. Even barring takeover (because of, say, a poison pill provision), a persistent abuse of shareholders interests must eventually result in bankruptcy. In either instance, assets will be stripped from the self-dealing board's control and surrendered to others who may be better able to enhance share values. Indeed, the recent spate of corporate scandals has, if anything, provided vivid testimony as to how quickly and efficiently this market process works in practice."

Jordan, Davis, and Gramm at least had professional credentials for serving on boards. Other directors, many of them athletes and entertainment celebrities, are selected simply because they are well known. O. J. Simpson served on the audit committee of Infinity Broadcasting and was a director of a company that imported Swiss Army knives before resigning from both boards shortly after being charged with his ex-wife's murder. Former NFL quarterback and television host Fran Tarkington served on the Coca-Cola Enterprises board and its audit committee before he settled with the SEC over allegations of an $8 million accounting fraud at a company he ran. Also a Coca-Cola Enterprises director at the same time was former Olympic ski champion Jean-Claude Killy. Lance Armstrong left the board of Morgans Hotel Group in early 2008 after missing every single one of the eleven board meetings the previous year and collecting $71,644 in fees and stock. Elvis's ex-wife, the actress and fragrance promoter Priscilla Presley, was a director of Metro-Goldwyn-Mayer Inc., where she served on the compensation committee.

Retired military leaders or former government officials may have useful contacts, especially for companies seeking federal contracts or other help in Washington, but most have little if any business experience to bring to the boardroom. Former general Tommy Franks and Admiral Joseph Prueher both resigned as Bank of America directors in June 2009 amid questions about board members' lack of financial expertise. Both had been on the audit committee, where they were charged with monitoring the integrity of financial statements, internal controls, and regulatory compliance. The convicted former New York City police commissioner Bernard Kerik made more than $6.2 million from stock options during his two and a half years as a director of the stun gun manufacturer Taser International. Former vice president Dan Quayle was on the audit committee of the toilet manufacturer American Standard. Former president Gerald Ford served on the Travelers Group board until he was eighty-five. Ford juggled numerous other directorships, reportedly with one nonnegotiable understanding—that the companies hold their meetings during the same week so that they would not interfere with his golf schedule.

AMERICA LACKS the traditional basis for social classes: tribal affiliations (if you stay off Native American reservations), a feudal system, monarchs and their kin, castes, state religions, and the like. While the American Revolution was fomented overwhelmingly by the merchant class, the mythology of our national birth rests on freedom and liberty, and the noble egalitarian philosophies of Locke, Rousseau, Hume, and Paine. Social class is almost unmentionable in America.

G. William Domhoff, a sociologist at the University of California at Santa Cruz, has studied American elites and power structures for forty years. "Americans as a group are reluctant to acknowledge the existence of the power elite," he says, "but the rich are in fact a very cohesive group that attends the same schools, goes to the same clubs, vacations at the same summer resorts, and shares a view of the world." In fact, in a nation of 300 million, great power is vested in about 3 people per 100,000. Admission to that group from the lower ranks is not impossible, but once having arrived, the newly elite are usually quickly assimilated and take on the attitudes and customs of their elite peers. Many of them end up serving at some point as public company directors.

It is instructive to look at the transfer of wealth upward since the Reagan years, carrying on through the Clinton terms, and accelerated by the Bush tax cuts. The promise was that a rising tide would lift all boats, but some proved too anchored to the bottom of the sea. Researchers at the Federal Reserve Bank of Chicago found that wealth in the United States "is highly concentrated and very unequally distributed: the richest 1 percent hold one third of the total wealth in the economy." This is the third-worst maldistribution among the thirty countries that belong to the Organisation for Economic Co-operation and Development (OECD). Almost all this wealth has been generated by corporate activities. Apart from any moral or ethical issues, the current recession has finally made it clear to everyone except the most doctrinaire free-marketeers that the magnitude of this maldistribution puts a tremendous brake on economic recovery. The people at the top simply cannot purchase enough to accomplish what is required.

In his 1956 book *The Power Elite,* C. Wright Mills presented an influential theory about the distribution of power in America. To Mills, most public policy decisions and many determinants of our quality of life stem from the actions and decisions of a small group of interconnected elites in the military, political, and corporate sectors. He saw no conspiracy. Rather, the commonality of goals, backgrounds, values, and views suffices to create the same effect. Mills focused particularly on what President Dwight Eisenhower termed the military-industrial complex in his famous farewell address.

Mills saw the corporate and political elites engaged with the military in a symbiotically supportive and unbounded relationship, with overlapping interests and interchangeable memberships, and he argued that this military-political-economic elite was ultimately driving all public policy decisions. He wrote:

> As the means of information and of power are centralized, some men come to occupy positions in American society from which they can look down upon, so to speak, and by their decisions mightily affect the everyday worlds of ordinary men and women.
>
> At the top of the economy, among the corporate rich, there are the chief executives; at the top of the political order, the members of the political directorate; at the top of the military establishment, the elite of soldier-statesmen clustered in and around the Joint Chiefs of Staff and the upper echelon. As each of these domains has coincided with the others, as decisions tend to become total in their consequence, the leading men in each of the three domains of power—the warlords, the corporation chieftains, the political directorate—tend to come together, to form the power elite of America.

In the years since, some analysts of the power structure in the country argue that the political and corporate spheres of power have come to dominate in this triumvirate. William Domhoff says, "In the post–World War II era, the military became part of the elite in terms of the way they work. But they are very secondary. The civilians at the top of DOD pick who will be a general. They pick where we are going to go. They pick the countries we go into. The power is between the corporate guys and the political guys." The secretary of defense must be a civilian at least ten years out of the service, and the congressional funding apparatus is entirely civilian as well.

Mills placed the military atop the other two elites—political and economic. Domhoff departs from Mills by pointing to the primacy of business over *both* the military and political sectors. By now, no one doubts the dominant role played by corporate campaign contributions and lobbyists in the American electoral, legislative, and regulatory processes, as well as the revolving door between public and private employment.

Corporations' share of defense spending remains enormous. America's top five defense contractors took in $135 billion in DOD funds in 2008. Defense spending was 43 percent of the overall federal budget's $1.14 trillion in discretionary spending, and these contractors got 28 percent of the defense budget. Two of them, Raytheon and Lockheed Martin, were dependent on the government for more than 90 percent of their revenue.

What has changed, however, is the depth of the corporate ties into the Pentagon, and the increasing direct dominance of businessmen over career military brass. While Mills's focus was on the soldier-statesman, today we see the ascent of the soldier-businessman. The career of Donald H. Rumsfeld is one of the starkest examples of how this operates. At Princeton Rumsfeld roomed with Frank Carlucci, another future secretary of defense and corporate leader. (Carlucci served on the boards of twenty for-profit companies and twelve nonprofits while also chairing the Carlyle Group, the powerful private equity firm that has made many of its investments in the defense industry.) Rumsfeld then touched all the bases described by Mills: naval aviator, congressman, White House staffer, NATO ambassador, defense secretary, and for a quarter of a century, the CEO of two corporations and board member for eight. When he first left government service in 1977, he became CEO of G.D. Searle pharmaceuticals. The patent on one of Searle's largest profit makers, the birth control pill Enovid, had lapsed. The company desperately wanted to get the artificial sweetener Aspartame through the FDA, even though the agency had been blocking the drug for fifteen years because of its alleged links to cancer. With help from the new Reagan administration the FDA fell into line and rapidly approved it. Rumsfeld oversaw the sale of Searle to Monsanto, and five years later went to General Instrument, a defense contractor, as CEO, and next became the board chairman at Gilead, a biotech company that holds the rights to Tamiflu, an antiviral drug that is stockpiled by the government in case of bioterrorism or epidemics, and whose board has included former secretary of state George Shultz, the former HUD secretary and U.S. trade representative Carla Hills, and Gayle Edlund Wilson, the wife of former California governor Pete Wilson. From there, George W. Bush chose Rumsfeld to run the Defense Department, where he attempted to put the defense of the nation on a more businesslike footing. Under Rumsfeld's tenure, private contractors came to outnumber soldiers in Iraq.

This was part of a much broader outsourcing. According to R. J. Hillhouse, an expert on espionage outsourcing, the ratio of contractors to employees at the CIA's National Clandestine Service—the "heart, brains, and soul" of the spy agency—is now 1:1, and many government employees are tasked with simply signing off on employment contracts with large corporations.

The revolving door from the private sector into government and back out again has continued to spin in recent years. The Clinton administration brought 16 corporate directors into top government positions upon taking office in 1992. The Bush administration brought in 73 who sat on 133 boards. The number of Washington lobbyists doubled in a decade to around 30,000 people, and the expenditures for lobbying have also doubled. They have gone from providing information and a lot of money to politicians, to dumping huge amounts of money and actually drafting large chunks of important legislation for congressional staffers. More than 230 former congressmen are registered lobbyists—

including almost half of those eligible who have left Congress in the past decade. The *Washington Post* reported that one lobbying firm said that it calculated that "for every $1 million its clients spend on its services, it delivers, on average, $100 million in government benefits." A much scuffed line divides lobbyists and legislators.

Favors and back scratching are difficult to trace if they are granted in private on boards, committees, at country clubs and social events. Or they can be official business. The Security and Prosperity Partnership of North America is led by the president of the United States and his counterparts from Canada and Mexico and was inaugurated in 2005 to increase cooperation among the three countries on security and trade. In 2006, the Partnership created the North American Competitiveness Council consisting of thirty CEOs, ten from each country, including the heads of Ford, Merck, General Electric, Walmart, and Chevron. The Council meets annually in closed-door sessions with government officials. Ron Covais, the president of the Americas for Lockheed Martin and a former Pentagon advisor to Dick Cheney, chaired one of the Council's early meetings and later told a reporter, "The guidance from the ministers was, 'Tell us what we need to do and we'll make it happen.'" Corvais suggested that rather than going through the legislative process in any country, the council's agenda would be implemented in incremental changes by executive agencies, bureaucrats, and regulators. "We've decided not to recommend any things that would require legislative changes because we won't get anywhere," Corvais said.

It is sometimes impossible to separate the corporations from the politicians who make policy. Take the case of the Pentagon contract for a new fleet of aerial refueling tankers. Through most of the past decade, the air force has been negotiating on the purchase of 179 of these aircraft to be built over twenty years for around $40 billion (though today's projected sticker price should not be taken seriously). Presumably the Pentagon would seek to buy the best aircraft at the best price for the taxpayers' huge outlay. After several years of wrangling, it awarded the contract to a combine of Northrop Grumman and EADS/Airbus out of Europe. Boeing took the news hard and launched the lobbyist Richard Gephardt, the former Democratic House majority and minority leader and now a director of five companies, to lobby for a change. In response, Northrop Grumman and EADS turned to the newly amicable Breaux Lott Leadership Group, run by Trent Lott, the Republican former Senate majority leader, and John Breaux, retired Democratic deputy whip of the Senate and Finance Committee member, who is a director at CSX Corporation, which was formerly run by ex-Treasury secretary John Snow. Breaux is a consultant to Cerberus Capital Management, which is now run by Snow and where former vice president Dan Quayle chairs an international division. Later in 2008, EADS upped the ante by naming Lott to the board of its North American subsidiary.

If this is beginning to sound like a phone booth stuffed with former politicians and thousand-dollar bills, it gets even more crowded. EADS also added to its board of directors Franklin Miller, a former Bush White House staffer and a "senior counselor" from former defense secretary William Cohen's Cohen Group lobbyists. The Cohen Group has a high-level alliance with the 3,700-attorney law firm DLA Piper. Senior counsel to DLA Piper is the same Richard Gephardt who was retained by Boeing to lobby against EADS, Lott, and Breaux for those tankers. DLA Piper's nonexecutive board chairman at the time was former U.S. senator George Mitchell. Mitchell is, or recently has been, a director of Disney, FedEx, Staples, Starwood Hotels & Resorts, Unilever, UnumProvident, and Xerox—and at one point was serving on at least eight public company boards at the same time.

If these people did not know one another through their prior government service (and indeed they did), their connections would suffice to advance almost any corporate initiative. If, in a hypothetical example, Richard Myers's colleagues at Northrop needed a favor in Japan, the CEO could call William Cohen or George Mitchell, who could call the head of Disney Japan, or FedEx, or Starwood, who would in turn get in touch with a person in charge of that company's Tokyo office. A call from the CEO's office, initiated by a former head of the Joint Chiefs and a board member, is usually received with a certain urgency. Follow-through would be an excellent career move, and in the scheme of things might generate an outstanding chit for later repayment. Critically important, the relationships transcend formal party affiliations. Cohen, a lifelong Republican, served in Bill Clinton's cabinet, and John Breaux and Trent Lott were often at loggerheads in a Senate that lacked cooperative leadership. Their subsequent relationships have somehow managed to overcome political partisanship.

The cost in the case of the aerial refueling tankers may be more than a matter of money. The contract became so mired in political wrangling that the matter has still not, as of late 2010, been concluded, which means that the manufacturing of the badly needed planes is being delayed. The battle took a dramatic turn when, in June 2008, a Government Accounting Office report backed Boeing's claims of a flawed bidding process. Some speculated that the decision was due to the fact that the air force had feared retribution from Senator John McCain, who reportedly helped terminate numerous air force careers over the F-22 fighter contract. Several McCain staffers have relationships with EADS/Northrop. Representative John Murtha, no stranger to scandal, then got involved and tried to get the contract awarded to both sides, but the air force feared that a nightmare of oversight would ensue. A year later, Secretary of Defense Gates reopened the bidding, and the battle was joined by more politicians and lobbyists. An air force officer commented, "For every year or two that we delay up front, that means that we fly these things past 2040 and that means the KC-135 [the current tanker] is over eighty years old. It's unconscionable that we're asking people to fly in combat in fifty-year-old airframes."

MEMBERSHIP ON A CORPORATE BOARD—or, as is so often the case, on several—offers one of the most coveted forms of connection into the inner circle of power. "A sparse network of a few powerful directors controls all major appointments in Fortune 1000 companies," Albert-Lászlό Barabási, a physics professor at Notre Dame who studies network effects, says with only slight exaggeration. "Understanding network effects becomes the key to survival in a rapidly evolving new economy." Of course, these networks are vastly deeper, wider, and more entangled than can be conveyed by the mapping of interlocking directorships. Other connections are made through colleges, fraternities, social and country clubs, industry associations, former board members, political action committees, think tanks, charities, common friends, and former work associations. Literally impossible to document or track, these links would not appear in most studies, and thus the estimates of board connectedness are probably seriously understated.

Researchers have tried to describe and quantify these sorts of relationships using the tools provided by the relatively new discipline of social network theory. The essential idea behind network theory was popularized by the film *Six Degrees of Separation* and what became known as the Kevin Bacon game, but it is also a full-fledged science that has been applied to problems ranging from epidemiology to the dispersion of inventions. Network theorists measure, for example, how many boards Person A would have to go through to reach a stranger, Person B, on some other board. The answer to that question, by the way, using only formal board interlocks, in 1999 was approximately 3.5, but it is, of course, actually fewer because of myriad informal connections. In the corporate sphere, academics have found solid statistical evidence of the influence of such links on questions such as what anti-takeover defense to use and which stock exchange to list on. The theory can be applied as well to charitable giving, political activism, business strategies, financial leverage, and hiring decisions, among other things.

For most of the twentieth century, bankers were the interlocks that glued boards together. J.P. Morgan bank directors held seventy-two board seats at forty-seven companies in 1914. In the twenty-first century, however, commercial banks have lost most of their "centrality" (or connectedness) in the board world. In 1982, nine of the ten companies with the most interlocked directors were banks, but by 1999 only one bank survived on that top-10 list. During that period, a third of the biggest companies had disappeared each decade, either through mergers, acquisitions, or bankruptcy. Vast numbers of directors retired. Only 2 percent kept their seats at the same companies. Nevertheless, the degree of connectedness among directors remained virtually the same. It's not very hard for one person on a board to get to someone on another board.

Boards are, by their very nature, tight networks that span outside the corporation. A 2002 University of Texas study of 4,000 people who served on for-profit and nonprofit boards, as well as on government committees, revealed "substantial linkages within organizations and elites within and across the three sectors." Interlocks grow from multiple affiliations, and these affiliations serve a purpose. "You're damn right it's helpful to be on several boards," one director told Michael Useem. "It extends the range of your network and acquaintances, and your experience. That's why you go on a board, to get something as well as give."

Many directors and executives take leading roles in the community and frequently apply their corporations' largesse to their own nonprofit organizations and those of fellow directors. Nonprofits are perpetually in need of money and consequently seek to staff boards with wealthy people who have wealthy networks. Money begets money, and power begets power. Sometimes, though, the charitable inclinations of those atop our corporate system are not quite what they seem. David Yermack, a professor of finance at New York University, studied million-dollar-plus charitable gifts by chairmen and CEOs to their own family foundations. By making such gifts, they could get tax write-offs, but keep voting control of the stock. By timing the gifts, they can maximize the value of the tax deduction. Yermack found "a pattern of excellent timing" and noted that on average these gifts "occur at peaks in company stock prices, following run-ups and just before significant price drops." The graphs of the contributions form an inverted V for two months around the gift date, suggesting either legal insider trading or illegal backdating. Stock gifts by chairmen and CEOs to all other recipients besides family foundations "are also well timed." Even here, the power of an elite corporate position affords advantages unavailable to other people.

THE AVERAGE BOARD at a major American corporation today has 10.8 members. For all the changes in the makeup of the population of businesspeople in the United States over the last half century, with so many more women and minorities reaching the ranks of management, a simple fact remains true: if you put one hundred board directors in a big paper bag and plucked one out at random, there would be about an 85 percent chance that you'd have a white male, probably about sixty years old.

The resilience of the culture of boards has held up despite efforts to substantially change their makeup. The biggest reform has been the requirement that boards must have a majority of outside directors—people who do not work for the company and can therefore bring independent and unbiased judgment to decision making. During President Eisenhower's day, only one in five directors was independent. Today, 82 percent of directors at S&P 500 companies are nominally "independent." But independence has always been a deceptive term. Traditionally, "outside" directors were patently interested parties: the company's lawyer, an ex-CEO or former chairman, a large customer or supplier, the firm's investment banker, possibly a founding family member, or a close friend of the CEO/chairman. Today, after the debacles at Enron, WorldCom, HealthSouth, and many other companies, people with major business relationships to a firm cannot be considered independent. In 2003, the SEC approved new rules by both the New York Stock Exchange and NASDAQ requiring a majority of outside directors, and various bodies required all-independents on nominating, audit, and compensation committees. In practice, however, the binding baseline definitions of independence as set by the exchanges are formal check-the-box criteria, and in this spirit do very little to guarantee independence of thought. If you were a quarterback at Princeton, and you wanted to nominate your running back, who had been the best man at your wedding and who golfed with you every Sunday for twenty years, your nominee would qualify as "independent" for purposes of the regulations.

James Westphal of the University of Michigan, who studies the behavior of directors, thinks the recent changes have actually altered very little. "My sense is that there has not been broad-based change," he said. "I still think a major rule in making selections is whether the person is a good fit with the group, someone the CEO can get along with." As Warren Buffett wrote in his letter to stockholders in 2003, "True independence—meaning the willingness to challenge a forceful CEO when something is wrong or foolish—is an enormously valuable trait in a director. It is also rare." Some directors don't wish to appear foolish by asking questions. Others don't want to rock the boat for fear of ostracism. Sometimes the desire for collegiality seems much more immediate than the need to represent shareholders who are not in the room.

Women on boards are under extra pressure to "get along." Cecily Cannan Selby, once the national executive director of the Girl Scouts of America, became Avon's first female director. Avon had marketed exclusively to women since 1886. Early in her tenure, amid a tense atmosphere at a premeeting dinner, one of the directors offered her a cigar. "When I accepted," she remembered, "I could feel them all relax."

The percentage of women directors, for all the talk of diversity, has stagnated during the past several years after making significant progress from single digits during the mid-1990s. A 2009 Catalyst survey of the Fortune 500 companies showed only 15.2 percent of board seats were held by women, a slight improvement from 14.8 percent in the prior year, while the number of companies with no women directors at all increased from fifty-nine to sixty-six. About 10 percent of S&P 1000 boards have no women directors, a third have only one woman director, and another 40 percent have but two. A 2006 study entitled "Critical Mass on Corporate Boards: Why Three or More Women Enhance Governance" found enormous benefits to boards from having at least three female directors because they would be less likely to be marginalized. According to the study, women directors make three key contributions that men are less likely to make: "They broaden boards' discussions to include the concerns of a wider set of stakeholders, including shareholders, employees, customers, and the community at large; they are more persistent than male directors in pursuing answers to difficult questions; and they often bring a more collaborative approach to leadership, which improves communication among directors and between the board and management." The number of companies with three or more women board directors increased from eighty-three in 2007 to ninety-two in 2008. Women of color held just 3.2 percent of all Fortune 500 directorships while making up slightly more than one-fifth of women directors.

There is a similar dearth of African Americans, Hispanics, and Asians on boards. According to a report issued by the Executive Leadership Council in July 2009, African Americans comprise only 7.4 percent of the Fortune 500 directorships (a percentage that has fallen from 8.1 percent in 2004) and 39 percent of the boards have no African American members.

Nineteen percent of boards are all white. Of the 278 African American directors at other companies, 67 serve on two boards and 28 on three or more boards. (Until 1964, when Samuel Pierce joined the U.S. Industries board, there were no African American directors whatsoever at Fortune 500 companies.)

Hispanics are even more underrepresented on boards than African Americans. A 2007 study conducted by the Hispanic Association on Corporate Responsibility showed that 71 percent of Fortune 500 companies do not have a single Latino or Latina on their boards. They hold only 3.1 percent of board seats despite representing 14.2 percent of the population, and only twenty-five of the companies have two or more Hispanic board members. A 2007 report on directors of Asian ethnicity showed that only 1.5 percent of the Fortune 500 board seats were held by Asians.

Once at the table, though, it's not necessarily easy for minorities. "When African Americans get on a board, we are finding that they are happy to be there but feel uncomfortable rocking the boat. They don't want to be typecast as a 'civil rights director,'" John W. Rogers, Jr., chairman of Ariel Investments and cofounder of the Black Corporate Directors Conference, said. "If the few of us who have the good fortune to be in the boardroom are uncomfortable bringing up race issues, they're not going to be raised and we won't make a difference."

That the average board member is about sixty-one years old makes a certain amount of sense. Board members are supposed to be chosen on the basis of relevant business knowledge and connections, and these qualities take time to acquire. In the past decade, the number of boards with an average age of sixty-four years or more has increased from 14 percent to 26 percent. New directors now start at an average age of fifty-seven. And getting people off boards is almost always a ticklish process. Boards have increasingly mandated retirement ages, and by the time a director reaches seventy-five years of age, there's a 90 percent chance he will retire. But boards can, and frequently do, bend the rules to extend the tenures of directors whom they want to retain. The record holder is likely Charles Stewart Mott, who was elected to the board of General Motors in 1913 (the year Ford introduced the first moving assembly line) and was still serving when he died, sixty years later. The age of directors, of course, does not necessarily mean that they slumber through board meetings, but older directors may not be as attuned to changes in the culture and market as would be desired. As MIT professor Peter Senge described the problem, "New insights fail to get put into practice because they conflict with deeply held internal images of how the world works, images that limit us to familiar ways of thinking and acting." He cited GM's leaders, who believed people bought cars based on styling, not quality or reliability. This flawed thinking opened up the door to Japanese imports.

Even as the times and business models have changed, elites have endured. It would be unrealistic, however, to believe every director's career is spent blissfully swapping favors and exercising power and influence. In fact, the job of corporate director has become much more intensive (if not always more meaningful), and it can occasionally trap well-intentioned people in dire situations. As a result, some potentially good candidates are now refusing board nominations and others are taking a much closer look at the companies recruiting them. A cautionary case in point is the nightmare experience of consummate Washington and corporate insider Roderick Hills when he joined the Chiquita Brands board and found that the September 11 attacks had temporarily disrupted the normal ties connecting the corporate and government elites, while exposing some of what remains business as usual.

Rod Hills has a gilt-edged corporate and government résumé replete with moderate Republican credentials. The quintessential A-list board member, he has been clerk to a Supreme Court justice, cofounder of a law firm with Warren Buffett's partner Charles Munger, White House counsel, SEC chairman at age forty-four, and former CEO of Peabody Coal Company. His wife, Carla, has degrees from Stanford, Oxford, and Yale, was secretary of HUD and the U.S. trade representative. She is now or has been on boards of Gilead Sciences, JPMorgan Chase, the Coca-Cola Company, Rolls-Royce, AIG, Time Warner, Chevron, and Lucent.

Hills bemusedly describes himself as a man who gets called in to clean up other people's messes. When the corporate giant WasteManagement overstated earnings by $3 billion, Hills was asked to join the board to straighten out the company's books and governance. He also helped tidy up Sunbeam and Federal

Mogul. As Drexel Burnham Lambert got itself into trouble, Hills was asked to join the board to run the audit committee. He has served on sixteen boards since leaving government service in 1980.

Hills entered the boardroom of Chiquita Brands in March 2002, after the Cincinnati-based company had emerged from Chapter 11 bankruptcy. Chiquita had borrowed large sums to expand capacity, gambling that the European Union would change its quota system to permit Chiquita to export more bananas. That didn't happen, and then Chiquita ran out of cash. Hills was asked to run the audit committee, and he immediately replaced management's choice of auditors with one he felt would do a better job. His routine cleanup was brief, because in April 2003 he received a call from the company's general counsel, Robert Olson, who apologized for dropping a "hot potato" in Hills's lap. Olson said that Chiquita had been making illegal payments to a violent, right-wing paramilitary group called the United Self-Defense Forces of Colombia (AUC in Spanish). Between 1997 and 2007, nearly 4,000 murders and sixty-two massacres were attributed to AUC. The payments had been going on since 1997, but on September 10, 2001, the federal government had designated the AUC a terrorist organization, which made the payments illegal. Chiquita had long disclosed the payments to its auditors; they were no secret to Hills or anyone else at the top. Olson claimed he had been unaware of the change in their legality until February 20, 2003, when an in-house lawyer found the bad news on the internet. The company had also made protection payments—legal at the time—to the left-wing radical group FARC (Revolutionary Armed Forces of Colombia), but claims to have stopped them in 1997 when FARC was put on a terrorist list. AUC carried out thousands of executions, rapes, and murders, and also moved from political violence into extortion and drug running. It would sweep in at night and butcher families or entire villages. Torture and decapitations were common. Some of these attacks were conducted against Chiquita employees on company property, and the group extorted payments for workers' safety.

As Hills explained it, the monetary payments were a way of life. "It was our clear understanding that every plantation owner in Colombia and many other companies were making the same kinds of payments that Chiquita was making. There were a lot of U.S. companies doing that." It did not help when the docks of Chiquita's Colombian subsidiary Banadex had apparently been used to route thousands of AK-47 rifles and millions of rounds of ammunition from Nicaraguan army arsenals through an intermediary and into the AUC's hands on November 8, 2001.

Shortly after learning of the situation, Hills used his contacts and tried to remedy Chiquita's problem in a way that had worked twenty-five years before: he walked into the U.S. Justice Department to "self-disclose" and ask for guidance. Hills had instituted such a gentlemanly procedure while running the SEC during the foreign bribery scandals of the 1970s. As his son-in-law was a high-ranking official in the DOJ's criminal division and had to recuse himself, Hills went to see the assistant attorney general Michael Chertoff, who would become more famous some months later for his role as head of Homeland Security. But Chertoff was already well known to Hills. He had served as an attorney at Latham & Watkins while Hills was a partner there in the early '80s. To this day, the two men disagree about key details of their discussions at their initial meeting in 2003 regarding the payments to AUC. Hills says the company offered to pull out of Colombia but wanted to minimize disruption. They talked cloak and dagger: a sting operation and collaboration with other antiterrorism agencies would provide more information about AUC, but it would take time to set up. If Chiquita pulled out, Hills said, it feared destabilizing the region and putting its workers at risk. Hills offered to go to the National Security Council, but Chertoff, Hills claimed, said he would do so himself. "They were looking for clarity and direction from that meeting, and they came away not feeling as though they got it," said a Chiquita attorney. "They left there feeling that the department was going to consider what was going on. They waited."

Chertoff never did get back to anyone, though. Within days of that meeting, he was named to the bench of the U.S. Third Circuit Court of Appeals, and from there he went on to become the head of Homeland Security. The Bush Justice Department decided to launch a legal offensive, and the four-year battle that ensued could have sent the distinguished Mr. Hills to prison for life in America or gotten him extradited to Colombia for trial as an accessory to murder.

Prosecution of the vigor Hills and Chiquita faced would have been utterly unimaginable to the United Fruit Company, Chiquita's original name. Its history shows us the concentric circles in which the elite have long operated. For most of the twentieth century, United Fruit and a few sister companies exercised a virtual stranglehold on the business in fruit, sugar, tobacco, and utilities in many Latin American countries. Their power dominated most aspects of life in those countries, and the term "banana republic" comes to us by way of an O. Henry story based on the actions of United Fruit.

Even then, United Fruit's power was abetted by its influence in the halls of the White House, Congress, the executive branch, and the CIA. During the 1950s, United's PR director had the good fortune to be married to President Eisenhower's personal secretary. John Moors Cabot was assistant secretary of Inter-American Affairs and the brother of Thomas Cabot, who had been another president of United Fruit. His boss, secretary of state John Foster

Dulles, had worked on United's business as an attorney at Sullivan & Cromwell and remained a major shareholder. Dulles's brother Allen, the CIA director, who also had worked at Sullivan, had served on United Fruit's board. In 1969, United Fruit was the object of a tender offer by Zapata Off-Shore Corporation, a company founded by George H. W. Bush and joined later by Ralph Gow, his Skull & Bones classmate. Gow's father had sat on the board of United Fruit when it was deeply engaged in CIA activities. Soon thereafter, Eli Black, the corporate raider, bested Gow's offer and bought out the Zapata interest at a premium. Having been renamed United Brands, the firm by 1975 was deeply in debt and Black was about to face indictment for bribing Honduras's dictator to reduce export tariffs on bananas. This Honduran episode catalyzed the passage of the Foreign Corrupt Practices Act in which Rod Hills played a hand.

The next phase of Chiquita's history is dominated by the wealthiest man in its hometown of Cincinnati: Carl Lindner, Jr. A perennially major benefactor of the GOP, and to a lesser extent the Democratic Party as well, Lindner became president of United Brands in 1976 and purchased a large and subsequently controlling stake through his American Financial Group (AFG) insurance company six years later. Lindner's attorney and subsequently his business associate at AFG was Charles Keating, later notorious for his role as the head of the failed Lincoln Savings and Loan, which cost taxpayers more than $3 billion and landed Keating in prison. Keating became a director of AFG in 1963, joined the firm as an executive vice president in 1972, and he and Lindner parted ways in 1976 when Keating resigned and assumed control of an Arizona home construction subsidiary spun off from AFG.

Lindner went on to build a multibillion-dollar empire and develop a large philanthropic base. While many directors serve on the boards of nonprofits, Lindner's largesse is almost larger than life. His name is all over his hometown. He even owned the Cincinnati Reds baseball team at one time and his company has the naming rights to their new stadium. Having raised at least $200,000 for Bush-Cheney in 2004, Lindner was probably influential in obtaining the use of the Reds' ballpark for a George W. Bush "Victory Rally" thirty-six hours before Election Tuesday. Two days later, Ohio delivered the margin of victory for Bush's second term.

Chiquita went bankrupt in 2001 thanks to a dispute with the European Union, and Lindner left the board the next year, though he remained a major stockholder in the company. As Lindner left, Jeffrey Benjamin filled a board seat. He came as a senior advisor to the Apollo Management private equity firm, which is run by Leon Black, the son of Eli. Leon is also an alumnus of Drexel, of which Lindner was a very large customer. Chiquita sold its banana holdings in Guatemala, by the way, to Del Monte in the 1970s, ending its relationship with that country. But in a bow to how the world has both changed and stayed the same, Del Monte is now owned by Kuwaitis, who named Marvin P. Bush, the youngest brother of George W., to its board in 1998.

As Lindner departed Chiquita, Rod Hills arrived. Meanwhile, for the next eleven months after its disclosure to DOJ, Chiquita continued the payments to the AUC, waiting for Justice to make up its mind. Hills and his colleagues met numerous times with Chertoff's successor, Deputy Attorney General Larry Thompson, who might have been expected to move effectively in dealings with the Chiquita directors, since he knew quite a bit about the shenanigans of corporate boards. As a federal prosecutor, Thompson had won some of the largest corporate fraud cases of the twentieth century, including that against Enron. It was disturbing, then, that just the year before he took the job as head of the DOJ Criminal Division he had exercised stock options for a gain of between $1 million and $5 million, according to his federal disclosure filings, as a director of Providian Financial, a specialist in high-interest credit cards sold to the very poor. Thompson cashed in a scant two months before the company shocked the business community by announcing it had severe financial problems. He had been chairman of Providian's audit committee and later said he was unaware of the difficulties sixty days before the bankruptcy. Thompson moved on from his DOJ job, at any rate, within two months after meeting Hills, when he became the top lawyer at PepsiCo. The Chiquita case ultimately passed through the hands of no fewer than three U.S. attorneys for the District of Columbia, a variety of assistant U.S. attorneys, and three deputy attorneys general at Justice.

The web of interconnectedness of those playing one role or another in the adjudication of this case is marvelously representative of the larger problem. Take, for example, the fact that Thompson's predecessor as deputy attorney general during the Clinton administration was Eric Holder, now the U.S. attorney general. When George W. Bush took power, Holder went into private practice, and he was hired by Chiquita to defend it in criminal and related civil lawsuits related to the AUC Colombian payments. Chiquita's audit committee also hired a former attorney general, Richard Thornburgh, to defend it.

By the time the case was resolved in 2007, the $4.5 billion fruit company wound up agreeing to pay a $25 million fine over five years as part of a plea agreement, and the investigation against Hills and another director was dropped. Today, AUC is disbanded and its leaders are in jail. From their cells, they are claiming they took payments from numerous Western multinational corporations. The truth is difficult to ascertain, a problematic fact in light of five civil suits in American courts filed by survivors of hundreds of massacre victims, plus another derivative suit on behalf of shareholders. Chiquita has subsequently sold all its Colombian operations.

Chiquita still defends its actions in making the payments because, the company says, doing so secured the safety of its employees and facilities. By continuing its business, it played a role in the larger economic health of Colombia. For Rod Hills, the question of justifying and supporting the payments to terrorists seems somewhat more complex. At a training workshop for corporate directors at Stanford Law School in 2008, Hills candidly discussed his predicament as openly as a lawyer can, when speaking to a sympathetic audience of two hundred directors under a huge tent.

Along with Hills, other speakers included Ken Langone, the financial backer and former lead director of Home Depot and a former director of General Electric, who spoke about the Horatio Alger promise of America, strongly defended the $140 million pay package he had approved as compensation committee chairman at the New York Stock Exchange for its former CEO Richard Grasso, and skewered their mutual nemesis Eliot Spitzer, who had resigned the New York governorship three months before and had sued both Grasso and Langone over Grasso's pay when he was the New York State attorney general. Langone left after his speech to have dinner with Angelo Mozilo, the former Countrywide CEO who had served as a director on Home Depot's compensation committee during some of the controversy over Bob Nardelli's enormous CEO pay package. Grasso also had served on that committee while a Home Depot director from 2002 to 2004, although at an earlier time than Mozilo. Another speaker, SEC Commissioner Christopher Cox, had been pilloried that day by Gretchen Morgenson in the *New York Times* for his lack of engagement during the final Bear Stearns negotiations. As the most prominent reporter who writes about board misconduct, the mere mention of Morgenson's name drew loud boos from the audience, while Cox received a standing ovation. His speech dealt with the promise of a web-based technology for financial disclosure, but did not get into the simmering scandals around lax SEC enforcement.

Of all the speakers, Rod Hills conveyed the deepest reflection and judgment. "Is it ever appropriate, proper, to pay money to a terrorist organization if you have reason to believe that that organization would kill or terrorize people later?" he asked the group.

> You have to acknowledge that if nobody ever paid ransom for kidnapping, if nobody ever made payments to terrorists like AUC and FARC, the kidnappings would drop and the AUCs and FARCs would not exist anymore.
>
> But I have to say that as a director of Chiquita, that thought really did not pass our minds. We had employees who were threatened, and we thought we had the obligation to protect them. It is very hard to be the first person to enforce the no-ransom ideal. Destroying AUC, disarming it, or abandoning the banana business in Colombia, was the only way that the killings and extortion payments would stop. And I must say to you that I must doubt an easy answer to the moral issue.

Played out against the history of United Fruit, the tribulations of Rod Hills and his Chiquita colleagues show how far business has come in some ways and how little it has progressed in others. Chiquita's directors still belong to elites. The elites still have access to one another and to leaders in government, finance, and nonprofits. Bushes and Blacks played a role thanks in part to inheritance. Others participated because of their sequential positions of power in government and business. Like the Chiquita board, there are no women in this story. Chiquita was able to call on at least one former and one future U.S. attorney general. A person is tempted to think that if Hills's chits were a bit more current, none of this might have happened.

Chiquita acknowledges its shady past forthrightly on its website in a section called "Our Complex History." The company freely confesses to its roles in the overthrow of Guatemala's democratically elected president in 1954; the use of its cargo ships in support of right-wing Cubans during the Bay of Pigs fiasco; and "the use of improper government influence, antagonism toward organized labor, and disregard for the environment. These actions clearly would not live up to the Core Values we hold today or to the expectations of our stakeholders." And indeed, directors today, in word if not always in deed, must acknowledge the existence of diverse stakeholders, including investors like socially responsible mutual funds, public employee pensions, church endowments, and the like. In addition, a new set of corporate watchdogs—such as Greenpeace, the Sierra Club, the ACLU, and Amnesty International—work to hold corporations and boards accountable for human rights, environmental, and social justice policies.

Rod Hills's perspective—whether to put the corporate interest ahead of the broader social interest in clamping down on terrorist groups—crystallizes one of the dilemmas inherent in the current system of governance in which he operates. Whom does Chiquita serve? Those who work on boards generally come from an age, a walk of life, a socio-economic class, and a political leaning that reject the notion that the boardroom is a pulpit from which to address social ills.

When Hills waxed philosophically about saving employees, he was engaging in the sort of introspection that seems rare in the public utterances of CEOs. His regard for the workers and the economy of Colombia, accepted at face value, invokes components of the stakeholder theory first espoused by Darden School business professor Edward Freeman in the 1980s: that corporations owe their loyalty to their customers, employees, the communities they serve, their vendors and suppliers, and their stockholders.

The role of elites in society has preoccupied philosophers for thousands of years. To whom much is given, much is expected. In subscribing to neo-Classical economics and Chicago School theory, directors enlist in a more limited vision of what the business elite should do for society. For some this has proved problematic, as recent events have overwhelmed not only Milton Friedman's theories, but also the debt-fueled consumer class that has been necessary for the smooth functioning of our system.

In this context, we're drawn back full circle to the corporate director as an elite, and to how our economic, political, and military realms have evolved to further facilitate that elite's self-interests, despite some inspiring exceptions. Consider, for example, the difference between five-star general George C. Marshall and navy captain Donald Rumsfeld. Both became secretaries of defense toward the conclusion of impressive careers. One remained a person of modest means throughout his life, while the other became a millionaire many times over. One authored a plan to rebuild Europe while the other, along with a former Halliburton CEO, authored the largely private-sector-driven plan to defeat Iraq. Both initiatives happened to further the interests of American business, but in much different ways. Marshall was considered by Franklin Roosevelt, Harry Truman, and Winston Churchill to be the greatest person of his time. He turned down numerous offers to serve in retirement on corporate boards. Rumsfeld served as the CEO, chairman, or director of ten different companies while shuttling among jobs at the highest levels of government and defense.

Under any system, elites always will run business. Even the Soviet communists proved that. The question is, whom do they serve? In our free enterprise system, at a minimum we expect them to serve us, the shareholders, more than they serve our hired hand—the CEO—and certainly more than they serve themselves. But the system as it exists today, together with the incentives and reforms instituted with the intent of making corporate governance more responsible and effective have ended up being perverted to serve the self-interests of the elite at the expense of the greater good.

4

Hand in Glove

ALTHOUGH IT'S NOT SUPPOSED to be the case, most CEOs exercise powerful control over their boards. They dictate or greatly influence the directors' selection and compensation, they set the boards' agendas and committee assignments, and they control access to information. Thus, many boards come to represent executives' interests rather than those of the shareholders.

The former Harvard Business School professor and governance expert Michael Jensen puts it bluntly: "In the publicly held corporate model, the CEO has no boss. We pretend that the CEO has a boss. We pretend that it is the board of directors. But it almost never is. Basically, the boards of directors of most organizations, even the so-called independent directors, see themselves as employees of the CEO. Mostly, the only times CEOs of publicly held organizations have a boss is when a sufficiently large crisis occurs. At that point boards often wake up, but by then it is often too late—much of the damage has already been done."

Too many boards are as complacent and inbred as the one Michael Eisner dominated when he was the CEO of Disney. Eisner was in office from 1984 to 2005, far longer than any of the CEOs at the twenty-nine other Dow Jones Industrial Average companies at the time. The Disney board included Eisner's personal lawyer (who chaired the compensation committee); friends such as the actor Sidney Poitier; the principal of the elementary school that his children had attended; the architect Robert A. M. Stern, who designed Eisner's 16,000 square foot log cabin near Aspen, Colorado, as well as many buildings for the company; the president of a university to which Eisner had given a $1 million donation; the former Disney chairman who had hired Eisner; and former U.S. senator George Mitchell, who had done consulting for Disney.

Largely because of the Disney board's glaring lack of independence, *BusinessWeek* named it the worst board in America in 1999 and 2000. Charles Elson, who runs the University of Delaware's Weinberg Center for Corporate Governance, commented at the time that the Disney board was "such a rat's nest of conflicts that the only thing to do is to clean the whole thing out. Let it start all over again." In 2004, the SEC imposed a cease-and-desist order on Disney for failing to disclose relationships between the company and its board members, such as that three directors had adult children employed at Disney and the wife of another director was paid more than $1 million a year at a company in which Disney owned a half interest.

Early on in Eisner's reign, Disney performed spectacularly, but it began to decline as he remained unchallenged and his decisions became erratic. Eisner's disastrous hiring of his friend Michael Ovitz as Disney's president, which cost shareholders more than $140 million in compensation and tens of millions in subsequent legal fees after Ovitz was dismissed, resulted in ten years of litigation by shareholders against Eisner and the directors. William B. Chandler III, the Delaware Chancery Court judge who heard the case, concluded in his 175-page opinion that "the Disney directors had been taken for a wild ride, and most of it was in the dark" as Eisner "stretched the outer boundaries of his authority as CEO by acting without specific board direction or involvement." The judge was especially scathing about Eisner's ego and management style, writing that he "enthroned himself as the omnipotent and infallible monarch of his personal Magic Kingdom."

Eisner and the board were cleared in the Delaware court because, under the business judgment rule, their actions did not meet the state's high threshold for having breached their fiduciary duties to shareholders. However, the judge's ruling made the case an object lesson in how the CEO-board relationship can go awry: "By virtue of his Machiavellian (and imperial) nature as CEO, and his control over Ovitz's hiring in particular, Eisner to a large extent is responsible for the failings in process that infected and handicapped the board's decisionmaking abilities. Eisner stacked his (and I intentionally write 'his' as opposed to 'the Company's') board of directors with friends and other acquaintances who, though not necessarily beholden to him in a legal sense, were certainly more willing to accede to his wishes and support him unconditionally than truly independent directors."

The judge was equally damning of "the unwholesome boardroom culture at Disney," which demonstrated "how ornamental, passive directors contribute to sycophantic tendencies among directors and how imperial CEOs can exploit this condition for their own benefit, especially in the executive compensation and severance area."

In mid-2009, some four years after the ruling, Eisner still seemed to be feeling the sting. One of us spoke briefly with Eisner after a panel discussion he had participated in and asked if he'd be willing to talk generally about corporate governance. He agreed to do so and handed over his card. Then an anguished look came over his face and he glanced down. "You know, I can't encourage you on that, it's still really hard to think about."

Governance problems are exacerbated when the CEO also serves as chairman of the board, as was still the case at 61 percent of the S&P 500 companies in 2009. Gary Wilson, who served on the Disney board and saw the problem firsthand with Michael Eisner, wrote in a 2008 *Wall Street Journal* opinion article that "entrenched management leads to empire-building, continued adherence to flawed business strategies, resistance to change, the stifling of healthy debate in the boardroom, and destruction of shareholder value." Eisner lost the chairman role after a shareholder revolt at the 2004 annual meeting—and left the firm the following year. Wilson noted that Disney's shares appreciated 30 percent in the four years after the chairman and CEO roles were split, while they had dropped 20 percent during the previous five years.

THE GREAT man theory of history—the idea that natural-born, charismatic leaders wield power decisively for good or ill and thus control our destinies—has powerful appeal. As corporations grew to enormous size and influence in the economic boom after World War II, chief executive officers moved to center stage in this drama and were celebrated throughout our culture. Ted Turner of CNN, Andy Grove of Intel, and Bill Gates of Microsoft—all both the CEOs and chairmen of their companies—joined world political leaders among the ranks of *Time* magazine's Man of the Year.

The economic cycle of booms and busts leads to an alternating deification and demonization of CEOs. In good times, we attribute much of a company's success to them, and the rewards in pay, power, perquisites, and prestige they reap are widely considered justly earned. When things go wrong, CEOs are vilified, and we call for new laws to restrain them. We need a better approach to understanding how to critique their performance.

The job of a CEO is heady stuff. Most CEOs get to where they are because they are strong, competitive, risk-taking personalities with a great deal of self-confidence. As shareholders and citizens, we want these traits in our corporate leaders because, if channeled properly, they can translate into growth and jobs and prosperity. However, when CEOs are ungoverned, especially over time, as they grow accustomed to being unquestioned within their companies and living in a rarified world of enormous power and wealth, those same characteristics can lead to disaster. While it is convenient to attribute the problem to greed or venality on the part of some CEOs, it is simply human nature for high-powered executives to fill the vacuum left by weak boards. Our political system ensures that the president is subject to checks and balances exerted by Congress and the courts, as well as by elections and term limits. In the absence of boards doing their jobs, no such constraints operate for CEOs, unless they are caught actually committing a crime. And as we've seen all too often recently, boards can be the last to wake up even then.

The classic example of late awakening among a company's directors was at McKesson & Robbins, the large pharmaceutical company. In 1938, Sidney Weinberg, the legendary head of Goldman Sachs who sat simultaneously on thirty-one corporate boards, including McKesson's, was summoned to an emergency meeting of the McKesson directors. The board had been told that the CEO, Dr. F. Donald Coster, was, in fact, a swindler and ex-convict named Philip Musica, who had faked the inventory accounts and disappeared after stealing $21 million in one of the largest accounting frauds of the mid-twentieth century. Musica had created a phony subsidiary in Canada to hide his thefts and fooled the board with claims that the directors should have caught if they were paying any attention at all. For example, the Canadian warehouses supposedly held several times the world's possible supply of certain drug ingredients, and documents referred to moving inventory from South America to China and Australia "by truck." During the emergency board meeting, word came in that Musica had committed suicide. Weinberg stood up and said "Well, come on, gentlemen, let's fire him for his sins anyway!"

Today even death triggers "golden coffin" provisions at some companies, giving executives an estate-planning benefit that often pays tens of millions in shareholders' money to their families. According to a shareholder statement in January 2009, the board of Shaw Group Inc., a Louisiana-based engineering and manufacturing conglomerate, approved paying its chairman, J. M. Bernhard, Jr., an estimated $38.2 million upon his death, together with an additional $15 million, plus interest, under an agreement that he "will not compete with Shaw Group after his employment is terminated, whether by death or otherwise." In spite of the obvious absurdity of the noncompete provision, at the 2009 annual shareholders' meeting the company resisted a proposal to allow shareholders even an advisory vote on such deals in the future, saying that doing so "effectively calls for shareholder intrusion into the management of the company, would restrict the flexibility and discretion of our board, and, in our board's view, would impede its . . . ability to recruit and retain qualified senior executives." The proposal passed by a two-thirds majority, but because the shareholders' decisions on such matters could themselves only be advisory under the rules then in existence, the company said it would take it under consideration.

A comprehensive study of the one hundred largest business failures from 1998 to 2003 found that autocratic leadership and a weak board were among the most prominent causes of the companies' declines. Tyco, WorldCom, Vivendi, Warnaco Group, Enron, Time Warner, and other firms included in the study had generally collapsed into bankruptcy or experienced huge drops in stock value immediately following what seemed to be the peak of their success. Here is how the CEOs and boards are described: "A powerful CEO holding multiple titles (chairman, CEO, president), receiving particularly high compensation, and often controlling large shareholdings dominated the examined companies. . . . Ineffective boards with directors mainly chosen through the influence of the CEO failed to provide the necessary checks and balances. . . . Almost without exception blessed with a charismatic and self-confident personality, the leaders used their autocratic position to pursue aggressive and visionary goals. The press, shareholders, and analysts praised initial successes with increasing rapture." These factors led to CEO hubris and catastrophic failure, often in the wake of overpaying for acquisitions.

The study describes a second group of failures, like Kodak, Kmart, Motorola, and United Airlines, which also had weak boards, but which were characterized by their past successes having led to an entrenched CEO who resists change, removes potential rivals, and is followed by ineffective successors who are rapidly replaced (like the five CEOs in seven years at Kmart following CEO Joseph Antonini). The company misses shifts in the market or makes strategic errors—like Kodak missing the switch to digital pictures—and eventually breaks down.

The good news, according to the study, is that a strong board can help prevent or cure both types of crises: "an independent and competent board of directors . . . is therefore essential for countermeasures to be introduced promptly." The bad news, as we have seen throughout recent corporate history, is that such boards are exceedingly rare because the CEOs prevent them from existing.

Some have argued that the reduced tenure of the average large company CEO demonstrates that boards have begun to assert themselves, especially in cases where CEOs have been fired for poor performance. A 2007 Booz Allen study showed that annual CEO turnover grew by 59 percent between 1995 and 2006 and that involuntary departures increased by 318 percent, with one in three exiting CEOs being forced out in 2006. In fact, most of the recent examples reveal the continuing dysfunction of too many boards: selecting inadequate CEOs in the first place; failing to advise and mentor executives; keeping incumbents in place until a problem has developed into a crisis; and avoiding realistic succession planning.

The post-Enron reforms were supposed to increase the independence of boards. The New York Stock Exchange requires that listed firms not only must have a majority of independent directors but also that only independent directors can serve on the compensation, audit, and nominating/governance committees. In addition the independent directors must meet in executive sessions separately from inside directors at least once a year. The rules focus on these directors having "no material relationship" with the company but leave it largely up to companies to decide and disclose what that means beyond a few specified financial conflicts (such as the directors and their immediate family members being paid more than $100,000 annually for direct services to the company within the prior three years). That, of course, leaves a loophole a mile wide.

Warren Buffett, in his 2002 annual letter to Berkshire Hathaway shareholders, focused on the failures of so-called independent corporate directors and pins the problem squarely on the makeup and culture of today's boards:

> Why have intelligent and decent directors failed so miserably? The answer lies not in inadequate laws—it's always

> been clear that directors are obligated to represent the interests of shareholders—but rather in what I'd call "boardroom atmosphere" . . . Over a span of 40 years, I have been on 19 public-company boards (excluding Berkshire's) and have interacted with perhaps 250 directors. Most of them were "independent" as defined by today's rules. But the great majority of these directors lacked at least one of the three qualities I value [being "business-savvy, interested and shareholder-oriented"]. As a result, their contribution to shareholder well-being was minimal at best and, too often, negative. These people, decent and intelligent though they were, simply did not know enough about business and/or care enough about shareholders to question foolish acquisitions or egregious compensation. My own behavior, I must ruefully add, frequently fell short as well: Too often I was silent when management made proposals that I judged to be counter to the interests of shareholders. In those cases, collegiality trumped independence.

CEOs can dominate their boards by selecting the nominating committee members, screening the candidates, and sometimes recruiting friends and business associates. Even if the CEO and a new board member don't know one another well initially, they quickly become close during their time together on the board. (This is why laws in England were changed so that directors are no longer considered independent after they have been on a board for nine years.) CEOs generally decide or greatly influence who chairs the other committees, as well. One experienced board member who has served on several Fortune 500 boards chuckled when we asked about the issue of domineering CEOs and said, "They usually pick the stupidest director to head the compensation committee and the second stupidest for the audit committee."

The board at Citigroup was widely criticized even before the financial meltdown for a lack of independence, and it fell under intense scrutiny as the bank began to lose tens of billions of dollars for shareholders. Nevertheless, Vikram Pandit, the new Citigroup CEO, who did not even serve as the board chairman, apparently controlled the process by which his long-standing business associate Lawrence Ricciardi was selected in 2008 to fill a vacant director position. The company didn't bother to give even the appearance of having conducted an independent selection process. And Ricciardi, while adding some sorely needed financial expertise to the board, hardly sounded like a tough watchdog in his first public comment as a newly minted Citigroup director. According to the *Wall Street Journal*, Pandit had "approached Mr. Ricciardi a few months ago about a seat on the board." The story further noted that "Messrs. Pandit and Ricciardi have known each other since 1989. Mr. Pandit, then a young investment banker at Morgan Stanley, was a member of a team working for RJR Nabisco Inc. where Mr. Ricciardi was an executive. Mr. Ricciardi says Mr. Pandit struck him as 'absolutely brilliant.'" How independent and objective is such a director likely to be in evaluating executive performance at a company that clearly needs better oversight—and that at one point in March 2009 set a world record by losing more than $270 billion in market value for its shareholders in less than three years?

Surveys in 2007 and 2008 of more than a thousand directors on the boards of the largest U.S. publicly traded companies found that 55 percent of board members felt that the CEO was still primarily responsible for setting the agenda for board meetings. More than half felt that there was a shortage of qualified board members. They also admitted shortcomings in some of their primary duties: only 51 percent said their boards were effective at monitoring their company's risk management plan, and only 53 percent believed they had an effective management succession plan. Nearly half found it difficult to evaluate CEO performance. And while 90 percent of directors agreed that board members should attend seminars for directors, only 40 percent of boards had a formal budget for board education.

Many board meetings assume the quality of well-worn rituals. The board secretary has distributed the board books in advance although many directors admit they don't read them until right before the meeting. These assiduously prepared documents contain reams of numbers, PowerPoint printouts, charts, legal documents, and the like. They can be slim and useful, or crafty CEOs can sandbag them with mounds of irrelevant data to camouflage unpleasant realities. The received wisdom for CEOs is to brook no surprises, so they have personally politicked individual board members around contentious issues in advance, to persuade and dampen dissent.

Sometimes board business is conducted informally at a resort or golf club. There might be a dinner the night before the official meeting. The formal meetings can therefore become perfunctory affairs highlighted, if that's the word, by interminable PowerPoint presentations by the CEO, CFO, expert gatekeepers, and occasionally other staffers who are permitted a star turn before the board. Frequently rushed, the agenda usually comprises a predictable cycle of budget discussions, sales projections, and bonuses. "It's all pretty boring, actually," summarizes Roland King, the cofounder of Southwest Airlines. The whole thing may well have a patina of "good news," unless some crisis or big issue arises: takeovers, CEO succession, and big acquisitions can break the routine. Committees meet before or after the full board meeting, which averages four hours. They report in.

These sessions can be useful, but frequently involve the recitation of the latest updates to numbers from the prior meeting.

These lengthy incantations frequently displace the discussion of strategy. The board secretary can easily ascertain and certify that all mandatory topical boxes have been checked, but in the meantime, the company can drift or even veer off course, because no one has had time to get to the more important issues. Those outcomes do not fit in a box that can be checked. People leave with both a sense of routine and also being rushed, and it's little wonder so many directors yearn for something more substantial, more strategic.

At the end of the meeting, it's standard practice for the board secretary to confiscate all handwritten notes at the door. They are summarily shredded to prevent plaintiffs' attorneys from gathering evidence in some potential future lawsuit. Instead, board minutes memorialize and sanitize the proceedings. The entire affair takes a day or two, including travel time—and will happen again, typically about ten weeks later.

Even though they are perceived as controlling boards, CEOs are, by and large, not pleased with board performance either. According to two consultants involved in a study on board effectiveness, CEOs "almost universally confide that they have at most one or two very effective directors who provide wise counsel, offer advice on key issues, and contribute both formally and informally to the direction of the company . . . Roughly, then, only about 10–20 percent of directors are seen by CEOs as effective. Further, say CEOs, their top management team often regards working with the board as a demotivating experience." A separate survey of CEOs found that only 56 percent agreed that nonexecutive directors are well prepared for board meetings, while 63 percent said directors must spend more time learning about the business, its people, and the industries in which it operates. Only 47 percent agreed that the directors often raise important new issues in board discussions.

But to those who are well qualified and well prepared, being on a board can be a frustrating business. A highly respected business professor, who also serves as a counselor to CEOs and chairmen of major global corporations, recalled that he agreed to be on a board after he had established what he felt was a gratifying relationship with a CEO. "I had a social connection with the CEO," he recalled. "We lived in the same neighborhood and we'd occasionally talk about what was happening at his company and I'd make suggestions. A couple of years later he asked me if I would be interested in joining the board, and I was. My real motivation is that I like to help—I'm on a lot of charitable boards, too." The man was excited about being able to deal with important issues—executive compensation, shareholder activism, CEO succession—as an insider dealing with thousands of people and billions of dollars. A few months into his tenure, however, he thought about resigning. "The problem is that the CEO doesn't really want help and has a board only because he's required to. If we said, 'Let's make the bathroom walls yellow,' he'd say no. We're just there for window dressing. I used to be able to give real advice and I thought maybe if I resigned we could go back to that, but I guess that couldn't happen, since I've moved to the other side of the table." He also said that the other board members seemed resentful that he had visited the company's facilities and reported on some issues he'd found. He was rueful and more than a little downcast. "I must confess that I don't really like being on the board," he said.

Isolation and ostracism are what tends to happen to many of the very directors American business needs most—the strong, experienced, and diligent board members who are willing to ask tough questions and truly represent the shareholders' interests. All too often, CEOs and other board members marginalize such directors, who eventually resign, fail to be re-nominated, or simply become discouraged at the futility of their efforts. The dilemma these ideal directors face was best articulated by the economist Albert O. Hirschman, whose 1970 book *Exit, Voice, and Loyalty: Responses to Decline in Firms, Organizations, and States* says that a responsible member of a dysfunctional organization has two options: walking out or protesting. In the boardroom, neither has helped—quitting may absolve the director of further complicity, but leaves the problem in place; speaking out internally or externally usually ensures that a director's tenure will be brief. While both options may call attention to the problem for a brief moment, the system is so resistant to change that nothing happens. A tree falls in a forest where no one is listening.

Shirley Young, for example, found herself kicked off a board for asking a simple question. Young is a highly respected Chinese American business executive who was the first woman appointed to the Target Corporation board and later served as a director for numerous S&P 500 companies including Verizon, Bank of America, Harrahs, and Salesforce.com. Target's cofounder Bruce Dayton, who, with his brother Ken, had pioneered many of what are now considered the best practices for corporate governance, calls Young one of the most intelligent and perceptive directors he has ever met. Over tea in her New York apartment, Young spoke of the single most shocking experience in her twenty-two years as a board member. After Bank of America was acquired by NationsBank in 1998, Young continued as a director of the combined company, which retained the Bank of America name. NationsBank's CEO and chairman Hugh L. McColl, Jr., who had built the company from a small regional bank into one of the largest financial services firms in the country, was a dictatorial former Marine who liked to hand out crystal hand grenades as mementos to favored employees. Within two years of the acquisition, McColl was under fire himself as the bank's performance deteriorated and it laid off 12,600 employees—over twice the number it had originally estimated. At the same time, his $76 million pay package for 1999 and allegations that he was packing the board with unqualified cronies was attracting the attention of activist institutional investors such as CalPERS. In a board meeting, Young raised the point that McColl's compensation presented at least a public relations issue under the circumstances and that the compensation committee should bring it to the whole board for discussion. Young recalls that McColl's friend William "Hootie" Johnson, who was a member of the compensation committee, interrupted her and snapped that such a discussion wouldn't be necessary. (Johnson was later to become infamous as chairman of the Augusta National Golf Club when he vociferously defended its policy of excluding woman as members.) "I think a lot of the minutes would be written before the meetings took place," Young said of McColl's management style as chairman. "Hootie Johnson was really there to act as his blocker with the board." Young was soon dropped from the board and only learned of it when the corporate secretary failed to send her the materials for the next meeting. When Young expressed concerns about the bank's governance practices at her final board meeting, they somehow failed to appear in the board's minutes. When she asked why, she was told it was because "we couldn't hear you." Two other board members without ties to McColl left the board around the same time. The board was reduced in size and they were replaced by Frank Dowd IV, a local pipe company executive who was the son of a former NationsBank board member.

While a few board members may challenge the authority of CEOs, in general they identify strongly with management and resist changes that might give any real power to the shareholders they theoretically represent. This attitude is rarely revealed directly except when directors are talking among themselves. For example, a group of compensation committee chairmen from companies such as Microsoft, Motorola, Wells Fargo, and Delta

Airlines was convened in early 2009 by an organization called Tapestry Networks, which sponsors such panels regularly and gets the directors to speak frankly because individual quotes are unattributed. The topic for the panel was the "say-on-pay" proposal, which would give shareholders a nonbinding vote on executive compensation similar to laws passed in 2002 in the UK and recently adopted by Aflac in the United States. Some panel members were cynical and greatly resistant to the idea of receiving even advice from shareholders. They also indicated that the reform, which has been strongly advocated by shareholder rights activists, will have little impact when implemented because it is merely advisory and thus easily ignored. "We're accepting of say-on-pay because it doesn't have any real effect," one of the chairmen said. "However, the next step might be 'Let's approve certain plans in advance.' Then we'd have an issue. I'm not fighting say-on-pay anymore, I just want to know if it's going to cause other issues to come up faster." Another director on the panel explained that his company had spent money actively opposing the plan "because if you don't show you're willing to fight, there's going to be something else, then something else, then something else."

What, exactly, are these directors afraid of? Because most of them have already joined the ranks of the extremely wealthy, they seem particularly sensitive to issues involving compensation and identify strongly with CEOs who, of course, are in the same position. The relationship between directors and CEOs provides fertile ground for logrolling when it comes to material benefits, and corporate leaders still enjoy a host of perks, despite the symbolic austerity displayed by some, such as the three automotive CEOs who drove to Washington, D.C., from Detroit for their second round of congressional testimony after their use of corporate jets had caused a public outcry at the initial hearings. Look, for example, at the *Corporate Board Member* magazine website's "Lifestyles" section from the fall of 2009 ("This is a page about your lifestyle, how you meld business and pleasure . . .") for a glimpse at the exclusive and seemingly recessionless world so many of these corporate leaders inhabit:

> Golf remains the quintessential prelude to closing deals and a stepping-stone to career advancement or even a board seat. Here are the leading links where the elite meet, greet, wine, dine and assess one another's talents and temperaments . . . Ready to wave good-bye to the airlines? Here's what it takes to choose—and pay for—a private jet. . . . The demand for yachts is greater than ever, especially those big enough to serve as vacation home and satellite office . . . Great places for a rich retirement . . . Directors ready to ease up on work can find a lifestyle that will fulfill their needs and dreams—and let them stay connected to their boards as well.

Boards identifying with the financial needs of a CEO can be taken to an extreme. The governance mess recently exposed at Chesapeake Energy Corp., the nation's largest independent producer of natural gas, combines the worst elements of mutual back scratching, grossly excessive compensation, and blatant conflicts of interest. It is a paradigmatic story of the capture of a board by a CEO. The Chesapeake story came to light in early 2009 because of the diligence of journalists like Michelle Leder, who runs footnoted.org, a website that takes a close look at what companies try to hide in their routine SEC filings.

In 2008, Chesapeake, which is based in Oklahoma City, had a very bad year. Everything had seemed fine in the first two quarters, as skyrocketing commodity prices boosted Chesapeake's income and stock price to record levels. But as natural gas prices plummeted in the late summer and early fall, the company's earnings for the year dropped by half and its stock by 59 percent. There was every reason to consider reducing executive bonuses at Chesapeake. In fact, according to calculations by compensation expert Graef Crystal, there perhaps shouldn't have been any bonuses at all. The company performed 23 percent worse than the S&P 500 Energy Index in 2008 and its returns had been substantially under the index since 2002. By the end of December 2008, shareholders had lost approximately $33 billion in value from the stock's high point in early July.

Chesapeake's cofounder and CEO, Aubrey McClendon, was pegged at No. 134 on the 2008 Forbes 400 list of America's richest people, with a net worth estimated at $3 billion in September, even after his Chesapeake shares had dropped some 44 percent. Chesapeake's board had granted McClendon $20 million in restricted stock in 2006, $21 million in 2007, and another $32.7 million in the first half of 2008. However, because McClendon had borrowed heavily to bet even more on his stock holdings, he got caught in mid-October's stock market crash with a margin call that forced him to sell 31.5 million Chesapeake shares over a three-day period—"substantially all" of his holdings, according to a company statement. In announcing his losses, McClendon noted, "My confidence in Chesapeake remains undiminished, and I look forward to rebuilding my ownership position in the company in the months and years ahead."

Thanks to the board, which McClendon had handpicked over the years, his bad fortune lasted only eighty-two days. The five-year employment agreement he had signed in 2007 was torn up and a new one drafted. On New Year's Eve, as investors were counting their losses and taxpayers were bailing out the nation's largest banks, the Chesapeake board bailed out McClendon with a $75 million bonus and new pay package. As a result, his $112.5

million compensation in 2008 was the highest among large public company CEOs as calculated by the Associated Press and was almost fifteen times the median pay within that group. His compensation went up more than 400 percent from the prior year, while the median for other CEOs dropped 7 percent. According to the proxy statement issued by Chesapeake in May 2009, McClendon's total pay for 2008 included $648,096 for personal use of company aircraft, $438,750 for retirement contributions, $577,113 for "accounting support," and $131,226 for "engineering support" related to his personal investments in wells under a "Founder Well Participation Program," a benefit the board had created to allow McClendon to invest selectively in Chesapeake's drilling projects and which he valued at $191 million at the end of 2008.

In the "Transactions with Related Persons" section, the proxy statement separately included a few more sources of money for McClendon approved by the board, such as the company's $12.1 million purchase of his antique map collection, which had been displayed in the headquarters lobby. A company filing asserted that the price represented McClendon's cost of acquiring the collection and that it was worth at least $8 million more, but it also said that the valuation came from "a dealer who had assisted Mr. McClendon in acquiring this collection." The proxy statement justified the purchase because "the Company was interested in continuing to have use of the map collection and believed it was not appropriate to continue to rely on cost-free loans of artwork from Mr. McClendon" and because of its value in "complementing the interior design features of our campus buildings and contributing to our workplace culture."

The company also paid $4.7 million in 2008–2009 to sponsor a National Basketball Association team that McClendon owned 19.2 percent of, and spent approximately $177,150 for catering services from Deep Fork Catering, which was affiliated with a restaurant of which McClendon owned 49.7 percent. The basketball sponsorship was justified in a letter released by Chesapeake's general counsel because "the Company believes the sponsorship provides valuable support to the local community and contributes to employee morale." The catering bill was similarly excused because "Aubrey is not involved in decisions to hire Deep Fork Catering and has requested that the Company's future use of Deep Fork Catering be limited."

The board defended its 2008 compensation for McClendon as being "in recognition of his leadership role in completing a series of transactions in 2008 that were valuable to the company and its shareholders" and necessary "because of other entrepreneurial opportunities that exist in the industry and Mr. McClendon's reduced company stock holdings." The board also emphasized that the $75 million bonus had to be invested in the Founder Well Participation Program, and if McClendon left Chesapeake within five years, he would have to return part of the bonus.

The Chesapeake board was insular and entrenched. It included no women and no minorities. Chesapeake used a staggered election system that kept shareholders from voting on more than three of the nine directors each year. In 2008, at the annual shareholders' meeting, 61 percent of the voting shareholders approved a proposal to have annual elections of all directors, but the board simply ignored the advice. In any case, there was no requirement that directors had to resign if they failed to receive less than 50 percent of the votes cast by shareholders. The board included two Oklahoma politicians with little business experience—former senator Don Nickles and former governor Frank Keating. The three-member compensation committee included Keating, whose son and daughter-in-law worked for the company and received total cash compensation of $274,569 in 2008. (Chesapeake's proxy disclosure stated that "Governor Keating recuses himself with respect to decisions regarding the compensation of his son and daughter-in-law.") Another director, V. Burns Hargis, was the president of Oklahoma State University, which received $1.2 million in contributions and athletic ticket purchases by Chesapeake in 2008. The audit committee that "approved or ratified" McClendon's payments for the map collection, as well as the basketball team sponsorship and catering costs, was chaired by Breen M. Kerr, who happened to be Aubrey Kerr McClendon's second cousin.

The full board met only four times and held thirteen conference calls in 2008, yet the independent members received an average of nearly $670,000, among the highest compensation levels for any public company board and over three times the average for large-company directors. In fact, the actual compensation was substantially more than that. The company accounts for directors' restricted stock grants over the following three years as they become vested. On July 1, 2008, based on "analysis and recommendations for adjustments" to directors' compensation, which the company's executives make each year, the board awarded each member $842,000 in restricted stock.

The directors and their families also had access to corporate jets, as noted in the proxy:

> [O]ur directors are provided access to fractionally-owned company aircraft for travel to and from Board meetings. For Board meetings and other Company activities at which the attendance of a director's spouse and immediate family members are also requested by the Company, we make tax gross-up payments to the director associated with the taxable compensation attributable to the spouse/family member travel. In addition, each non-employee director is entitled to personal use of fractionally-owned company aircraft seating eight passengers or fewer for up to 40 hours

of flight time per calendar year in North America, the Caribbean and Mexico.

The small-print footnotes describing the accounting for the personal use of aircraft showed that only the variable operating costs were counted. The far greater fixed costs, such as the purchase cost of the plane and maintenance, were ignored. Comparable jet charter services cost about $5,000 to $6,000 an hour, so the actual cost to shareholders for this director perk could total as much as $240,000 a year in the real value of a director's compensation.

Apparently, the board felt that it would be unseemly not to allow the top executives similar privileges with company aircraft. Chesapeake's 2009 Compensation Committee Report justified the cost to shareholders with these words: "Feedback from our executive officers indicates that access to fractionally-owned company aircraft for personal use greatly enhances productivity and work-life balance which we believe may impact their willingness to work to or beyond normal retirement age."

Compensation committees at almost every large company use an expert consultant to evaluate and help in negotiating pay for senior executives. At Chesapeake, those recommendations come from McClendon, his chief financial officer, and chief operating officer, who according to the company's filings "are responsible for analyzing, developing, and recommending base salary adjustments, cash bonuses, and restricted stock awards with respect to the executive officers, *including themselves,* for review, discussion and approval by the Compensation Committee at its regularly scheduled meetings in June and December of each year" [emphasis added].

The compensation committee was chaired by Frederick B. Whittemore, who has served as an independent member of the board for sixteen years and who had reason to be empathetic to McClendon's plight. According to Chesapeake's general counsel, Whittemore himself had to sell more than $5 million in Chesapeake stock to meet margin calls the same week McClendon sold his shares. Whittemore is the son of a wealthy New Hampshire industrialist and was a senior banker for many years at Morgan Stanley, where he ran syndications and was known for a hail-fellow well-met personality that earned him the nickname "Father Fred." The job required coordinating the dozens of other banks that participated in financings that Morgan Stanley was running, and Whittemore's friendly demeanor was well suited to the task. Whittemore retired from Morgan Stanley in 1989 and became an advisory director for the firm. He remained active in the affairs of the company and was a prominent member of the "Gang of Eight" former Morgan Stanley executives who helped oust CEO Philip Purcell there in 2005. Morgan Stanley has been a lead bank on a number of Chesapeake's financings since its 1993 initial public offering—when Whittemore joined Chesapeake's board. Morgan Stanley has reaped millions in fees from Chesapeake over the years, all disclosed and, of course, all perfectly legal. A presentation by a Morgan Stanley energy analyst in 2005, for example, disclosed five different categories of services the firm provided to Chesapeake that year, as well as that the bank owned more than 1 percent of one or more classes of Chesapeake's stock. In January 2009, the firm helped lead a $1 billion debt financing for Chesapeake.

Two public pension funds filed a shareholders' suit in Oklahoma to require Chesapeake to produce books and records relating to McClendon's compensation. Others sued, claiming a breach of fiduciary duties by the board. Jeffrey Bronchick, an investor whose firm owned 1.18 million Chesapeake shares, wrote to the board on April 23, 2009: "I sat in silence for ten minutes contemplating my 25-year career in the investment management business . . . I have never seen a more shameful document than the Chesapeake proxy statement. If I could reduce it to one page, I would frame and hang it on my office wall as a near perfect illustration of the complete collapse of appropriate corporate governance."

Remarkably, the board and McClendon would not acknowledge that anything was amiss, although at the shareholders' meeting on June 12, 2009, they came under harsh criticism. Jan Fersing, a shareholder from Fort Worth who said he would be selling his stock immediately after the meeting, was particularly vociferous in addressing McClendon:

> So, your $2 billion fortune was not enough; you wanted more. But this time your hand got stuck in the cookie jar, and you couldn't let go until your own cookies were taken in the process. And after your embarrassing losses, but with a carefully picked and extremely well compensated Board of Directors, Chesapeake shareholder funds were partially used to cover your losses . . . We essentially covered part of your bet, but our interest, I don't believe, was served in the process. The abuse of corporate responsibilities was endorsed by this Board of Directors who ignored their own corporate responsibilities. Instead of shareholder interest, they corrupted the process and represented their own interest. This lack of ethics, in my opinion, has a chilling effect on both potential and existing shareholders like me, whose investments were fashioned the old-fashioned way; we earned it.

But shareholder lawsuits and the opportunity to let off steam at annual meetings aren't likely to bring about much change. As McClendon said in response to another shareholder's comments at the 2009 annual meeting: "I have learned over time that a short memory and a thick skin will do you quite well in this position."

ELIOT SPITZER TOLD us he sees the crux of the problem as the insularity of boards and their resulting inability or unwillingness to deal with difficult issues: "It's always been an inside game and boards do not tolerate dissenting voices." He continued, "Boards do not represent shareholders, they represent the plutocracy and the status quo, the comfort and self-satisfaction of having arrived. . . . And they don't make decisions—they are led by the nose by CEOs and those who are in power." He recalled that when he was the New York State attorney general and the board of the New York Stock Exchange was confronted by the growing scandal over its CEO Richard Grasso's enormous compensation package, the board's chairman John Reed came to Spitzer's office and asked him to handle the situation. "We don't want to deal with it," he recalls Reed saying (although Reed has said his recollection of the conversation differs).

GIVEN ALL THE CULTURAL and practical constraints on board oversight of CEOs, can a board ever really be in control? What about a case in which the presiding director of a company whose CEO seems literally out of control is a tough, smart, experienced, and highly respected person like Ann McLaughlin Korologos at Fannie Mae? Korologos knows her way around both Washington and boardrooms and has assisted in dismissing five CEOs at various organizations when they didn't meet her high standards. But a report by Fannie Mae's regulator in May 2006 on problems at Fannie Mae alleged a litany of board failures, such as approving a compensation system easily manipulated by executives, following managers' scripting of board committee meetings, permitting earnings management that hit growth targets often to the penny, ignoring a whistleblower, claims of accounting irregularities, and allowing millions of dollars of contributions from the Fannie Mae foundation to be paid to charities affiliated with board members.

A section of the report described how the board missed an accounting maneuver that improperly shifted $200 million in expenses from one fiscal year to another, thus allowing executives to claim the maximum bonus payout of $27.1 million in shareholders' money when they should have received no bonus for the year. The report also spotlighted the dysfunctional culture and "tone at the top" set by the CEO and chairman Frank Raines and condoned by the board. It quoted from a speech that Fannie Mae's chief risk officer—the corporate financial watchdog—gave to the internal auditing staff regarding a $6.46 earnings per share goal established by Raines. The plan, when achieved, would trigger more than $100 million in special employee stock options grants approved by the board:

> By now every one of you must have 6.46 branded in your brains. You must be able to say it in your sleep, you must be able to recite it forwards and backwards, you must have a raging fire in your belly that burns away all doubts, you must live, breathe, and dream 6.46, you must be obsessed on 6.46 . . . After all, thanks to Frank, we all have a lot of money riding on it . . . We must do this with a fiery determination, not on some days, not on most days but day in and day out, give it your best, not 50%, not 75%, not 100%, but 150%. Remember, Frank has given us an opportunity to earn not *just* our salaries, benefits, raises, ESPP [Employee Stock Purchase Plan], but substantially over and above if we make 6.46.

The board did spring into action after the directors saw they had been misled. Raines "retired," the roles of chairman and CEO were separated, and the board stepped up oversight of management. But a great deal of damage to Fannie Mae's reputation and to its shareholders might have been prevented had it done so sooner.

Korologos served as the secretary of labor under Ronald Reagan and is one of the most experienced board members in America. She was a director at Fannie Mae from 1994 to 2005 and was the presiding director during its accounting and management crisis in 2004. A veteran of boards ranging from Microsoft and General Motors to American Airlines and Kellogg, she is described by the Corporate Library's Nell Minow, a scathing critic of many boards, as an exemplary director. Korologos said that Raines's personality and the arrogance of institutional leadership at Fannie Mae should have "caused my nose to twitch and see the signs early, but I can't say I picked it up. And I didn't pick up that the relationship between Frank and Fannie Mae's regulator was devastatingly bad."

The board had also missed warning signs when management assured them that there were no accounting problems like those that had recently been uncovered at Freddie Mac, its rival in the government-sponsored mortgage financing business, and that a whistleblower's allegations had been thoroughly investigated by management. Stephen Ashley moved up to become Fannie Mae's new board chair when Korologos left after delaying her planned departure for an extra two years to see the company through its crisis. Ashley spoke later to graduate students about how disastrous business leadership problems can develop. "It usually comes back to some of that core value where you get off the track on your internal gyroscope," Ashley said. "What's right, what's wrong. You begin to think that you're the smartest person in the room and you don't have time to listen to anybody else."

"Fannie Mae was a good example of how management can control the flow of information to the board, while the board allows itself to be manipulated and not assert its responsibilities," said Armando Falcon, the former head of the Office for Federal Housing Enterprise Oversight, Fannie Mae's regulator. "In one case, a board member asked someone in the company for a piece of information and Tim Howard, the CFO, found out about it. He sent a blistering email to the manager, saying that any inquiries should be referred to him and that no one should talk to the board members directly. It wasn't so much an ego thing—he just wanted to control what was going to the board."

Falcon waged a David-versus-Goliath battle with Frank Raines, in which he felt "the board just seemed to be a cheerleader for management" and that Fannie Mae was spending enormous resources on lobbying the Congress and the White House to thwart his investigation. According to the Center for Responsive Politics, Fannie Mae spent more than $27 million on twenty separate lobbying firms from 1999 to 2002. In a series for VanityFair.com on the hundred largest culprits to blame for the current economic mess, Bruce Feirstein wrote one of his longest entries on Raines. He cited Raines's four separate "Friends of Angelo" Countrywide special VIP mortgage loans, his $90 million in compensation over six years that included $52 million in bonuses tied to earnings that had been overstated by billions of dollars, Fannie Mae's efforts to get Falcon fired, and the tap-on-the-wrist settlement of OFHEO's suit against Raines seeking to recover more than $84 million. In April 2008, without admitting wrongdoing, Raines settled by "giving up near-worthless stock options, making a $1.8 million donation to charity and a $2 million fine to the government that was covered by Fannie Mae's insurance policies."

Falcon agrees that Fannie Mae's problems stemmed from organizational arrogance: "It was clear that Fannie Mae had cultural issues that emanated from the very top of the organization," Falcon said. "The reports discuss at length problems with the tone at the top, and the arrogance and huge egos of senior management and how that fostered a culture where no one questioned management. It was always just groupthink and if you ever raised a dissenting voice, your career would be over. Ego and arrogance was visible everywhere, in everything the company did: how it treated counterparties in the marketplace it dealt in, how it was able to throw its weight around politically, the way it spent money to curry political loyalty, the arrogance that permeated everything that the company did, including ultimately the accounting misconduct and the lack of any kind of corporate ethics. The arrogance and egotism allowed them to convince themselves that they were doing nothing wrong."

After Raines left Fannie Mae in December 2004, the company had to make a $6.3 billion restatement of its earnings. With new management in place and a board that was chastened by the accounting and leadership scandal, Fannie Mae seemed like it might be on the mend, but it never really recovered. With more than $3 trillion in mortgage-related loans and guarantees outstanding in late 2007, Fannie Mae began to hemorrhage tens of billions in losses as loans defaulted and homes were foreclosed. Its stock dropped more than 90 percent in less than a year. Nevertheless, the new CEO, Daniel Mudd, told analysts in a May 2008 call that Fannie Mae would be in great shape after raising just $6 billion in new capital, especially given the reduced competition in the mortgage business. "We will feast off this book of business we're putting on for many years to come," he predicted. Only four months later, after further losses threatened insolvency, the Federal Housing Finance Agency placed both Fannie Mae and Freddie Mac into conservatorship, dismissed their boards, replaced their CEOs, and wiped out most of the remaining value in their shares.

The Fannie Mae shareholders, represented by the board, lost more than $90 billion.

MANY OBSERVERS POINT to executive compensation as both a litmus test for whether a board is able to stand up to a CEO and as a leading indicator of other, less apparent governance problems involving CEO succession, ethics, business strategy, and risk management. Take the case, again, of Countrywide Financial, which had a board that was glaringly incapable of standing up to the astonishing arrogance of Angelo Mozilo. The company's compensation committee report in its 2007 proxy statement says that "the Company has historically targeted our Chief Executive Officer's base salary, annual incentives and long-term performance awards at or above the 90th percentile for his peer group. This target positioning was based on Mr. Mozilo's status, knowledge and reputation as a top leader in the industry . . ."

The problem of excessive pay is pervasive, but it's more excessive at some companies than others, and Mozilo ran roughshod over his board. Not including gains on his existing stock holdings, he received more than $200 million in salary, bonuses, and stock during the 2001–2006 real estate bubble that Countrywide did so much to help inflate. In 2006 alone, just as the company's plunge into subprime mortgage origination was sending the company over the edge, Mozilo was paid more than $48 million, including such perks as personal use of company aircraft, country club fees, use of a car, tax and investment advice, executive physicals, and reimbursement for personal taxes he owed on certain of these benefits. Mozilo's son and son-in-law received a total of $734,674 that year as company executives. Mozilo had taken home even more in 2005 when his direct pay and gains from exercising prior years' stock options totaled nearly $165 million.

When a shareholder at the annual meeting in 2006 questioned Mozilo's pay as being "out of whack" in an era when investors were losing faith in corporate leaders after so many scandals, Mozilo replied that "People like me, entrepreneurs, are not going to come into the public arena if . . . their reputation is ruined because they did well" and declared such objections as "obscene, ridiculous, and absurd." Mozilo delayed his planned retirement as CEO in 2006, after his chosen successor Stan Kurland abruptly resigned after objecting to Mozilo's insistence on remaining as chairman of the board for five years. The board then sought assistance from a compensation consultant in an apparent attempt to stand up to Mozilo and renegotiate his pay. The consultant pointed out that Mozilo's contract should be restructured because the proposed performance targets could be met too easily. Unhappy with the process, Mozilo told the board to hire a second consultant, which they, remarkably, agreed to do. The result? Mozilo won again. As a U.S. House Oversight Committee analysis concluded, "The discrepancy between Mr. Mozilo's compensation and Countrywide's performance is striking. In 2007, Countrywide announced a $1.2 billion loss in the third quarter and an additional loss of $422 million in the fourth quarter." The company's stock dropped 80 percent from its peak in February to the end of December. "During the same period, Mr. Mozilo was paid $1.9 million in salary, received $20 million in stock awards contingent upon performance, and sold $121 million in stock."

Mozilo thought he had been shortchanged. The committee found an email exchange with the second compensation consultant in which Mozilo writes: "I appreciate your input. . . . Boards have been placed under enormous pressure by the left-wing anti-business press and the envious leaders of unions and other so-called 'CEO Comp Watchers,' and therefore Boards are being forced to protect themselves irrespective of the potential negative long-term impact on public companies." In a later email, Mozilo complained bitterly about not being reimbursed for the taxes he owed when his wife traveled with him on the corporate jet.

The board's generosity with shareholders' money didn't stop with just Mozilo and themselves—and it lived on even after Countrywide was sold. As one example, the Gulfsteam IV jet was still getting a workout in mid-2008, this time on the Bank of America's shareholders, thanks to the employment agreement Countrywide's board had approved for David Sambol, the company's forty-eight-year-old president and chief operating officer. Sambol was pushed out by Bank of America executives under pressure by federal officials later that year and took home a $28 million severance package after being paid $10.3 million the previous year. He used the jet one last time to take his family on a three-week summer vacation to Africa just before he left. "This is a personal matter involving my family and I would like to protect my privacy," Sambol told a *Los Angeles Times* reporter, adding that "everything I am doing is in connection with my agreements with the company."

Countrywide and Chesapeake are hardly the only companies to allow the use of corporate jets for nonbusiness purposes. Apologists for the practice say it's relatively small potatoes in the great scheme of things, but the costs to shareholders do add up and it has enormous symbolic significance in demonstrating just how absurdly out of control executive compensation in the United States has become. Remember that this is *personal* use by the executives—if it were possible under any stretch of the staff or gatekeeper imagination to have it categorized as business use, there's little doubt that it would be. There can be no legitimate justification for this use of shareholders' money—and, from our own observation of its effects, it is perhaps the single most corrosive perquisite in fostering elitism and a sense of entitlement among corporate leaders.

There is strong evidence that the practice hurts shareholders beyond its direct costs, as well. A 2005 study by David Yermack of New York University looked at ten years of data for 237 large firms that reported CEOs' personal use of the corporate jet. He controlled for various other factors and found that, on average, these firms underperformed market benchmarks by a full four percentage points. He also found a strong association with the perk and a CEO's membership in golf courses far from their homes.

In 2007, the Corporate Library issued a report on the private use of corporate jets entitled "Up, Up and Away," which showed that more than half of the 215 CEOs studied were allowed to fly in company planes for nonbusiness purposes, almost always with security cited as the supposed justification. Each of the top twelve CEOs on the list, most of whom also served as their companies' chairmen, took personal flights costing more than half a million dollars during 2006, with David G. Hanna, the CEO of CompuCredit Corporation, coming in at slightly more than $1 million and Michael McGrath, the CEO of i2 Technologies, Inc., at $942,565. Twenty-one of the CEOs got tax gross-ups, including Meg Whitman of eBay at the time, who made $773,467 worth of personal flights and received $230,992 in tax reimbursements. ChoicePoint's CEO Derek Smith will receive personal use of the jet for ten additional years even if he leaves the company when his employment agreement ends in 2010—at a cost estimated at $3.3 million in current dollars.

One reason for board support for such excessive perks and pay is surely reciprocity; CEOs tend to return the favor. For example, when Bob Nardelli was running Home Depot, he was almost as generous to his board as it was to him when it paid a fortune in shareholders' money to lure Nardelli after he lost out on the CEO job at GE. "The Company . . . pays the travel and accommodation expenses of directors and, when requested by the Company, their spouses to attend Board meetings, conduct store visits and participate in other corporate functions, together with any taxes related to such payments," the 2006 proxy statement explains. The board approved an employment contract with Nardelli that guaranteed a minimum of $3 million in annual bonuses no matter how the company performed and compensated him for taxes due on a high-end luxury car, his own family's travel on Home Depot aircraft, as well as forgiveness of a $10 million loan. In one year alone, Nardelli received $3 million in tax gross-ups. His total compensation during his five-year tenure as CEO amounted to approximately $240 million, despite the company's stock price remaining flat while its main competitor Lowe's more than doubled.

By far the best analysis of why excessive compensation is such an intractable problem is made in *Pay Without Performance* by Lucian Bebchuk and Jesse Fried. They write that "the 'smoking gun' of managerial influence over pay is not high levels of pay, but rather such things as the correlation between power and pay, the systemic use of compensation practices that obscure the amount and performance insensitivity of pay, and the showering of gratuitous benefits on departing executives." Bebchuk and Fried calculated that CEO pay is 20 percent to 40 percent higher if the CEO is also the chairman of the board. They cite "camouflage and stealth compensation" such as well-above-market-rate interest paid on deferred compensation, extremely generous pension plans and postretirement perquisites, tax gross-ups and "reloading" of options to increase their value if the stock price has dropped. Bebchuk, in a separate study with Robert Jackson, showed that two-thirds of the S&P 500 CEOs have executive pension plans with an estimated average value of $15 million—amounting to about a third of their total compensation—that is rarely counted in the public's view of CEO pay.

When asked what, other than imposing regulations on pay

or hoping for some sort of miraculous change in the dysfunctional culture of boards, could be done to reform the system, Fried smiled. Would better compensation consultants make a difference? "I know a compensation consultant who goes to a board with ideas that are in the shareholders' interests," Fried said. "The board gets excited about them and goes to the CEO who says, 'No fucking way!' and nothing happens. So the problem isn't compensation consultants, it's the board and their unwillingness to stand up to the CEO." Fried said that requirements for longer-term stock holdings by executives would help. "The current system creates a culture of 'how much money can we make right now' and not one that looks at how decisions affect the company five to ten years down the road." Another problem is that "few investors with power have a long-term view." He was hopeful that say-on-pay and shareholders being able to nominate directors would make incremental improvements but was ultimately pessimistic: "In bad economic times boards work harder to do the right thing for shareholders, but if we're in a booming economy ten years from now, expect to see relapses to the bad behavior of the past by boards."

Bebchuk and Fried conclude that there is nothing today that effectively deals with the CEO problem at a given company other than what they call the "outrage constraint"—basically the point at which public exposure gets people angry enough that it shames a board into taking action.

Sometimes even shaming doesn't work—especially if the executives are so shameless that they would keep millions of dollars from what amounts to an error by the board. A case in point is FPL Group Inc., the parent company of Florida Power & Light Co., where some of the directors apparently didn't know that they had approved a compensation policy with a major loophole in its provisions regarding merger bonuses after a "change in control." In early 2001, after an $8 billion merger with Entergy Corp. fell through, the board discovered that $92 million in cash bonuses had already been paid to seven hundred managers for the deal, with two-thirds going to the top eight executives. In an entirely unusual provision, FPL Group's compensation policy said a bonus was due when the transaction was approved by shareholders, instead of when it was completed. The deal had died in a squabble over financial projections and who would be in charge, but after the shareholders had voted in favor of it. Shareholders were duly outraged and sued. The board—or at least a few of its members—was shamed, but after a sixteen-month study by a special three-member board committee, the directors decided that the bonus could not be recovered. A sum of $22.6 million had gone to the CEO and chairman James L. Broadhead, who was friends with at least three of the independent directors. The year before, according to *BusinessWeek*, Broadhead's pay had been doubled, despite the stock's total return having dropped 27 percent.

Three years after the deal collapsed and millions more were paid with shareholders' money for legal fees, the judge in the shareholder suit ruled against the company on a number of points. He noted that the board committee investigating the payments had been selected by the CEO and that two of its three members had served on the compensation committee that had structured the awards. In addition, the law firm initially chosen by the committee to assist in the investigation had been the same firm that reviewed and approved the compensation plan—and had been recommended by the firm's general counsel, who himself had received a large deal bonus. The suits were later settled on a technicality with the executives returning only $9.75 million and insurers paying another $12.5 million (the insurance premiums, of course, had been paid by the shareholders and no doubt increased significantly after this payout). The outrageous amount managers kept for wasting time and millions of shareholders' dollars on a failed transaction was more than $82 million—truly money for nothing.

The outrage constraint seems to have had a real effect in at least a few cases, such as that of the retirement package GE's board granted to its former CEO Jack Welch as part of a retention agreement. The package included voluminous perks, such as access to GE aircraft for unlimited personal use and for business travel; exclusive use of a furnished New York City apartment worth at least $11 million; a leased Mercedes-Benz; bodyguard service during speaking engagements; dry cleaning; office space in New York City and Connecticut; and communications systems and networks at Welch's homes, including television, fax, phone, and computer systems, with technical support (and more). The SEC charged GE with failing to disclose the agreement's details to shareholders, and Welch said he would reimburse GE for the costs of the perks, estimated at $2 million to $2.5 million a year, and would only accept a free office and administrative support (together with a $9 million annual pension). He wrote in an explanatory op-ed piece for the *Wall Street Journal* that "One thing I learned during my years as CEO is that perception matters."

Deals like Welch's, however, continued to be made through the 1990s and beyond, as weak boards routinely approved whatever consultants said was the new standard for CEO employment agreements. In fact, compensation consultants told us that Welch's agreement itself was Xeroxed and used for people like John Snow at CSX—and there are few reports that any of those are being reimbursed like GE's after the "perception problem" was rectified.

IN 2001, when S&P declared the Tyco company the number one performer in the country, Tyco's CEO and chairman, L. Dennis Kozlowski, was on the cover of *BusinessWeek*. Kozlowski was interviewed for the *BusinessWeek* story at Tyco's modest, two-story wooden headquarters in New Hampshire. "We don't believe in perks," he told the magazine. "Not even executive parking spots." *Barron's* had featured Kozlowski in a cover story in 1999, portraying him as the next Jack Welch. Kozlowski had built Tyco's sales from $40 million to nearly $40 billion and had increased its value by seventyfold. Not long before, he had written a fascinating piece for *Directors & Boards* magazine about the relationship of CEOs and boards. "Considering the recent, well-publicized strife and scandal with several prominent CEOs and boards," he wrote, "it is no surprise that the integrity of the corporate governance process is on trial. Boards of directors can expect a higher degree of public scrutiny, and skeptical critics will challenge them with renewed rigor . . . So, as a CEO, I want a strong, competent board; one that can advise me and my staff how to continue succeeding . . . Is the CEO's criteria for a board of directors any different than the shareholder's? I don't think so. Effective corporate governance comes down to one word: accountability . . . With competent directors, shareholders can be confident of sufficient control over CEOs to guard against abuses."

It was an impressive and concise statement of what ought to be the case at more companies. Unfortunately, very little of it actually applied to Tyco. For exactly the reasons cited in the study of the one hundred biggest business failures of the era, the roof fell in on Tyco and Kozlowski in January 2002, just as it seemed at the peak of success: a charismatic, ambitious, visionary and autocratic CEO with a weak board, overpaying for an acquisition, aggressive goals, multiple titles, large compensation, extensive shareholdings, fawning press coverage—the whole package. A conflict of interest incident involving Kozlowski and Tyco's lead director triggered an internal investigation that exposed a culture of corruption, waste, and fraud. Kozlowski and Tyco's CFO, Mark

Swartz, were eventually convicted of grand larceny, securities fraud, and falsifying business records while taking compensation worth $170 million without the approval of Tyco's directors, abusing an employee loan program, and misrepresenting the company's financial condition to investors to boost the stock price while selling more than $430 million in stock. They were each sentenced to 8⅓ to 25 years in prison.

What was little remarked upon at the time was the astonishing negligence and flagrant conflicts within the Tyco board. Without any disclosure, Tyco had purchased houses from two different directors, one for $875,000 and the other for $2.25 million. Kozlowski had personally invested $5 million in another director's venture capital fund. Yet another director—who had been on the board for some thirty-four years—was being paid $360,000 a year for vaguely defined legal services.

But by far the worst conflict was with the "lead director" Frank Walsh, who had previously chaired the compensation committee and controlled two companies that did business with Tyco. Kozlowski had given Walsh a $20 million finder's fee for Walsh's role in what turned out to be a disastrous acquisition of CIT Group, Inc. When the rest of the board found out about the fee six months later and demanded repayment, Walsh refused, stalked out of the meeting muttering "Adios," and later quit the board. Kozlowski told the board that he had talked Walsh down from a $40 million fee. It was this fee incident that triggered an independent investigation and marked the beginning of the end for Kozlowski at Tyco. In their few public statements later and their testimony at the two Kozlowski and Swartz trials, board members said they hadn't been told what was going on. Or they were misled. Or they thought the lawyers and auditors were supposed to be catching this kind of thing. In reality, this was a board that wasn't asking questions and didn't want to. Abraham Zaleznik, a retired Harvard Business

School professor and trained psychoanalyst suggests Kozlowski was "a narcissistic personality who comes to believe that he and the institution are one." He summed up the board's relationship with Kozlowski this way: "There is a peculiar psychology at work. The members of the board feel that if they question him, it puts them in jeopardy. Standing directors don't want to lose their job. It's their job to speak up, but they become wimps. That is the short of it." He further noted, "They have the feeling that if they lose the CEO or stop him, that will create chaos. There is a fear of this and a desire to maintain stability."

The author and shareholder activist Robert Monks served on the Tyco board for ten years. He had been instrumental in Kozlowski's becoming the CEO because he respected his business skills and felt the company needed strong leadership. He resigned in 1994, early in Kozlowski's tenure, after sending him a memo expressing frustration that the board had "no defined role, no mission, no explicit benchmarks against which the board can be evaluated." Despite that, Monks stayed in touch with Kozlowski and found the actions that led to Kozlowski's downfall curious. "Kozlowski wouldn't have needed to steal a penny," Monks said, "because that board would have given him anything he asked for. He was a very detail-oriented accountant who was meticulous in everything he did with acquisitions, so it's kind of strange for him to have been so utterly careless in this."

Until at least March 2014, Dennis Kozlowski is Inmate #05A4820 at the Mid-State Correctional Facility in Marcy, New York. He gave us an interview there shortly after his appeal to the U.S. Supreme Court had been turned down. Kozlowski earned a dollar a day working in the prison laundry and, like most well-known, white-collar inmates, was isolated for his own security from the general population and kept in the protective custody unit, where he is surrounded by child molesters and prison snitches. Kozlowski seemed bright, charismatic, and well informed—he kept up with business publications—and grateful for the chance to talk: "Not much chance for intelligent conversation here." He was charming and inquisitive, and seemed open and sincere, convincing even. It was easy to picture him as a CEO, even in the drab surroundings of an empty prison visiting room. He said his retirement deal was, in fact, patterned exactly after Jack Welch's when his CFO had gotten a copy of it. "I was thinking of leaving for a private equity job, but several directors said they wanted to give me a retention agreement to hang around for seven years." He was surprised that the board agreed to a package amounting to $250 million to $300 million, when he had expected them to balk at a fraction of that amount. "If I was on somebody's board, I wouldn't have gone for that," he said.

Kozlowski said that he considered himself a victim of the times and a weak board. He felt he had become the poster boy for excessive pay in the wake of public anger over the Enron, WorldCom, and other scandals. He claimed that some Tyco board members actually had suggested he should be paying fees to all the directors like the one Walsh had received for the CIT deal. "I think it was a jealousy thing." He also felt his case should have been tried in civil court as a pay dispute with a board that wanted to get out of the agreement it had signed. "After Enron blew up in 2001, boards started taking a hard look at the contracts, figuring 'We owe him $300 million, we'd better fire him.'" He said he got irate when thinking about the directors at his two trials who testified that they had been kept in the dark about his compensation: "If they did not know what was going on, they certainly should have. I just don't buy that."

Kozlowski said that he felt that his compensation was justified in relation to what hedge fund managers were getting for creating considerably less value: "We were getting a one percent formula for bonuses, unlike hedge funds with their two [percent fees] and twenty [percent bonuses]." He admitted that things had gotten out of hand personally: "I was spending too much money. I could have kept things a lot simpler in my personal life, a hell of a lot simpler." He said he was focusing too obsessively on growing the company, getting into the office at six a.m. every day and working until nine p.m. "If I had it to do all over again, I probably would have been happier with slower growth and maybe twenty-five percent of the compensation I was earning. I would have had a better quality of life from a personal standpoint, and I wouldn't be sitting in jail right now."

Kozlowski didn't think much of the Tyco board. "I treated some of the directors as an afterthought because there's only so much time in the day," he recalled. "There were only two or three directors who if they nodded yes, chances are the other directors were going to go along with it. I guess I should have been as diligent about selecting directors as we were about acquisitions." He reflected with regret that if any of the directors had been strong, he might have had somebody to stick up for him instead of running away and claiming ignorance when things had gotten tough. He mentioned Ken Langone, who had been the head of the compensation committee at the New York Stock Exchange and defended its CEO Dick Grasso when he was under fire about his compensation. Kozlowski talked about serving on six public company boards—and said he'd had no problems asking tough questions as a director. "But I don't know why anybody in their right mind would go on a public company board today," he said. "Why risk that?"

When Wendy Lane, a director who had only joined the Tyco board in 2000 and had served on the audit committee, was asked in 2003 by *Corporate Board Member* magazine what she would do differently if considering joining another board, she replied: "I'd ask the CEO, 'What do you see as the role of the board and your relationship to the board? What kinds of decisions do you want them to help you with, and how far do you want them to go?' I don't want to be a board member who simply approves things. I want to be able to say, 'I don't agree yet; persuade me,' and have some give-and-take with the CEO. I would look closely at the strength and character of the management team on which the board relies."

Kozlowski said that he wasn't sure if or when things started to spin out of control: "I don't know, maybe when we started making the lists of the top twenty companies in the world and all that. I just started believing some of that press."

In the end, though, it's clear that Kozlowski and his directors shared the same flawed relationships that have plagued so many other boards. For Kozlowski, the board faded into irrelevance compared to the power, prestige, and satisfaction provided by the acquisitions he engineered. Perhaps with a stronger board to keep his talents within legal bounds, Kozlowski today might still be on top of the world instead of washing inmates' clothes at the Mid-State Correctional Facility. The highest praise he could muster for his board was exactly what had contributed so much to the company's downfall and to their—as well as his own—disgraces. He paused a moment, thinking how best to articulate it, and concluded: "They didn't slow me down."

5

Extraordinary Delusions

THE COLLECTIVE BRAINS of a ten-person board of directors weigh about thirty pounds, twenty-three pounds of which is water. Say about three pounds are lipids and another two pounds are proteins. Toss in some carbohydrates, soluble organic substances, and a dash of inorganic salts, and you have the recipe for higher-order judgment. With quality ingredients like these, why is it that so often CEOs and boards make glaringly bad judgment calls about running their businesses? The fact that they so often serve one another's interests at the expense of shareholders is troubling enough, but the problems in their decision making go deeper than conscious self-dealing. A fascinating range of research about human decision making addresses the largely unconscious sources of many of their bad decisions. Some of this research is evolutionary and anthropological, such as studying whether boards and banks followed the herding instinct all the way off the cliff. Other studies rely on ingenious quantitative analysis, such as seeking correlations between financial results and the presence of independent directors. Still other researchers travel into the human skull, to see which parts of the brain light up when people make risky decisions in a world of uncertainty. Above all, this diverse body of research tells us that apart from the obvious monetary incentives, a host of deeply ingrained, subconscious psychological proclivities and biases contribute mightily to companies going off the rails.

A survey of the literature on economic decisions introduces us to someone we'd never want to meet: the "rational economic man" who spends his working hours "maximizing utility," making logical choices to maximize his gains—in profit, efficiency, and market share. Not to worry about meeting him: he doesn't exist, though regrettably, he is the basis for a lot of our economics. Economic theorists readily grant that rational man is self-interested to a fault, but popular free enterprise mythologists like Ayn Rand and Alan Greenspan have assured us that this is not a problem; self-interest truly is good for us all. It creates millionaires. It's what drives the world's-worst-economic-system-except-there-is-none-better.

Rational economic man enjoys perfect access to information and calmly considers each alternative course of action. He (it's usually a "he") uses a cash-flow model to discount perfect information to current value and an arsenal of other analytical methods, weighing each decision carefully and maximizing returns. The reality, though, is much more complex: human beings act in perversely irrational ways much of the time and not the least in C-suite corner offices and boardrooms.

Garden-variety greed plays an undeniable role in leading people to less than ideal choices, but that only begins to tell the story. Pathbreaking research into the psychology of decision making over the past several decades has revealed the prominent role of social pressures, personality characteristics, and cognitive biases that lead to corporate leadership breakdowns. Business failures and scandals often stem from "conscious choices" that are really not conscious, as well as emotional reactions that we unknowingly justify with "reasons" a microsecond later. Why did so many of the best and brightest bankers continue to take on massive debt and take fatal risks while JPMorgan Chase's Jamie Dimon (and the heads of numerous smaller regional banks) heeded the signs of the economy imploding—or while Goldman Sachs and a number of hedge funds made a fortune betting on the housing collapse?

To say that these were "smarter" is a glib answer. It's more than IQ. After all, why do, in the face of withering criticism, American boards pay CEOs in the biggest companies not just exorbitant amounts, but 900 percent what their Japanese counterparts make and 300 percent what their European peers do? Why do many captains of industry become meek church mice when they sit down at someone else's board table? Why do otherwise intelligent and well-intentioned men and women, accomplished in their fields, selected for their leadership and acumen, too often fall prey to confusion, illusion, and delusion in making calls about corporate governance? Researchers have come up with a host of explanations.

People who research executive decision-making love to study the mergers-and-acquisitions market, possibly because the litany of misguided corporate moves in this one area is so lengthy: AOL/Time Warner, Sprint/Nextel, Quaker/Snapple, Daimler/Chrysler, ATT/NCR, ATT/TCI, Yahoo!/Broadcast.com, Citibank/Travelers, to name just a few. Bright people on boards constantly okay mergers when they also know most mergers fail, and these failures can be spectacular. On a percentage-lost record, perhaps the record for overconfidence and acquisition miscalculation would belong to VeriSign for its $21 billion acquisition of

Network Solutions, the internet domain registrar, in 2000. (The VeriSign CEO sat on Network Solutions's board and thought he saw the synergies too clearly.) Three years later, VeriSign dumped its prize at a corporate tag sale for a 99.5 percent capital loss.

One study of the effects of acquisitions, conducted by Columbia University professors Mathew Hayward and Donald Hambrick, found that acquisitions generally "tend to damage acquirers' performance, as reflected by shareholder wealth." They concluded that "not only did acquiring firms tend to lose value in general, but the larger the premium paid, the greater the loss (over a one-year postacquisition period)." Numerous studies have shown that approximately 80 percent of acquisitions fail to deliver on the projected per-share gains and that a great many fail spectacularly.

Acquisitions don't—or at least shouldn't—"just happen." Rather, they are the fruit of careful deliberation by the staff, CEO, and directors of our biggest companies. These people attained their positions through an employment tournament where the cream supposedly rises to the top. A minority of M&A transactions are done for good reason and succeed. M&A definitely plumps up the top revenue line of a corporation, and the elevated gross sales figure of the newly larger company catapults management into a new, higher class of "comparable companies" that the compensation consultants find very impressive when it comes time to boost executive pay. Some managers also love M&A because it creates a world of new squirrel holes in which accountants can hide nasty stuff. There are many stories of acquisitions—and the temerity with which CEOs and their boards have pursued them—that are explained more fully by insight into the dodgy thinking that's involved.

In virtually all corporations, the CEO is the mother, father, and obstetrician of all mergers and acquisitions. M&A activities occur *because* of the CEO and never in spite of him. For all the publicity they garner, multiple acquisitions, and particularly binge acquisitions, are usually bad business for everyone involved. If Company A decides to acquire Company B, it means one of two things:

a) The market is a bunch of fools who have undervalued Company B, and only Company A has the Athenian wisdom to see through this, pounce, and take the prize for the benefit of its shareholders. It's like going to Cartier and finding a diamond ring marked $1,000 instead of $10,000 after hundreds of shoppers have pawed through the wares. After all, why would you spend someone else's money to buy something for more than it's worth?

Or,

b) Company A is so well run, and the benefits flowing from a merger or acquisition are so great, that Company A's management, through the force of its brilliance, will be able to earn the premium overpaid out of shareholders' money tendered to acquire Company B. It's an alluring idea.

In the typical takeover, the CEO has convinced himself and his board that his perspicacity has identified an easy mark. Say the target company is currently selling for $20 a share. He cannot offer $19 a share. Nor can he offer only $21. As he begins to bid up the price to $25, $28, $30 with the help of willing investment bankers (who are paid by the size of the deal) and lawyers (who are paid by the hour as the mating dance turns into a complex dance marathon), the foundations of the price begin to heave and buckle away from reality. Competitors often join the bidding, thus driving it up more. Speculators start buying up the stock. The stakes rise: $32 . . . $34. The CEO and the board deliberate the next offer. Inexorably, they are drawn into a trap.

DESPITE SO MUCH EVIDENCE of the dangers of mergers and acquisitions, many CEOs, always green-lighted by their boards, pursue not just one but multiple or even simultaneous deals. Some even become like Tyco during the period that "Deal-a-Day Dennis" Kozlowski earned his nickname. One of the illuminating areas of research that helps to explain this perverse phenomenon concerns the cognitive bias of overconfidence, which some researchers refer to as "hubris."

CEOs are not known for their introspection, and most wouldn't agree to sit down on a psychiatrist's couch. Nor have these behavioral researchers the funding to dispatch squads of traveling shrinks to corner offices around the world. Instead, they often look at externally observable quantitative data to infer conclusions, using mathematical models as proof. For example, what's the relationship between narcissistic CEOs and company strategy and performance? If they cannot interview a CEO's mother to find out if she cooked special oatmeal to gratify his whims and thus contributed to his narcissistic personality, there are other routes to take. In one study, the academics measured the placement of the CEO's photograph in the company's annual report, the CEO's prominence in the company's press releases, the length of the CEO's *Who's Who* entry, the frequency of the CEO's use of the pronoun "I" in interviews; and the CEO's pay relative to the next-highest person's.

The CEO-hubris-acquisition connection was explored by a UCLA professor named Richard Roll during the Reagan years. In more recent times, before it exploded, the financial rocket was powered by an unstable fuel called collateralized debt. But in that bygone era, Wall Street's rocket scientists used junk bonds, a peculiarly unstable form of alchemy that shared the curious property of turning lead into gold (and later, back into lead).

In the 1980s, acquirers were funded not by cash in the bank, but by "fully confident letters" from Drexel Burnham Lambert signaling that they could come up with a junk bond financing. Corporate shopaholics spent that funny money with an élan that evoked Imelda Marcos in the shoe department of Neiman Marcus. Roll captured the spirit of the times this way:

> Although some firms engage in many acquisitions, the average individual bidder/manager has the opportunity to make only a few takeover offers during his career. He may convince himself that the valuation is right and that the market does not reflect the full economic value of the combined firm. For this reason . . . the takeover phenomenon can be termed the "hubris hypothesis." If there actually are no aggregate gains in takeover, the phenomenon depends on the overbearing presumption of bidders that their valuations are correct. . . .

Eleven years later, Mathew Hayward and Donald Hambrick studied 106 acquisitions in one of the largest studies ever made seeking evidence of hubris in the acquisition process:

> CEO hubris, manifested as exaggerated pride or self-confidence, plays a substantial role in the acquisition process, particularly in the decision of how much to pay. We have found that several sources of hubris have their own independent and additive effects on the premium the acquirer is willing to pay. First, the better the recent perfor-

> mance of the acquiring firm, the more that is paid for an acquisition. This represents a tendency to attribute organizational success to the CEO and for the CEO to deem that success as applicable to managing additional entities. The greater the CEO's confidence in his or her own abilities (as well as those of subordinates), the greater the benefits the CEO believes he or she can bring to an acquired entity and the higher the price paid.

The biggest merger of all time, Time Warner and AOL, may forever rank as the biggest such blunder of all time. Two days after the announcement of the merger, the market hacked $20 billion from the value of the company. Gerald Levin, Time Warner's CEO/chairman at the time, wrote it off as "a shuffling of shareholders" and "some [normal] dislocation in a deal of this size." Ultimately, more than $196 billion of shareholders' money went up the chimney as the combined market capitalization dropped from $280 billion when the merger was announced in 2000 to $84 billion by 2004. Steve Case was removed as chairman in 2003, quit the board in 2005, and relocated back to Hawaii, where he is now the state's second-largest landowner.

Hambrick and Hayward went on to correlate higher premiums paid in acquisitions not only to recent organizational success, but also to such factors as:

- Recent media praise for the CEO;
- The CEO's sense of self-importance (his or her pay compared to that of other executives in their firm is a particularly revealing indicator);
- The CEO also filling the chairman's seat.

Think of Dennis Kozlowski appearing on the cover of *BusinessWeek*, being hailed as the next Jack Welch, having a board that gives him a $300-million-plus retention package, and dominating what he felt was a weak set of directors. Then think how predictable something like Tyco's acquisition in 2001 of CIT Group for $9.2 billion might be. Tyco sold CIT the next year at a loss of around $4.6 billion.

In another study, professors Ulrike Malmendier and Geoffrey Tate from Stanford and UCLA respectively came up with a measure of CEO overconfidence. For evidence, they looked at Fortune 500 CEOs who held options in their own company's stock until the years of their expiration. "Previous literature in corporate finance shows that risk-averse CEOs should exercise stock options well before expiration," they maintain. By exercising options early, a CEO can diversify his portfolio. "Holding an option until its final year . . . indicates that the CEO has been consistently 'bullish' about the company's prospects," they maintain. "The CEO is repeatedly betting his personal wealth on the company's future returns."

They then studied CEO merger decisions and they found that overconfident CEOs felt the urge to merge with other companies much more strongly than their less self-assured counterparts. These CEOs also made these acquisitions more often with internal funds, rather than going to the equity market, in part because the market would not value the projects as highly as they would. Overconfident CEOs use twice as much available marginal internal cash than do less confident CEOs. "These CEOs tend to think that under their glorious leadership the stock prices will keep going up, so they keep holding on to their shares and their options," Malmendier reasoned.

THE STUDY of psychological motivations complements the findings about the role of CEO hubris in interesting ways. A leader in this field was a Harvard professor named David McClelland, who was best known for developing the scoring algorithm for the Thematic Apperception Test (TAT) and the theory of motivation or drive. The TAT has become a mainstay of psychological testing, something like the now-iconic Rorschach inkblot test. Since it has Freudian underpinnings, cultural bias, and other problems, the TAT has legions of detractors, but it still enjoys a large base of trained proponents who keep it going strong. To the extent that the TAT is accurate, it derives its validity from the fact that the subject's drives are revealed indirectly and subconsciously. The test is much harder to "game" than many of those in the psychologists' toolkit. Subjects look at simple drawings and are asked to invent stories about the scenes that are depicted: "What are they saying?" "What happens next?" The content of their stories is supposed to reveal the relative strengths of their drives, their motives, and internal conflicts. McClelland identified six basic drives: power, achievement, affiliation, aggression, deference, and autonomy. The first three hold particular relevance to the behavior of corporate leaders.

The "power" drive includes the needs to be strong and influential and to have an impact. McClelland found that executives tended either to aim their power toward aggrandizing themselves ("personal power") or outward toward the organization ("altruistic power"). The latter kind tend to build good organizations, while "ample evidence" was found that the former group is more likely to be "rude to other people, they drink too much, they try to exploit others sexually, and they collect symbols of personal prestige such as fancy cars or big offices."

Those high in "achievement" want the latitude to exercise personal responsibility and the freedom to take at least a moderate amount of risk. These executives perceive too little risk as lacking in challenge, and therefore in limiting the opportunity to demonstrate superior performance. They enjoy competing, and getting positive feedback, often through measurement. Perhaps this explains why some CEOs can bear the intense pressure of quarterly earning announcements and daily fluctuations in their company's stock prices, and can get themselves and their teams energized to meet goals. "Affiliation" includes the needs for cooperation, friendship, and acceptance. Tellingly, McClelland found that a high need for affiliation could be problematic for business executives, since it led to making exceptions for individuals, which could result in chaos. This might explain why so many CEOs seem comparatively aloof and self-centered.

Executives were found to have stronger needs for power and achievement than the average population, and successful executives had an even higher need. Perhaps unsurprisingly, among successful executives the need for affiliation often appears relatively low, whereas the need for social power is high. Acquisitions are a highly appealing method by which corporate leaders may satisfy their drives for power and achievement. For one thing, they are among the riskiest actions a company can take. Acquiring other firms is an ultra-macho activity and CEOs see acquisitions as tests of their mettle. They also offer more rapid achievement. One can quickly become a bigger fish in a bigger pond without taking the time or enduring the struggle of tending to organic corporate growth. The increased rewards in pay, perquisites, and prestige can be enormous and intoxicating.

Acquisitions thus provide a seductive external measurement of where a CEO stands among his peers. McClelland found the desire for such validation is much more prevalent among high achievers than it is among the rest of the population. It may account, as well, for why CEOs who are already wealthy beyond most people's wildest dreams still seek ever greater compensation—

to them it's less about what the money can buy than it is about keeping score.

Almost every business executive, particularly after the economic meltdown, will freely admit that "risk" is at the heart of business. Mergers and acquisitions are ways to put a *lot* of other people's money at risk very quickly, and boards know that, statistically, most of these efforts end badly. Yet they think things will be different for them, that they are somehow better, smarter, or more destined to win. Against what ought to be their better judgment, boards have condoned this behavior tens of thousands of times, and will do so again when the current economic wreckage is cleared.

ANOTHER REVEALING AREA of research, which underscores the irrational mechanisms so often at play in the decision making of corporate leaders, explores the role of emotions in hijacking thought processes. CEOs are well paid because, allegedly, they can think about and motor through the dangerous landscape of risk more swiftly and surely than lesser mortals. Directors, in theory, help with the navigation and copiloting. But research has shown that the ways in which people evaluate risk are often anything but dispassionately rational.

Scientists are looking at psychology but also neurobiology. Jack Stuppin, who spent thirty years on boards at Silicon Valley startups, has observed the sort of behavior that researchers are referring to when they postulate that the hormone dopamine may influence corporate decision making. Stuppin points out that one of the most difficult decisions corporate leaders face is how long to keep pushing capital into the losing slot machine of a given business investment. How long should they continue to invest in projects or divisions that are not returning the expected profit payoffs?

"Particularly with new technology," Stuppin says, "you get an order here and an order there, and a big one from a prestigious or potentially large customer makes everybody's thinking about it more optimistic—that it will really take off. I am getting orders from places that I think are important . . . but I don't have any volume. One doesn't know if this is the beginning, middle, or end. What do you do?"

In his college psychology class years ago, Stuppin read about experiments with rats that provided him with insight into why corporate leaders often continue to put good money after bad. "You put a rat in a cage," he said, "and you put a bar in there, and the bar is set to give the rat a pellet of food every time, or every fifth time he hits it. The rat will eventually learn to hit the bar to get the food pellet. Over a period of an hour, the number of hits will reach a certain plateau and level out. That's 'fixed ratio' reinforcement."

A soda machine gives you precisely one can, immediately, each time you insert one dollar. A slot machine may give you nothing, or a million dollars, and the time between payoffs is seemingly somewhat variable. To a point, people engage in a behavior much more—whether it's hitting a bar, pulling a slot machine handle, or investing in failing projects—if the rewards vary in size and frequency. "In business, this sort of variable intermittent reinforcement is dangerous," Stuppin said, "because it is much stronger than any other kind of reinforcement you could get."

Researchers at the University of British Columbia found clues to the behavior Stuppin recalled from his college psychology class. Dr. Catharine Winstanley at UBC says that the neurohormone dopamine "hijacks" the parts of the brain "associated with planning and forming strategies." Dopamine has been shown to play a powerful role in risk evaluation, reward and motivation, perception, mood, cognition, and learning. It can trump the brain's natural, moderate reward system, green-lighting a gambler to wager away the monthly mortgage payment or a CEO to blow the pension fund on a pet project.

"Rats given the choice of an activity with small but consistent rewards very quickly learn to maximize their benefits," Dr. Winstanley explains, "but when dosed with amphetamine to simulate the rush of gambling action, they begin to prefer the high-risk option of bigger, infrequent rewards." These sorts of findings are, of course, from rats, but they are undertaken to correlate human and rodent behavior. For corporate boards, this might be a humbling thought.

Motorola put sixty-six satellites in earth orbit for the Iridium phone project. Over twelve agonizing years, time after time, it poured more shareholder money in—$5 billion in total—bit by bit, waiting for that big return. After a dozen years, Motorola had found fifteen thousand customers in the world willing to shell out $3,000 for a brick-sized one-pound-plus phone that cost $7 a minute to use. In 2000, when the capital investment reached $90,000 per customer and user acquisition stalled, Motorola sold off Iridium for one-half cent on the dollar for its investment. This is not higher-order thinking.

Another hormone, epinephrine, also plays a role in decision making by triggering the fight-or-flight response when stressful challenges arise. Fight or flight was discovered by Dr. Walter Cannon, who had a chance to see both in action a few years later when he also made important discoveries in the treatment for wounds and shock during World War I. Through some of Professor Cannon's work, we know that when a CEO reads a letter from a $1,000-an-hour hostile attorney informing him that his firm is the target of a takeover, the CEO's eyes send a signal to the visual cortex in the back of his brain. From there, the image of the squiggles on the page is pushed forward to the midbrain and frontal lobes and translated into words, which are interpreted as being very disturbing. Alarm bells go off in the hypothalamus, which manufactures dopamine, which in turn sends all-points bulletins to the pituitary gland, which then sends a jolt down the spinal cord to the adrenal glands that sit on top of the kidneys. This happens at lightning speed, but the result is that epinephrine squirts into the blood. Fight or flight. Epinephrine-rich blood causes a boost in the hormone cortisol, which causes stress. These hormones trump the homeostasis (smooth steady-state body functions, another Walter Cannon discovery) that facilitates higher forms of thinking or judgment. These higher cognitive processes might lead us calmly to consider a hostile takeover bid or to refrain from swearing in the presence of a *Fortune* magazine reporter who's sitting in the room at the moment. Under the influence of the hormones it's not so tidy.

PROFESSOR JENNIFER LERNER of Harvard's Kennedy School of Government is the only psychologist on the School's faculty and studies how emotional reactions affect high-level decision making among leaders. She has spent much time studying fear, anger, and the willingness to take on risk.

Lerner runs the Harvard Decision Science Laboratory, which was created in December 2008 to conduct research at the nexus of economics, psychology, and neuroscience. Some three thousand executive education students come through the Kennedy School each year in addition to the enrolled students and some volunteer to get wired up with electrodes. Dr. Lerner said that army generals are particularly willing and curious. The volunteers are often shown a scary or enraging video (such as September 11 news footage to induce anger) to prime certain emotions and then are asked to perform tasks that involve evaluating risk or the prices of things. The stimuli and responses are measured against those of control groups. "Emotions become perceptual lenses through which we perceive information," Dr. Lerner says.

According to Lerner, Americans tend to exhibit anger more readily than those in many other cultures, and the effects of being in power closely resemble those of being angry. Her findings indicate that executives who are angry have substantially larger appetites for risk and more optimism about outcomes: "Not feeling you need more information. Underperceiving risks. Being prone to taking risks. Attributing causality to individuals rather than situations. Simplistic thought." Fear has the opposite effect: frightened people shun risk and are more pessimistic.

We may speculate that these emotions have kicked in when executives are engaged in a hostile takeover bid—like Oracle versus PeopleSoft or Microsoft versus Yahoo—and assault each other with full-page newspaper ads (anger). Livelihoods and prestige are at risk (fear). Actual outcomes suggest that cooler heads may not prevail. Sometimes companies take a position that locks them into a future course of action after emotions subside. The stakes can be billions of dollars of shareholder money and comparable effects on other stakeholders. Given that anger is the more prevalent emotion among executive decision makers, what can be done to prevent its harmful effects? Lerner suggests that changing the context and the environment in which the executives are operating can improve outcomes, particularly through what she terms "predecisional accountability to an audience with unknown views." In an experiment, angry decision makers who knew they would have to explain themselves to a knowledgeable group with unknown opinions made far more careful, nuanced, and well-thought-out decisions than those who did not have such accountability. The ramifications for corporate boards are clear: if we require greater accountability to shareholders, directors should make better decisions and reduce the risk of disastrous governance failures.

Researchers from Cambridge University have correlated traders' profitability with their morning levels of testosterone.

> A trader's morning testosterone level predicts his day's profitability. We also found that a trader's cortisol rises with both the variance of his trading results and the volatility of the market. Our results suggest that higher testosterone may contribute to economic return, whereas cortisol is increased by risk. . . . Our results point to a further possibility: testosterone and cortisol are known to have cognitive and behavioral effects, so if the acutely elevated steroids we observed were to persist or increase as volatility rises, they may shift risk preferences and even affect a trader's ability to engage in rational choice.

One researcher even went so far as to suggest that steroid feedback loops may contribute to market waves. It is surely curious to think of men's hormones washing around the world and roiling stock exchanges. (The economists have a world-class term for this financial condition: autoregressive conditional heteroskedasticity.)

NEUROCHEMICALS ARE NOT, by any means, the only forces distorting decision making. Even when the pituitary gland is behaving itself, we often don't think straight. Thinking has itself been found to be prone to abundant systematic errors, most often called cognitive biases, and many of them, undoubtedly, exercise effects on the decisions of CEOs and boards. Some of this research was pioneered by two psychologists, Daniel Kahneman and Amos Tversky, under the heading of "prospect theory." Thanks to the great insight their findings brought to the understanding of business and economics, Kahneman was awarded the Nobel Prize in Economics in 2002. (Tversky had died by then.)

The following experiment illustrates the sort of distortion in thinking that Kahneman and Tversky discovered:

Subjects were asked to pick one from Column A and one from Column B:			
Column A: Choose one		*Column B: Choose one*	
1. Sure gain of $2,400	2. 25% chance to gain $10,000 and 75% chance to gain nothing	3. Sure loss of $7,500	4. 75% chance to lose $10,000 and 25% chance to lose nothing

Eighty-four percent of the subjects chose Choice 1: it's risk-averse. Eighty-seven percent picked Choice 4: it's riskier, and has the same expected monetary value as Choice 3. Seventy-three percent of the people choose the combination 1 and 4, which has an expected value of a $5,100 loss. Three percent chose 2 and 3, which has an expected value of a $5,000 loss. In reality, the combination of 2 and 3 is the best because your loss is the smallest. The selection of 4 is riskier than 3, because you could lose more.

Kahneman and Tversky then reframed the choices as follows:	
Column C	*Column D*
25% chance to win $2,400 and 75% chance to lose $7,600.	25% chance to win $2,500 and 75% chance to lose $7,500.

This time, all of the subjects chose Column D. Column D is *the same deal as 2 and 3 above*. By altering how the same deal was presented, the *preference grew from 3 percent to 100 percent*. The findings from this study contradicted the prevailing economic assumption that people are naturally risk-averse, while also showing that the way a decision is framed influences its outcome. Kahneman and Tversky discerned in the results what they called the cognitive bias of "aversion to a sure loss," which leads a majority of people to opt for the riskier choice when they confront the fact that they are likely to lose no matter what they do. Our rational cognitive machinery pops a gear and breaks down.

Another such bias that is relevant to corporate decision making is the "optimism bias." Our decisions are highly sensitive to whether options are presented in a positive or a negative light. Tversky and Kahneman demonstrated this bias in action by asking subjects to choose between two public health policies: an Asian disease epidemic is breaking out and is expected to kill 600 people.

Program A: Would save 200 people.
Program B: Stands a 1:3 chance of saving 600 people, and a 2:3 chance of saving no one.

Subjects chose the less risky program, Program A, by a 4:1 margin. Then the frame was flipped:

In **Program C:** 400 will certainly die.
Program D: There's a 1:3 chance no one will die, and a 2:3 chance that 600 will die.

By the same 4:1 margin, the same group of subjects picked program D, the *more risky* choice. Suddenly it's much more acceptable to run a 2:3 chance of killing 600, than a 100 percent chance of killing 400. By flipping the frame, the 80:20 low-risk vote became a 20:80 high-risk vote. But *the choices are identical.*

Consider how this might influence an investment project. A CEO and the board might be paying a big premium to acquire a company to expand their product line and take over a market. Alternatively, they might defensively be acquiring a competitor to keep it from depressing their profit margins. The board might approve a different purchase price limit depending on how the board heard the presentation, even though the target company is the same. Because the CEO usually controls how such proposals are framed, this bias goes a long way toward explaining why boards so often seem to be rubber stamps. If you are on the Time Warner board and you are given a presentation showing the synergies and unlimited potential for a combination with AOL at the height of the dot-com bubble hysteria, what would you do?

In another phenomenon called the *Monte Carlo fallacy,* superstition and overconfidence are introduced into decisions. Prior experience is mistakenly taken as an omen for the next outcome.

People often think they have a better chance of getting heads on the fifth flip of a coin if they have gotten heads in the prior four. They see a pattern where there is none and correlations that don't exist in a series of random events that appear similar. Thus: "I am especially confident in this, my fifth acquisition, because the prior four went so well." The CEO might not see that this one is vastly different (which also invokes bounded rationality—the need to simplify problems, sometimes to the point of error).

One of the cognitive biases most relevant to the boardroom is "fundamental attribution error," which has to do with overweighing the influence of a person's internal disposition, or character, on an outcome, when in fact situational factors might have much more to do with it. A board might give undue credit to a CEO for a good year, when in reality it was the rest of the company or the market environment or sheer happenstance that was responsible. The media-fueled CEO superstar culture feeds this bias. Conversely, the CEO might get undue blame for a failure when no one could have saved the ship. Professor Lee Ross, who coined the term *fundamental attribution error,* performed an experiment at Stanford University in which he asked students to make up tough questions and present them to other students in the class. Everyone, including the student observers, was then asked to rate the knowledgeability of the person asking the questions and the one who answered them. Overwhelmingly, the questioners were rated as being more knowledgeable. The context of the situation—that one of the subjects was asking questions he or she had made up—was ignored.

Self-serving bias is a term used to describe the tendency of people to attribute failures to the outside environment rather than to themselves. Max Bazerman, a professor at Harvard Business School, has done self-serving bias experiments with auditors. In 2002, he gave five ambiguous auditing case studies to 139 auditors at the Big Four accounting firms. Half of them were to judge the accountants' work as if they had been hired by the company being audited. The rest took on the role of representatives of a company doing business with the audited company. By a 2:1 margin, the auditors working for the company approved the auditing decisions. Twice as many subjects in the other group found problems with the audits as approved them—the opposite ratio. This bias appears, for example, when boards hang on to a CEO longer than the situation warrants. No director enjoys the hassle of a firing and a search, but the bias can be invoked to justify the decision: "It's a bad economy; it's not his fault."

What happens when people see someone else screw up? If it's not someone they identify with, they tend to blame the person for the failure and to discount the environment. That is the opposite of the standard they apply to themselves. A board that identifies with a CEO instead of the shareholders can absolve itself, and the CEO, of responsibility or blame for failure and perhaps even go as far as the Chesapeake Energy board did in overcompensating Aubrey McClendon. In the midst of an SEC investigation Krispy Kreme blamed the lo-carb diet fad for its problems, even though Dunkin' Donuts did not suffer the same reversals.

Conversely, when good things happen, it's because of the leaders' brilliance in anticipating the opportunity and exploiting it to the fullest. In the spring of 2006, in a context of artificially easy money and a bubble economy, self-serving bias and attribution error were beautifully articulated by the secretary of the treasury, John Snow, who was also the former CEO of the CSX railroad and a former chairman of the Business Roundtable. Snow implicitly defended the work of many boards in ballooning the wage differential between CEOs and workers from 30:1 to about 275:1: "What's been happening in the United States for about twenty years is [a] long-term trend to differentiate compensation. Look at the Harvard economics faculty, look at doctors over here at George Washington University . . . look at baseball players, look at football players. We've moved into a star system. Across virtually all professions, there have been growing gaps. In an aggregate sense, [compensation] reflects the marginal productivity of CEOs. Do I trust the market for CEOs to work efficiently? Yes." So CEOs were responsible for the productivity increases of the decade.

Yet thirty months later, when he testified about the financial crisis, Snow laid the blame on "the financial community," "housing finance value chain participants," "traditional risk management activities," "market participants," and a host of systemic factors. At some point between the two speeches, the role of the star CEOs simply disappeared: self-serving bias.

Confirmation bias refers to the tendency to interpret information so it conforms to one's preconceptions. For example, Merrill Lynch looked around in 2006 or so and made a strategic decision to chase Goldman-style returns by getting into the subprime business late in the game, when adverse selection left only the worst borrowers in the market. The bank pursued this strategy to its doom. The management and board assumed Merrill was just like all the other banks, could replicate their success, and made a facile decision to jump in late.

Conversely, Ralph Whitworth, who manages Relational Investors fund and sometimes goes onto boards to change failing corporate strategies, joined the Sovereign Bank board in 2006. When he heard how popular their new auto loan program was, alarm bells went off in his head. He knew the bottom-of-the-barrel customers could get loans nowhere else, and he tried to exit the business as fast as he could. He did not succumb to the confirmation heuristic.

Yahoo's extended parting with chairman/CEO Terry Semel and founder Jerry Yang illustrates a board showing a great deal of confirmation bias. Semel's departure had been under consideration for a long time, and was finally triggered by 30 percent withhold votes against numerous directors. Yang suffered a similar fate the following year, again catalyzed by an external agent: a Microsoft takeover bid. Until that happened, the board was stuck in confirmation bias because the group didn't understand their performance or didn't see it for what it apparently was, until the votes and the bid knocked the motes from their eyes.

Additional biases appear in intriguing ways in the context of the merger-and-acquisition problem discussed earlier. For example, numerous studies have documented the existence of a cognitive bias known as *winner's curse*. The idea is that people will tend to radically inflate the value of something, sometimes by as much as tenfold, as they pursue it. And after they own it, thanks to the *endowment effect*, they believe the value to be much greater than it truly is. In repeated demonstrations of winner's curse, the Harvard professor Max Bazerman over a decade has separated his MBA students from $17,000 by auctioning $20 bills in class. The rule is this: the two top bids must pay, though only one wins the $20. In more than two hundred auctions, the top two bids always totaled at least $39, and in one case totaled $407. Although never a student in Bazerman's class, Robert Campeau bankrupted most of the North American retailing industry by chasing Federated Stores up from $33 to $73 a share in his 1988 takeover bidding duel against Macy's. All of his money was borrowed on top of the junk bonds he'd just borrowed to acquire Allied Stores, and of course the whole thing collapsed in bankruptcy two years later, bringing much of the retail sector down with it. For a CEO or a board on an acquisition tear, this bias can self-justify past actions and legitimize future overpayments. This can also mean digging in, defending an acquisition long after it's obvious that someone made a mistake.

Another kind of irrational thinking that would clearly contribute to the misguided pursuit of acquisitions was discovered by

Dr. Barry Staw at the University of California at Berkeley. He found that people have an innate resistance to weighing sunk costs, which is the already-invested money one cannot recover when one must make a new decision whether to invest more.

In a business simulation, he observed business students committing much more money to a failing company if they themselves had funded the original investment in it, rather than just having inherited the problem. In another experiment, he examined what NBA teams did with their highest-drafted players. His statistical analysis showed that they played more minutes and stayed with the team longer, even after controlling for on-court performance and other factors. Two other researchers went to a thoroughbred racetrack and asked 70 people who *had just placed* a bet how likely they thought they were to win. On a 7-point scale, the average answer was 4.81. Another 70 people were asked just *before* placing their own bets, and their estimates averaged 3.48.

The line between optimism and arrogance has never been clear, but we often commit ever more resources to a course of action that we ought to see as a lost cause. The Iridium satellite, the Concorde jet, and nuclear power plants tormented boards for years. Metro newspapers are currently bedeviling boards for the same reason.

BY NO MEANS do these subconscious biases and judgment errors tell the whole story behind the irrationality that often creeps into the thinking of CEOs and boards. Another set of findings in psychology that relates closely to the problem of biases has to do with the phenomenon widely known as *groupthink*. A Yale psychology professor named Irving Janis popularized this concept, which he defined as "a deterioration of mental efficiency, reality testing, and moral judgment that results from in-group pressures."

Janis identified eight symptoms of the phenomenon, including: "illusions of invulnerability (excessive optimism and risk taking); illusions of unanimity; illusions of group morality; rationalizations to discount warning signals; stereotyping of the 'enemy' as weak, evil, or stupid; self-censorship by members; mind-guarding (keeping negative feedback away from the group); and direct pressure to conform and accept stereotypes."

The collapse of WorldCom presents a clear example of groupthink. The company grew by sixty-five acquisitions over six years, but beneath that "success" lay an ever expanding accounting fraud. When the crimes were discovered and it came time to clean house, four hundred people were fired. Few of them saw the whole picture, but plenty knew something was very rotten. Yet no one stepped forward. Why? WorldCom's board later investigated and issued a report: "The answer seems to lie partly in a culture emanating from corporate headquarters that emphasized making the numbers above all else; kept financial information hidden from those who needed to know; blindly trusted senior officers even in the face of evidence that they were acting improperly; discouraged dissent; and left few, if any, outlets through which employees believed they could safely raise their objections."

For all the irrationality that occurs when a director is sitting alone in a room, the presence of other people can amplify it. The introduction of social or group dynamics invokes a new level of complexity. Playing a role are an array of insidious influences that have been studied: people's self-image, games of power and influence, assessments of social standing, information hoarding, submission to authority, polarization of opinions toward extremes, social conformity, pluralistic ignorance (when group members pretend no one knows anything about a problem), the delusion of group efficacy, and much more.

The economist Hersh Shefrin, who pioneered the field known

as behavioral finance, has studied group effects. "One key question is whether group behavior mitigates or amplifies the cognitive errors to which individuals are prone," Shefrin writes. "Researchers have found that groups often amplify individual errors. This is an especially important finding for corporate managers, in that most major corporate decisions are made in group settings. In this respect, research suggests that senior managers working in committees are even more prone to escalate their commitment to projects whose outcomes may have become questionable."

One of the most creative and rigorous scholars of board psychology is Professor James Westphal, from the University of Michigan. In a twenty-year career he has conducted a stream of studies that measure with abundant statistics many of the foibles of CEO and board behavior. He has shown, for example, that kissing the boss's backside (Westphal's term is "ingratiatory behavior") wins board seats at a disproportional rate for men who didn't go to prestigious colleges; that CEOs actually seek less advice when more independent directors are at the table; that boards with higher percentages of independent directors are less likely to challenge the CEO; that women and minorities who brownnose other directors and CEOs still don't move up the board ladder as rapidly as white men do; and, perhaps most important, that directors who "gave honest feedback to management, provided tight oversight, and lobbied for close evaluation of executive proposals did not reap the same benefits [as those who did not]. In fact, behaviors that promoted shareholder interests were punished."

In discussing his insights into breakdowns in decision making by our corporate leaders, Westphal shows how group effects—specifically that of a possibly unconscious allegiance to a social group—contribute to the insidious bias of attribution error: "The two critical factors that explain the most variance in governance failure are social ties between top managers and directors, and attribution bias. In this case, homogeneity of the managers leads to very serious attribution biases in which outside directors will tend to take an excessively sympathetic view of the causes of performance problems or the motives for executive behavior. They will tend to discount problems or attribute them to extraneous causes and attribute them to top managers' mistakes." Executives, in turn, attribute disappointing performance to market conditions without examining their own culpability. Too often, the decision is to pursue the same strategy with more resources and vigor, leading nowhere.

Ralph Whitworth of Relational Investors tells a story of how on one occasion he overcame pluralistic ignorance:

> After some negotiation, I went on a board of a large technology company. The company had a lot of governance issues that it was facing. Shortly before I went on the board, the company named the CFO as the new CEO. I think they wanted to get this appointment made and out of the way before I came on board.
>
> Before my first board meeting, we had, as often happens, a board dinner the night before. I asked the question at the dinner about why they chose the CFO rather than the president, who was the other obvious candidate. Someone said, "Well, let's have the chairman answer that." The chairman said, "It was my recommendation." I told the board that I had gotten to know both of the executives and that both were good individuals, but that considering what the company's mission is and where it is headed it seemed that the president was more suitable.
>
> One of the other directors said, "I felt that way, too." And another director said, "That is how I saw it." It went like that around the room. At that dinner we decided to

> change the succession configuration, even though it had been publicly announced, because we determined that a majority of the board members thought that the president was a better choice.

Whitworth added that there was no duplicity involved. The group simply got caught up in pluralistic ignorance and named the wrong man to run the major company.

If at times members silently disagree, at other times they can loudly and publicly agree, to a fault. This is the bias known as *group polarization*. Polarization does not mean that the board splits into two opposite, hostile camps. Rather, polarized groups tend to adopt a more extreme version of a viewpoint they may separately have held prior to meeting as a group. If the members are predisposed toward risk aversion, they will become even more risk averse when they meet in a room. If they are prone to gamble, they will seek even more risk when they get together, bidding up the offer price on an acquisition, loading up with even more debt, or approving audacious market expansion plans.

As if these group effects weren't insidious enough, there are also many negative effects due to social pressure felt within the boardroom. For instance, there are ways in which dissenting board members are subject to retribution, some quite subtle, by the other board members and the CEO. James Westphal explored the consequences of directors opposing the wills of CEOs and actually advocating the interests of the shareholders who elected them. "When corporate directors threaten the interests of top managers by participating in changes that increase board control over management, they may experience social costs that offset the potential financial benefits from enacting the changes," he wrote. Offenses could include advocating the separation of the positions of CEO and chairman, trying to install independent directors in committee chairs (before that was required), and opposing poison-pill antitakeover measures. Westphal looked at public data and learned that rebellious directors subsequently had a harder time getting onto other boards, and if they did, they were likely to be at smaller companies. Many directors look at increasingly important board memberships as climbing a ladder into the stratosphere of prestige and power. Thus, the pressures for conformity and silence, so long as it avoids legal liability, are many.

In the selection of board members, those who won't rock the boat have an advantage. Sitting board members frequently suggest prospective new directors. Board search firms' influence may be rising, but all of them naturally seek candidates who, at a minimum, will comport themselves in a friendly way. Also, no matter how a candidate's name originates, he or she must gain the approval of the CEO before being selected for automatic election. Thus, CEOs effectively exercise veto control over board nominations. They are free to favor those whom they believe will be supportive of their views. "The board is the agent of the CEO," Hersh Shefrin notes. "Structuring boards is not so easy. You do need a board and a CEO that have a positive working relationship so the organization can function. On the other hand, the trouble is that board members are as susceptible to these psychological issues as anyone else."

Once our congenial candidate gets on board, what will he or she do? Nell Minow summarizes it succinctly: "The primary qualification for board members is people who can walk into a room, immediately size it up, and fit in. Boards are seeking consensus builders. But when you have nine consensus builders and one bossy guy who controls all the information going to them, it's a recipe for disaster."

As Michael Useem of the Wharton School has shown, when a new director begins to advocate unpopular or iconoclastic opinions, even in a friendly way, he tests the boundaries of the "permission space" set by a CEO and chairman (often the same person) and the culture of the group. At that point, an amiable but independent-minded board member can be regarded by the rest as one of two things: a constructive maverick or a pain in the backside. Ultimately, whether the person is perceived as the former or the latter is not entirely under his or her control. Useem's research also established that corporate boards serve the purpose of socializing leaders to protect the autonomy and final decision-making authority of top managers. For the most part, he found, the strongest unifying factor was encroachment on the CEO or board's authority by outsiders such as regulators or potential acquirers.

What happens when a director publicly advocates on the inside the sorts of opinions that come from the outside? Fundamentally, the group pushes him to the outside: the opposite polarity from cohesion is *social distancing,* otherwise known as ostracism. It can appear in overt or subtle forms. Perhaps no one wants to sit next to the odd man out at the board dinner. His comments are ignored. He's not invited to golf anymore. There might be exclusionary gossip.

Facing up to a hubristic CEO can be a challenge, even for a competent, knowledgeable director. An arrogant CEO who doesn't want to be told "no" can become defensive and heavy-handed. Warren Hellman, a former president of Lehman Brothers and a founder of the successful Hellman & Friedman private equity firm, tells a story from a different company that is typical of dissenting directors:

> I was on the board of a financial company. The CEO wanted to make three acquisitions. Another director and I looked at it and said, "This is awful. These are not good companies. We should not be doing this deal." We expressed our

point of view at a board meeting. The CEO sent his "development" people out of the room. Then he said to us, "You are really hurting the morale of my entire management team by being so openly hostile." I said, "We are at a board meeting. What are we supposed to do? You say you are buying this at eight times earnings, but if you really put everything in, you are buying it at twenty times earnings." Basically, the two of us were singled out: he sent all the investment bankers and the lawyers to talk to us. He said, "You are disturbing the whole structure of the company." Well, we lost. We did vote against the acquisitions. They were a disaster. They just blew 160 years of net worth through these three acquisitions.

The other guy and I got off the board. But you just sat there and said to yourself, "Oh my God. They're not even listening! They have this whole packaged presentation. They have made up their minds." To me that is a classic example of a tautology.

Relying on survey results from more than 1,300 directors and CEOs, as well as interviews, James Westphal found a correlation between "elite-threatening" behaviors of specific directors and social distancing or ostracism on their boards. Bad news travels. When a director favored a shareholder proposal or sanctioned an executive or fellow director for bad behavior, he or she was less likely to be named to the boards of other, larger companies, or get plum executive or committee assignments.

Michele Hooper, a veteran of many boards, says that boards can turn against a CEO when the group believes it has been "used" and thereby put in an awkward position. The increasing complexity of the business (frequently in an industry that is not their own), along with asymmetric access to information between the

CEO and staff versus the board, contributes to the problem. The CEO's information advantage leads many board members to be reluctant to speak up and risk looking like fools. This may be the main motivation when CEOs work with a board that is seemingly unqualified. Lehman Brothers' board, with five directors over seventy years of age and lacking current financial experience, provides an example. Donald Langevoort, a law professor at Georgetown who studies the psychology of boards, noted that "another silencing mechanism arises because in groups of high-status, high-self-esteem individuals who seek power and influence there is a strong incentive to avoid appearing inferior."

> In the face of ambiguity and grossly incomplete information, directors will often not understand completely either the facts or the implications of a matter under consideration. Many people, however, are loath to speak up and say that they do not understand for fear of displaying ignorance or confusion to the others (and slowing down the pace of the meeting). This ego defense allows those in control of the available information to gain approval simply because they display confidence in their knowledge that others refuse to contest. They call Enron's Jeff Skilling "a master" of this, implying that his preferred interpretations were so obvious that anyone who would even raise questions "just didn't get it."

The truth is, there's much more to lose than to gain by bucking the system. In any event, CEOs frequently work out decisions with board members individually over the phone so that when items finally get to the formal meeting, the attendees already have been lobbied and won over, or their opinions may have shaped the proposal. Although it's unusual, one board member of a media company told us he could not recall a single dissenting vote in six years.

Many boards are active, engaged, and informed, and some even go so far as to take on the painful task of dismissing a CEO. Indeed, if the relationship between a CEO and the board is healthy, the group can function well. But the part played by the psychological foibles that are inherent in human behavior must not be discounted. As Professor Hersh Shefrin says, "Psychological impediments are just hardwired and huge. So the question is, is there anything we can do to deal with them? I think there certainly is something we can do. And it will start in the same way you do in a twelve-step program—admitting you have a problem."

Self-awareness is only the first step. If it is too much to expect boards to control these natural biases by themselves, it follows they could use outside help. Even though shareholders are not monolithic—different kinds of shareholders frequently have different expectations—in theory, as a class they could reduce the damage wrought by these all-too-human frailties and foibles. In general, shareholders provide neither check nor balance to this system. The reasons range from apathy to ignorance to self-interest. But something else is going on: boards work in a system designed to limit the rights of shareholders, and other forms of outside interference. Our current economic predicament is nothing new. Human error and this flawed system permit, indeed encourage, both boom and bust.

6

The Myth of Shareholders' Rights

IN 1935, during the first term of Franklin Roosevelt, Will Rogers's plane disappeared in Alaska, the first Major League Baseball night game was played, Huey Long was gunned down in Louisiana, the Gershwin brothers premiered their new musical *Porgy and Bess*, the government launched something called Social Security, and Babe Ruth returned to Boston playing first base with the Braves. Some ninety miles west of Braves Field, in Springfield, Massachusetts, Prestley Blake and his little brother Curtis had no time for baseball because they were launching the Friendly Ice Cream Company.

Late in the second term of President George W. Bush, this same Pres Blake concluded a successful seven-year battle to oust the management and board of Friendly. As he saw it, the company was no longer in the business of scooping ice cream and frying hamburgers to please customers and earn a good profit. Rather, he believed the company existed to pay the costs of a huge burden of debt and, above all, to enrich its management.

By 2007, Friendly's (the name was changed in 1989) was pumping millions in red ink every year and shelling out $32 million annually in debt service on $230 million in IOUs. The company had burned through all of its equity and earnings and had blown an additional $100 million hole in losses on its balance sheet. Worse yet, all the important numbers were going the wrong way. Back in the day when Blake ran Friendly, the company took on no meaningful debt, owned its restaurants outright, and even owned the land under them. Under Blake, the company didn't franchise any stores, an unusual and highly conservative strategy. His Friendly came of age in the old American business world, which has all but vanished due to the machinations of financial wizards.

The Friendly's story represents the collision of two styles of management—the traditional value builders (Blake counted Thomas Watson and J. C. Penney among his friends and mentors) versus the buyout groups that take existing companies private, seeking eventually to resell them for huge gains. In the worst cases, these latter groups weigh companies down with debt to the point of drowning them or exploit the companies through conflicted dealings with other companies they control. When that happens, sometimes other investors get skinned, employees are laid off, communities collapse, and the overall market system can sustain lasting damage.

The story also highlights how very difficult it is for shareholders—even those who own large blocks of stock—to change the leadership of an obviously foundering company, or even to gain access to management and information about companies' books. Shareholders wield little influence on leadership, even when they are consistently underperforming. And our legal institutions tend to rally around management.

In Homer's *Odyssey,* Odysseus returns to Ithaca in disguise after twenty years' absence, yearning for the bride he left, his farm, and his old way of life. At home he finds a band of insolent, greedy suitors gorging on his food and wine, despoiling his property, and lusting for his wife. When Pres Blake reappeared as an avenging founder at Friendly's two decades after retiring, his effort to clean house launched him on his own kind of odyssey, a tortured journey through the governance and legal system. Friendly's headquarters are near the Berkshire foothills of Massachusetts, but Massachusetts corporate law borrows heavily from management-friendly Delaware. If Odysseus showed up today in the Delaware Chancery suing for repossession of his home from the gang of usurpers encamped there, it is likely his suit would be tossed out on the first day.

The state of Delaware is famous for four things: DuPont chemicals, red chickens, Joe Biden, and corporate law. The last makes the state ground zero for corporate governance reform because 60 percent of America's corporations are chartered there. Many other states' corporate rules—and even those of foreign nations—are heavily influenced by two centuries of Delaware case law. While the critics of the state's legal system are legion, to tangle with Delaware-based law is to pick a fight that will be long and expensive, and probably lost from the start while often imposing insurmountable burdens of cost and proof on plaintiffs. Antishareholder decisions accrete through the years, discouraging many potential lawsuits. Armor-plated legal protections entrench the management of companies that are so ill-governed that they may be failing over the course of many years. The state provides elaborate defenses to shield CEOs and directors from outside influence and from liability.

In the arc of the seven decades between his founding of Friendly Ice Cream and his launching of a shareholder lawsuit, the business had grown from a room with a freezer, which Pres Blake and his brother started with $547 borrowed from their mother, to 740 restaurants employing almost 34,000 people at its peak. In 1968, the company went public, and in 1979 the Blakes sold it to Hershey for $164 million and retired. Soon the firm began showing signs of the benign neglect so common in takeovers by giant corporations. Quality deteriorated, and the chain lost many customers.

In 1988, a leveraged buyout CEO with a gilt-edged fast-food pedigree came along and paid—some would say *overpaid*—$375 million, or 1.5 times the book value for the company. Previously in his career, Don Smith had helped bring the carbo-cholesterol extravaganza known as McDonald's breakfast into the world and then held top positions at Burger King and Pizza Hut before moving on to serve as the CEO of the entire PepsiCo-owned cluster of fast-food restaurants. In 1985, he had founded a holding firm called The Restaurant Company (TRC) to acquire and turn around troubled restaurant groups, such as Perkins Restaurants.

Pres Blake says that he was told that Hershey set a price for Friendly so high that they expected Smith to walk away. Instead, Smith borrowed heavily to raise the funds to meet Hershey's asking price, putting up a relatively small amount of his own money. This common takeover technique has wreaked a great deal of havoc on American business, because such highly leveraged companies are unstable, like a person perched atop a high ladder. A slight wind, in the form of lower than forecasted earnings, for example, can bring them toppling down. But the person who invests just a little of his own money stands to multiply his stake many, many times over, *if* the risky maneuver works. This creates an extremely enticing incentive to make these deals, to underestimate the risks involved, and to run the company as lean as possible.

Smith initially owned 10 percent of Friendly outright, and 30 percent of TRC together with two other investors. He made himself both chairman and CEO, and selected five new directors.

Under this regime, Friendly did a good deal of business with other firms in which Smith had an interest, and one of these companies even owned Friendly stock. Smith and two Friendly board members also served on the boards of TRC.

By 1992, diners at the establishment now called Friendly's were too often confronted with a dirty restaurant staffed by sullen employees. *Consumer Reports* placed Friendly's dead last in its ranking of fourteen family food chains that year, citing customer dissatisfaction. Smith had tried numerous operational maneuvers to upgrade the chain, such as adding staff, altering floor plans, and improving the menu. Yet every time he came close to success, it seemed like some outside factor depressed sales and profits. Hefty interest payments to the bondholders who had funded the takeover cut into the funds for improvements, and by 1997, Friendly's began shutting restaurants, and Smith and his board took the troubled company public to raise cash.

The share price debuted at $18 and rose to $26 by June of the following year, but it cratered four months later to $5, weighed down by debt and poor results. For the next two years, Pres Blake watched with dismay as the share price of Friendly's kept sinking. Finally he had seen enough. He hated the mountain of debt the company had taken on; he was appalled by the announcement of 140 store closures in 2000; and he was mortified to see the share price dip to $1.70 by December 2000. Peering into the reports about the company's finances released after the IPO, he was particularly irked by numerous "related party" transactions involving Smith, TRC, and his inner circle on the board.

Blake expressed his displeasure to management, and in early 2001, Don Smith flew to Florida to visit with Blake, seeking to assuage him. Sitting in his car at the airport as he awaited Smith, Blake was perturbed to watch Smith alight from an $8 million Learjet. As three automobile CEOs were to learn at congressional hearings some years later, the spectacle of a money-losing company's executives stepping off a private jet does not sit well with people whose stock in the company has just dropped off a cliff. To Pres Blake, that pricey jet was more than just an irritant.

"The airplane really did get under his skin," James Donnelly, Blake's lawyer, recalls. "When we first focused on the airplane we didn't understand its true significance. It was the string that, when we pulled it, caused other things to unravel. The more we began to look, the more we became concerned about the fact that Smith was holding himself out as the CEO of TRC and Friendly's, but he had much a much bigger interest in one than the other. He was not providing effective leadership at Friendly's.

"When Pres first began to look at that airplane, it was as simple as 'Mr. Smith was taking advantage of an expensive perk,' and we assumed it was Friendly's airplane and he was just using it as Friendly's airplane. Then we began to realize fairly soon it wasn't Friendly's airplane—it was TRC's airplane and that Friendly's was paying a lot of money to TRC for its use. Then we began to realize it wasn't the only money that Friendly's was paying to TRC. There were a series of related-party transactions. It was hard to piece it all together. The information was not clearly disclosed in the SEC filings."

It later came to light through lawsuit depositions and other means, that Friendly's gave a $112,500 credit to Smith's sons for food products their franchises used, as something called "unearned development fees." Friendly's also paid $2.9 million in management fees to TRC between 1994 and 2000. In addition, Friendly's leased and subleased properties from Perkins Restaurants. Blake was also concerned about payments for an office the company maintained near Smith's Chicago home, despite the fact that Friendly had no business within hundreds of miles.

At the Florida meeting in Blake's sunroom Smith was tape-recorded telling the Friendly's founder: "I don't spend hardly any time at Friendly's anymore. I go in two days a month, I go to board meetings, I'm available and we talk once or twice a week on the phone, but make no mistake about it—I really do not run Friendly's anymore." He conceded the jet had no place in a money-losing company and vowed to sell it." Smith's admission of lack of leadership didn't sit at all well with Blake, particularly given that Friendly's board had committed to pay Smith almost $500,000 in salary and bonus in 2001 for his nonchalance. Worse yet, in the contract negotiated by Friendly's compensation committee, Smith's bonus was calculated based on the company's profits *before* deducting the massive interest payments required by its debt. Thus, Smith did not share in the financial pain of that hit, and the pay scheme offered little incentive for him to work to reduce interest payments, even though the $30 million-plus in annual interest charge obliterated all operating income for the company.

Taking advantage of the rock-bottom share price, Blake acquired 900,000 shares, about a 12 percent stake in the company, and announced his intention to force changes. "I believe in the company and things are not rosy. I won't say I'm going to work any miracles, but I am going to try . . . I'm not worried about the big stockholders. They can take care of themselves. I'm doing this for the employees and the smaller stockholders who don't have anyplace else to go." The business press generally portrayed Blake as a somewhat loopy and quixotic figure, and given the obstacles that block the path of any dissident investor, that might have been justified, were it not for his extraordinary willpower and shrewdness.

A few months later at the May 2001 annual meeting, at age eighty-six, Blake decried the company's management: "The biggest problem is the board. It's too bad Friendly doesn't have a full-time CEO." He demanded company records (which the company refused to furnish) and an investigation into the costs of the jet and other related-party payments. The company looked into things and reported no evidence of wrongdoing.

The following year, at the 2002 annual meeting, Blake called on Smith to resign and asked for another investigation and the right to inspect records concerning the jet and the Chicago office. Though he was a 12 percent owner of Friendly's, he was denied this access to the company documents. Instead, Friendly's directors created a "special committee" to look into the allegations. This group comprised Friendly's internal counsel who reported to Smith, got his raise or bonus through Smith, and also had been the lawyer for TRC. The committee also included three of the directors who had been picked by Smith. The law firm that assisted the committee also represented Smith personally. The special committee issued a three-page preliminary report finding no evidence of any wrongdoing with the jet and didn't pursue the matter further. It ignored the office expense issue entirely. Pres Blake had had enough.

If a shareholder like Pres Blake wants to hold directors accountable, he can turn to the board election process or to the courts or both. None of these gives him much leverage. The board election system has been so completely biased for so long that responsible people have compared it to the governance of the Soviet Union, Cuba, and Iran. It's really not an election system as much as a self-perpetuating, self-selection system. If an irate investor nonetheless wants to try his luck in an election, he can try to replace either *all* of the board (usually impossible) or only a few directors (difficult but sometimes attainable) through the proxy voting process, proxies being votes cast by shareholders or their surrogates at the annual meeting under the one-share, one-vote rule.

Should a shareholder—or group of shareholders—opt instead to go to court, there are two options: class-action suits and the less well known derivative suits, which are fiendishly complex long shots. In derivative suits a stockholder asks the company to sue its own directors or managers. When the directors and managers predictably refuse to sue themselves ("demand refusal"), the stockholder petitions the court for the right to do it himself on the company's behalf, fronting all the legal fees. Cost is one of many reasons derivative suits are an ineffectual remedy. They usually drag on over many years, during which lawyers charge $700 to $1,000 per hour.

The task of winning a derivative suit is daunting, and the odds of success are very long. A court reviews the directors' decision to determine if there was fraud involved in the demand refusal, or lack of good faith, or if there were no rational business purpose behind rejecting the demand. If the answers are no, as they most often are, the suit usually ends, although it may be years later.

Courts rarely grant plaintiffs the right to sue, and even then, the plaintiff must scale a mountainous burden of proof. If he wins, the company must remedy the situation raised by the suit, and he recovers legal fees and infrequently damages from the company usually paid by D&O insurance. But then, the company can always appeal, and the investor must pay the bills again and wait more years. A particularly determined plaintiff does, however, have one other option: he can claim "demand futility." This amounts to a catch-22, in which the plaintiff must prove "*with particularity*" that it would be futile to go through the process of asking the company to sue itself, because the defendants have a personal interest in the outcome that is antithetical to the company's interests. In Delaware, you must document these particulars by going through the discovery process. But you generally cannot get a green light from the court to go through the discovery process unless you already have the particulars to justify doing so. Game over. This is one of the innumerable ways in which Delaware law appears fair, but is biased in favor of corporations. But the law doesn't stop there.

If a plaintiff does manage to emerge from this gauntlet with court approval to sue, remarkably the next step is that the *board* takes charge again and creates a "special litigation committee" (SLC). Such committees usually retain outside law firms to prepare their reports, but the lawyers are paid by the board, which might be considered a conflict of interest. The SLC is composed of outside directors and is meant to perform a rational, good-faith inquiry into the charges, reporting objective findings back to the court. The court then decides whether the defendants' actions violated the standards of "business judgment," determining whether the plaintiff should be allowed to represent the company in the suit.

This "business judgment rule," as it's commonly called, sounds sensible, although in reality the latitude given judges by its three-pronged standards—care, loyalty, and rational business purpose—is so broad that it amounts to a get-out-of-liability-free card for boards and executives. As governance experts Robert Monks and Nell Minow point out, "The Delaware courts have bent over backwards to defer to the business judgment of the directors. Without compelling evidence of self-dealing, the court will not interfere with the board's decision."

Take the case of a derivative suit brought against Citigroup, which was until the 2008 financial implosion the most valuable financial institution on the planet. By early March 2009, its stock had fallen more than 97 percent, and $263.8 billion in shareholder value was vaporized—the largest such loss in corporate history. To continue operating, Citigroup required $45 billion of taxpayer bailout funds and a further government guarantee for $301 billion of its most dubious mortgage-related securities. A group of investors believed that the board should bear responsibility for failing in their fiduciary duties to shareholders. They brought a derivative suit in the Delaware Chancery Court, alleging that the board did not exercise good faith in permitting the bank to take on so much risk. The judge threw out most of the case immediately, stating that "to establish oversight liability a plaintiff must show that the directors knew they were not discharging their fiduciary obligations or that the directors demonstrated a conscious disregard for their responsibilities such as by failing to act in the face of a known duty to act." In other words, the directors would have had to harm shareholders intentionally or to have known they were disregarding their duties. Furthermore, he said, oversight duties are not designed to subject even expert directors to personal liability for failure to "properly evaluate business risk."

At the next annual meeting, two months later, all of the management-selected directors were reelected, even though RiskMetrics, the largest institutional proxy advisor, had recommended that the three directors who were on the audit committee should lose their jobs: "The pattern of chronic oversight failure at Citi and the magnitude of the corresponding shareholder losses warrant removal from the board of directors most responsible for risk oversight."

The law is also riddled with loopholes that torpedo derivative suits. In October 2008, for example, a federal judge citing Delaware law tossed out a derivative suit lodged against Countrywide executives. The plaintiffs alleged they were induced to buy $2.37 billion in Countrywide stock because the defendants had presented inflated characterizations of the firm's prospects at the same time these same defendants were unburdening themselves of $337 million of their own shares. The judge dismissed the suit because the plaintiffs filed it after Countrywide collapsed, and thus they had no legal standing as shareholders. The defendants kept their $337 million.

Professor Jonathan Macey of Yale Law School writes with understatement: "Empirical research shows that defendants are frequently successful in challenging plaintiffs' futility claims . . . [T]he number of derivative actions brought on behalf of public companies is small. This may be because the demand requirement and the possibility of reentry into the suit by management through a special litigation committee discourages plaintiffs from bringing derivative lawsuits."

Despite these obstacles, Pres Blake was up for the fight. On January 3, 2003, he rang in the New Year by launching a derivative lawsuit against Don Smith and Friendly's, charging breach of fiduciary duty and misappropriation of corporate assets, demanding access to records pertaining to the company jet and the Illinois office, and restitution to the company of financial damages the defendants had allegedly caused. Blake avoided a first-round knockout only because Massachusetts law diverges from Delaware's in one key way: the plaintiff's attorney can depose witnesses and go through a limited discovery without proving particularity in advance.

If actually allowed to proceed past the first round, a derivative suit can at least sometimes bring information about the management of the company to light. "We started with a lawsuit to try to protect the company's interests," attorney James Donnelly recalls. "That lawsuit quite obviously began to expose information [indicating] there was a governance problem. The board was just not doing its job at all. One consequence of that, because of their inattentiveness and all the problems, [was that] the market was punishing the value of Friendly stock. We kept pursuing the litigation, and the litigation made available information that probably should have been disclosed to stockholders in the first place. But it wasn't."

The disclosures from the lawsuit combined with all of Blake's hectoring finally began to shake things up. In 2003, Don Smith resigned as CEO but stayed on as chairman. Friendly's got rid of the office near Chicago a month after Smith moved away from the city, and it sold the jet. The primary problems with management had not been solved, however, and the stock was trading at a bargain basement price, so Blake continued to press his case. The depositions he conducted turned up a new set of allegations. The new information was powerful enough to make him want to amend the suit. Many involved TRC and the other directors, so he sought to include them as codefendants.

One deposition disclosed payments to a man named Rich Estlin who intermittently appeared around headquarters and on the Friendly's payroll. The CFO said Estlin was an " 'FOD' or Friend of Don . . . these types of folks had shown up before . . . I asked Estlin what exactly are you doing and what is your goal? And he looked me straight in the eye and said, 'My goal is to play two hundred rounds of golf a year,' and kind of laughed."

Pres Blake would ultimately allege that $12.3 million had been transferred from Friendly's to TRC for airplane expenses, consulting fees, real-estate transactions, and food purchases, of which only $9.8 million appeared on TRC books. He began to suspect that Smith and his family used the jet personally, and that Friendly's had paid as much as $3 million to support it. Friendly's had apparently committed to pay as much as $2.4 million in management fees to TRC over a period of three years, in addition to Smith's board and Friendly's compensation of almost $500,000 a year. The terms or purposes of these payments were never set forth in a three-paragraph unsigned letter authorizing the payments.

As head of Friendly's, Perkins, and TRC, Smith had an opportunity to shift assets between the companies to his own advantage, and to force divisions to purchase supplies at inflated prices. Blake wanted documentation to prove his suspicion. To relieve some of Friendly's financial burden, Blake offered the corporation a low-interest $50 million loan. When it was refused, he suspected a conflict of interest with certain board members and a financial institution.

In July 2005, the court refused to let Blake amend his suit. The reason given was that the Friendly's leadership had now indicated that it wanted to pursue *its own investigation*. In this situation, the law requires that the case be sent for consideration to a special litigation committee of Friendly's board, selected by the board, to investigate Smith and the board. While the Friendly's special litigation committee (SLC) appeared to be investigating, Donald Smith decided to sell his 70 percent stake in TRC to a private equity firm, personally reaping $170 million. He retained his position as Friendly's chairman, however. In the meantime, Prestley Blake was spending a small fortune of his own to continue his battle. He sold sixteen of his vintage Rolls-Royces to keep the suit going.

Finally, in October 2005, the Friendly's SLC issued its report: Blake's suit had no merit and was "not in the best interests of the corporation." The committee asked the court to agree and toss the suit out. But in 2004 the Massachusetts legislature had passed a law that imposed a two-part test on corporations moving to dismiss such suits. A majority of the overall board of directors must be independent at the time of the determination by the independent directors, and the independent directors must make the determination not to pursue the suit while acting in good faith after conducting a reasonable inquiry.

The judge assigned to the case in Massachusetts Superior Court, John Agostini, took six months to study it before ruling. Unlike Delaware's justices, state superior court judges don't specialize in corporate law, so Judge Agostini had to become a scholar of this arcane process, working nights and weekends, while simultaneously trying murder cases and the like. In Delaware, the ten

Chancery and Supreme Court judges work intensively on corporate cases and have developed great expertise. This is just one of many factors contributing to Delaware's perpetual dominance of this field.

The odds that Agostini would rule in Blake's favor were not good. In the entire history of such suits in Delaware, a judge had disagreed with a special litigation committee only four times. However, taking into account the new 2004 Massachusetts provisions, Judge Agostini slammed the board's independence and the reasonableness of its inquiry. He noted that one director, Michael Daly, played a "passive, largely nonresponsive role" on the 2002 special committee. "Other examples of [Daly]'s ignorance abound. Equally ludicrous is Daly's denial in his deposition that under some circumstances, Friendly payments to TRC could benefit Smith or TRC." Daly "remained oblivious and failed to apprise himself of reasonably available, material facts. . . ." Board member Steven Ezzes gave depositions "marked by evasion, surliness, and memory loss . . . that portrayed a stunning degree of ignorance, whether feigned or real." Director Burton Manning showed a "lockstep loyalty approach to his responsibilities."

Finally, as of May 24, 2006, thanks to Agostini's ruling, five and a half years after Blake picked up Don Smith at the airport, the case was on the runway, clear for trial. But even if Blake ultimately won, he would have to go through a lengthy appeal, and he was by now pushing ninety-two. Nonetheless, he said he had seldom felt better. He was also about to make a valuable ally.

In the summer of 2006 a twenty-nine-year-old Iranian emigré, Sardar Biglari, who had acquired nearly 15 percent of Friendly's stock through the Lion Fund private investment fund, which he ran, contacted Blake. Biglari's fund had been working on turning around another failing restaurant chain, and he saw an opportunity to do the same at Friendly's.

Earlier in 2007, Biglari had negotiated with Smith for two seats on the Friendly's board, but the talks broke down, and as the date for the annual meeting approached, Blake, Biglari, and a number of other significant stockholders, who together held over 30 percent of shareholder votes, prepared for a proxy fight that Biglari would spearhead. A week before the battle date, Smith indefinitely postponed the annual meeting to "explore strategic initiatives," a tactic frequently used by management to sap the momentum of dissidents. In this case, though, the tactic failed. As Biglari worked to line up votes, Sun Capital, another private fund, joined the fray with $337 million of cash, offering to buy all of Friendly's outright. Its $15.50 per-share offering price represented a 9 percent premium over the market value of Friendly's stock, and a 31 percent increase over the prevailing price two months prior. Shareholders approved the deal, though Sun's lawyers prevented Blake from keeping his promise to give some of his shares to employees. The entire board was replaced, and the lawsuit was dropped. Friendly's insurers reimbursed part of the legal fees Blake had risked, in return for an agreement to end further probes. Today Blake proudly points to a Harvard Business School case about his victory.

In the case of Pres Blake and Friendly's, a persistent shareholder managed to play a powerful role in inducing change. Donnelly speculates that the growing pressure from the lawsuit and its discovery process figured heavily in Smith's agreement to sell the company. But this kind of outcome is rare, because in most cases the legal process is over early. Most investors have neither the resources nor the stomach to stick with such a long and bitter fight. They sell their stock and walk away from the mess. Boy Scouts are trained to leave campgrounds cleaner than they found them, but investors are not Boy Scouts. When frustrated investors take what is called the Wall Street Walk, bad boards and directors are left free to inflict further damage.

Barring the reform of Delaware's laws, this pattern is unlikely to change. "Everyone knows where the gutter is, and the gutter rolls right down to Delaware," says Lynn E. Turner, the SEC's former chief accountant and an author of Sarbanes-Oxley reforms. "That state knows that. It collects huge sums of money for letting people get away with murder."

North Dakota is trying to become the Anti-Delaware by being shareholder-friendly, but as of mid 2010, just one company has set up shop in Bismarck. Nevada, meanwhile, has tried to out-Delaware Delaware, copying its law, increasing the veil of secrecy and nondisclosure around corporations that it charters, and levying virtually no corporate taxes. To date, Nevada has made no dent in Delaware's superiority.

"The Delaware Chancery court has a strong interest in keeping Delaware an attractive place to incorporate," Jesse Fried, Berkeley School of Law professor, says of those administering Delaware law. "There *are* good reasons to incorporate in Delaware: they have intelligent judges who understand business, and there's more certainty with a body of case law. On the other hand, it's overly favorable to management." Fried believes Delaware has become "a little tougher on corporations," since the big scandals earlier this decade, in part due to the pressure on the federal government. "Sarbanes-Oxley affected committee structures and who gets on boards," Fried says. "I think that scared the shit out of Delaware." But the jury is out yet on how much real change is under way.

Fortunately, the other type of suit that can be brought against companies, class-action, is often carried out on the federal level. Class-action litigation, even if only the threat of the suit itself, has caused many boards to make positive changes, but the process is far from ideal. Class-action suits represent entire groups ("classes") of individuals who stand to receive payouts if their legal arguments prevail. These suits are predicated on the idea that many people have been damaged by a company; the argument is that while individual losses may be small—too small to justify a suit—the sum of collective damages is substantial.

Frequently, companies settle these suits out of court, agreeing to payments and sometimes also to changes in the company governance. For good reason, many executives say that the "plaintiff's bar" that brings these suits is nothing but a gang of extortionists who engage in a wide range of unethical and shamelessly opportunistic behavior.

Dynergy not only forked out $468 million to settle a suit regarding an accounting scandal in 2001, but also agreed to add two directors from a slate proposed by the University of California Regents. A few other companies, such as Ashland Oil and Hanover Compressor, have allowed plaintiffs to nominate board candidates. But most of these cases are really about money.

Settlement and court-imposed penalty payments can involve triple damages, and they usually come out of insurance paid for by the company on behalf of itself, directors, and officers. This amounts to a transfer of wealth from the shareholders of the insurance company to the shareholders of the defendant company, offset by higher future insurance premiums for the defendant company. And massive amounts are skimmed off the top by lawyers. Plaintiff attorney's fees often total 25 percent of the cash settlement, though they can go down to 10 percent if the amount is enormous. William Lerach, the lead counsel in a class action against Enron, earned $688 million in the $7.4 billion settlement. In a case against Cendant, attorneys walked away with $262 million. Meanwhile, in a typical class-action suit the mom-and-pop shareholder might get a check for a few dollars, because there may be thousands of plaintiffs. The average plaintiff in a class-action suit against Seagate Technologies, for example, received $294, while the lead counsel earned $1.5 million.

Class-action suits are, therefore, mostly a sideshow in terms of effecting real governance reform.

THERE HAS BEEN much talk of late of a shareholders' democracy movement and advocates hope it can force significant reform. But one of the ironies of the last few decades of American business is that as the demographic base of stock ownership has expanded so significantly—with 50 percent of American households now owning stocks—the balance of power between common stockholders and management has stayed pretty much the same. Real power has flowed to the institutional intermediaries who usually have greater loyalty to corporate management than to the investors they are supposed to serve.

In the 1930s, when Pres Blake and his brother founded the Friendly Ice Cream Company, the volume of stocks traded on the NYSE was about a million shares a day. Now, a daily volume of three *billion* shares is not unusual. But as the number of shares traded has ballooned, the average period of ownership of a share has plummeted from about eight years in the 1950s to just nine months today. This has undermined the incentive of most stockholders to research, or even to care about, the governance of companies. The more the stock market becomes a casino, the less it provides an incentive for the majority of investors to police corporate leadership. Even more problematic, those shareholders who are willing to put in the time or are highly motivated to do so, such as hedge fund managers and the managers of large pension funds, face a formidable array of limitations on their power.

For decades prior to 2008 U.S. corporations had withstood

attempts by shareholders to secure the rights afforded them in many other large economies. British shareholders, for example, can call for a special meeting with only 5 percent of shares voting for it. Once convened, with a majority vote, they can remove directors. Five percent also is the threshold for getting an item onto the proxy for a vote. In the United States, by contrast, many companies' bylaws forbid special meetings altogether, or impose impossibly high vote thresholds to approve them. Japan, too, has stronger shareholder rights. As one American expatriate told us, "Japan is not a board-level governance regime; it is a shareholder-meeting regime," adding that Japanese shareholders have "incredibly strong" legal rights. In Germany, half the companies permit employees to elect directors. In Canada, 5 percent of shareholders can convene a meeting, gain proxy access, and with a majority, pass resolutions that are binding.

Meanwhile, although shareholder democracy has gained a certain traction lately among American investors and in the press, many people in the business, political, and judicial communities dispute the very idea that shareholders should have any rights over the running of companies. UCLA law professor Stephen Bainbridge maintains, "While notions of shareholders rights permit powerful rhetoric, corporations are not New England town meetings. Put another way, we need not value corporate democracy because we value political democracy. . . . What is most striking about shareholder voting rights is the extensive set of limitations on those rights."

Martin Lipton is Wall Street's analog to the legendary oil well firefighter Red Adair. Lipton is the person whom CEOs turn to when their firm is under attack. As with the oil industry and Adair, companies will pay enormous sums for his services. Lipton names them a flat fee in advance, in the millions, and with the CEO's approval, the shareholders foot the bill. His attitude toward the power of those shareholders has sometimes bordered on the dismissive: "They own securities—shares of stock—which entitle them to very limited electoral rights and the right to share in the financial returns produced by the corporation's business operations." They "have no more claim to intrinsic ownership and control of the corporation's assets than do other stakeholders."

UCLA law professor Lynn A. Stout agrees that shareholder democracy is a "myth," and she argues it should remain so. "After all, there are many myths—vampires, alligators in the sewers of New York City—we would not want to make real. Why assume, in the face of a century of American business history, that it is suddenly desirable to make shareholder control of the boards of public corporations a reality?"

Shareholder democracy is an "oxymoron," says George Mason University law school's dean emeritus Henry Manne, who sees the overall stock market as being not just an exchange for shares, dividends, and capital gains, but also for votes. People buy shares to get votes and will pay a premium for them if they wish. By this process, he says, "The votes and control move into the hands of those who, because they are best able to profit from them, are willing to pay the most for them. That is how efficient markets function."

According to this strict corporatist view, shareholder activism and many regulations imposed on companies are uneconomical and impractical. The corporation should be seen as nothing more than a "nexus of contracts," and people who own stock have certain predefined contractual rights. That's all.

Critics of the push for more shareholder power also argue that it is misguided because executives have overwhelmingly superior knowledge of their businesses. This makes them far abler to maximize profits, particularly if they are freed from certain exterior constraints like zealous regulators in Congress and the SEC. It follows, they argue, that stock prices provide the best mechanism to distinguish between good and bad management, to reward the worthy and punish the errant. In order for this mechanism to work effectively, though, the argument goes, managers must be free to control the day-to-day affairs of the business without enduring second-guessing. Takeovers are the ultimate disciplinarians. Virtually all company bylaws and state courts affirm executives' freedom to act, and their political lobbies seek to diminish outside control.

In fact, it's widely agreed that shareholders should not be mucking around with day-to-day operations. How would one draw a bright line between day-to-day and strategy? In light of this question, courts have generally drawn that boundary very far to management's favor, reasoning that management and directors must be free to undertake risks and maximize profits, and do so without fear of lawsuits.

This widespread perspective among corporate leaders provides the justification for a host of techniques used by CEOs and boards to thwart shareholder interference, some of which are patently absurd. Take, for example, annual meetings, which have become a form of Kabuki theater. The annual meeting is meant to provide shareholders with an opportunity to communicate with CEOs and boards face-to-face, but many are ridiculously ritualized and give extremely short shrift to shareholders. They are generally kept on a tight schedule. A recent annual meeting of DuPont, for example, lasted a total of forty-five minutes, which is not at all unusual. Meetings are also generally long on formality and short on substantive dialogue. At the TDS/U.S. Cellular meeting in 2009, for example, the CEO and his brother, the chairman, flat out refused to answer shareholder questions about strategy.

The highly ritualized and utterly vacant nature of these affairs is well represented by ExxonMobil, which has followed the same basic script for its annual meeting for years. After the formal presentation by the chairman/CEO about its triumphs in a challenging business environment, selected shareholders can speak for three minutes apiece about the nonbinding resolutions they might have gotten onto the ballot. For years now, the company's meeting has featured a group of climate change deniers who congratulate the chairman, climate change believers who excoriate the chairman, a woman who wants two directors to quit the male-only Augusta National Golf Club, and a group of people who want ExxonMobil to exit the oil business. In an elegy about his final ExxonMobil annual meeting, governance expert Robert Monks in 2009 sized up the process: "Exxon's view is that the shareholder meeting is an utter waste of time which they are legally compelled to endure."

Most of the shareholder-initiated resolutions suffer landslide defeats even before the annual meeting, due to a special tool in the hands of management. Management can legally count proxy votes as they come in, in advance of the meeting, and votes are not anonymous. (Dissidents have no such rights.) So management can call institutions that vote against its interests and persuade them to reverse their vote. They will take to the phones with the company's full financial war chest if an unfriendly resolution stands a chance of passing or a friendly one looks like it's in trouble. Thus, for example, over eight years and at a personal annual cost of $100,000 a year, Monks has failed to get ExxonMobil to separate the roles of CEO and chairman, but has gotten support as high as 40 percent. For six years Caterpillar has been pushed not to sell bulldozers to Israel, and for eight years Calvert, a socially responsible investment group, has asked Avon to disclose its policies on nanomaterials and potentially hazardous ingredients, also to no avail.

CEOs can display astonishing disregard at meetings for shareholders' concerns. Consider this now-classic exchange between GE CEO Jack Welch and activist GE shareholder Sister Pat Daly, a perennial moral gadfly:

SISTER PAT: The EPA continues to list PCBs on its suspected-carcinogen list. For you to be saying that PCBs are perfectly harmless is not true. I really want our company to be a credible mover on this. We all remember the images of the CEOs of the tobacco companies swearing that they were telling the truth. Do they have any credibility in the United States today?
WELCH: That is an outrageous comparison.
DALY: That is an absolutely valid comparison, Mr. Welch.
WELCH: It is outrageous.
DALY: Mr. Welch, I am sorry, but we need to have the independent scientific community decide this, not the GE scientific community.
WELCH: Twenty-seven studies, twenty-one of them independent, have concluded that there is no correlation between PCB levels and cancer, Sister. You have to stop this conversation. You owe it to God to be on the side of truth here.
DALY: I am on the side of truth. The other consideration here is that this is not just about carcinogens. We are talking about hormonal disruptions, fertility issues, and developmental problems in children. Those are real issues, and certainly those are the issues that my sisters are seeing in schools all along the Hudson River. That is exactly what is going on here.
WELCH: Thank you very much for coming, Sister.

Occasionally, the venting from shareholders becomes a good deal less polite. Two European bank annual meetings in 2009 were marked by the tossing of various missiles—coins, shoes, tomatoes—from the audience.

Some firms go to great lengths to escape confrontation with

shareholders. One tactic is to move the annual meeting to a location that is expensive or impractical for shareholders to reach. Sempra Energy of San Diego held its meeting in London a few years back, with the result that only fifty people attended, more than half of whom were directors, executives, and their spouses. MAXXAM, a Houston-based forestry, real estate, and dog racing company that attained notoriety for cutting down ancient redwoods, moved its meeting to the tiny town of Huntsville, Texas, and rented all the hotel rooms for miles around, which inconvenienced dissidents. One group of shareholders responded by renting an RV. Farmer Brothers Coffee, fleeing activists, held its meeting the day after Christmas. The Weyerhaeuser Company once required questions at the annual meeting to be submitted in writing. CEO Steven R. Rogel announced that the company would spend only fifteen minutes answering them and then gaveled down a number of shareholders who attempted to ask questions from the floor. When another shareholder tried to raise a point of order, he was ejected from the meeting by a security guard.

Home Depot in 2006 permitted no vote counts during the meeting and made no outside directors available. "The only director who attended was Bob Nardelli, the company's chairman, president, and CEO," AP reported. "Nardelli refused to acknowledge comments, answer questions, or stick around longer than thirty minutes. The company allowed shareholders to speak about their proposals, but it put a strict time limit on their comments, which were tracked by a giant clock." Home Depot later said that "it should not be seen as a lack of respect for shareholders or a lessening of its commitment to sound corporate governance and transparency."

One of the only potentially powerful weapons shareholders have for forcing change is the proxy fight, but the odds are stacked against them. Lewis Gilbert and his brother John were the original corporate gadflies, the first shareholder activists in the modern sense of the term. In 1932 Lewis became incensed over New York's Consolidated Gas Company's refusal to take questions from the floor at the annual meeting, and he and his brother embarked upon a fifty-year proxy vote war in which they lost more than 2,000 resolutions in a row.

The case of Harold Mathis of Richmond, Texas, demonstrates just how absurd the shareholder voting process can be. Having retired from his career in boatbuilding for offshore oil rigs, Mathis owned 810 shares of the drilling equipment company Baker Hughes. In 2000, he began sponsoring proxy resolutions to change the company's classified board structure so all directors would be elected at once, one way of making it easier to take control of a board. He won a majority of the vote in that first year, but management simply said it would "take the vote seriously" and then made no changes. Mathis put the resolution forth again in 2001. That year he won 76 percent of the vote, but management still did nothing. Mathis wasn't finished. In 2003, he garned 85 percent in favor of the resolution.

This time the company's management issued a statement that the resolution was "not in the best interests of the shareholders." The next year Baker Hughes actually said that if the measure received "at least the same support" as it did the prior year, it would introduce a binding resolution in 2005 to enact the measure. But when Baker Hughes counted the vote, it asserted that the proposal won "only 81 percent" of the vote, four points less than the prior year. Showing extraordinary determination, Mathis demanded a recount of the votes and found that he had actually won 90 percent, at which point Baker Hughes finally relented.

Despite being arduous and so often futile, proxy fights—or even just the threat of them—can be an important tool. Sometimes companies will avoid the negative publicity by settling the issues privately in advance of an annual meeting. In recent years, a quarter to a third of the 1,400 or so resolutions filed for inclusion have been withdrawn before the annual meeting, usually because the shareholder is satisfied with the company's response. Sometimes a vote that fails to win a majority can create enough attention to problems like an underperforming CEO and thus shame the board into taking action.

Companies, however, have many means of derailing shareholder proposals and about 95 percent of shareholder resolutions filed are nonbinding, in any case. Companies can appeal to the SEC in a "no action" request that, if granted, allows them to omit a resolution from the proxy. Companies can also impose thresholds for resubmission of resolutions that require at least 3 percent of the votes the first year, 6 percent the second year, and 10 percent the third year and thereafter. Until 1993, shareholders were actually required to have the SEC staff review and edit any communication they sent to more than ten other shareholders supporting a proxy resolution.

Even with that rule gone, shareholders are handicapped in seeking votes. While companies are required to put a shareholder's summary discussion of resolutions on the proxy, they have long enjoyed a huge advantage in influencing votes by using the company's resources to mail out proxies and other literature, hiring PR firms and proxy wranglers to lobby institutional shareholders, and launching campaigns through phone banks and the internet—all paid for with the shareholders' funds, of course. Combating such formidable campaigns can be extraordinarily expensive. In his failed 2009 attempt to seat five directors on Target Corporation's board through a proxy battle, hedge fund manager Bill Ackman spent at least $10 million. Target's exceptional record of having pioneered many of the best practices in governance, as well as shareholder suspicions regarding Ackman's motivations, helped them win the contest. The Target fight did have one very positive development that may be a harbinger of future board-election practices, if true proxy access ever materializes. A few days before the vote, both sets of director-candidates made presentations in a webcast sponsored by the proxy advisory firm Institutional Shareholder Services. It wasn't exactly a debate, but the arguments on both sides were enlightening, and it was a unique demonstration of how contested elections could help boards develop greater accountability to their shareholders.

The rules governing shareholder access to the proxy for directly nominating director-candidates were liberalized in late 2010. Despite the change being a step in the right direction (and one that has been squelched in the past), it seems unlikely that it will result in major changes in the composition or culture of boards because of its limited scope and the fairly high threshold requirements. Shareholders could make nominations for only a quarter of board seats (or one for a three-person board); they must have owned 3 percent of the stock, depending on the company's size, for at least three years; and they would have to certify that they are not seeking to gain control of the company and will hold their shares at least through the annual meeting. Given the power of large institutional shareholders who tend to vote with management, the chances of dissidents winning many of these votes will probably remain quite low except in the most extreme cases.

In 2001, the shareholder activist Les Greenberg did manage to alter the governance rules and influence management changes at Luby's Restaurants, through a grassroots campaign that cost only $15,000. However, this success has not been replicated. In commenting on why such battles are so hard to win, they enumerated a list of just some of the tasks required to launch such a vote:

- Locating other potential director nominees and conducting related due diligence;
- Drafting a charter for a committee;
- Deciding how to finance/allocate the out-of-pocket expenses (e.g., legal document drafting, printing and distribution costs);
- Obtaining a copy of the corporation's bylaws and articles of incorporation;
- Learning details of applicable state corporate law, federal securities laws, and various SEC rules;
- Dealing with the corporation and its transfer agent, which stall, often requesting thousands of dollars for a copy of the shareholders list, which costs them little to produce;
- Being willing to file a legal action in Delaware or other state courts to get the shareholders list;
- Being prepared to expend funds and effort in defense of a frivolous legal action by the corporation to exhaust challengers' funds and energies;
- Dealing with the SEC's response to draft filings;
- Making sure that the appropriate parties are notified that the election is "contested";
- Verifying that proxy statements have actually been mailed to "beneficial holders" of the stock and that votes have been counted properly;
- Locating and attempting to communicate with the proxy voter at large institutional investors;
- Learning the rules to be employed at the annual meeting without the cooperation of the corporation.

The management advantage comes most into play when a vote will be close, and Professor Yair Listokin of Yale Law School found strong evidence that close votes are rigged. In studying voting results "from the relatively small number of votes on management-sponsored proposals that are competitive," as he described his sample, he found "stark discontinuities." Management won in fifty-six out of a total of sixty-four close votes (those decided by 1 percent or less of votes). "Such a distribution should occur by chance less than one in one billion times."

Another distorting factor in proxy votes is that so many institutional stockholders, investment funds, and stock brokerages lend huge blocs of stock, along with their voting rights, to one another. In this little warp of the universe, almost all of the shares in the market are available for the purpose. A University of Pennsylvania professor studied stock lending patterns at two major banks and found that the number of shares out on loan jumped by 21 percent to 26 percent above the norm on the day the ownership of the stock is recorded—the "day of record." In fact, shares can be moved—and thus potentially voted multiple times—on the day of record. A trade association of stock transfer agents examined 341 shareholders votes in 2005 and found evidence of duplicate voting in 100 percent of them.

Stock lending is big business. One report says big brokerages and banks earn $8 billion a year from loaning (mostly other people's) stocks, keeping all the proceeds. Other institutions make out too. CalPERS realized a profit of $124 million by lending its shares in 2006–2007. The real owners often are unaware their stock is being borrowed, so this can lead to double voting as well. Borrowers generally pay 1 percent interest and put up Treasury bills or stock as collateral.

Thirteen percent of shares in El Paso Corporation—an enormous volume—were borrowed in 2003 just before the annual election, thus enabling management to beat back a slate of nine dissident directors by a margin of just 2.8 percent. The French insurance behemoth AXA Financial fought a bitter eight-month battle in 2004 to take over the Mutual Life Insurance Company of New York, known as MONY, for $1.5 billion. Just before the big proxy election, 6.4 million shares were loaned and the takeover won by only 1.7 million votes.

The fact is that ownership of stocks and the rights to control their votes are now effectively divisible. "This decoupling . . . is often hidden from public view and is largely untouched by current law and regulation," Henry T. Hu and Bernard Black of the University of Texas wrote.

> Hedge funds, sophisticated and largely unfettered by legal rules or conflicts of interest, have been especially aggressive in decoupling. Sometimes they hold more votes than economic ownership, a pattern we call "empty voting." That is, they may have substantial voting power while having limited, zero, or even negative economic ownership. In the extreme situation of negative economic ownership, the empty voter has an incentive to vote in ways that reduce the company's share price.

Corporate leaders can exert pressure on companies that hold shares to vote their way. Thanks to the now-infamous leaked voicemails and the conference call tape that surfaced in the Delaware trial *Hewlett v. HP*, this common practice finally attained much deserved notoriety. The sons of HP's founders, who sat on the board, opposed CEO Carly Fiorina's effort to push through a merger with Compaq in 2002. Fiorina observed that Deutsche Bank had voted its 1.3 percent of shares to oppose the merger, and that HP had an investment banking relationship with Deutsche Bank. A series of phone calls ensued and a voicemail was leaked in which Fiorina instructed her CFO to "bring Deutsche over the line," as she mentioned the possibility of "doing something extraordinary" if the vote went the wrong way. She next told Deutsche that the vote "was of great importance to their ongoing relationship." Ultimately, Deutsche Bank switched its 17 million votes in favor of the merger, which passed by two percentage points, and the Deutsche switch alone accounted for most of that margin. Fiorina maintained her language was misinterpreted and she intended to place no undue pressure on the bank. Many others strongly disagreed.

As of now, perhaps the most promising way to force reform of a company's governance is to follow the example of a small number of dissident investors who specialize in working with boards—either as fellow directors or outside advisors—to improve operational and governance performance for long-term gains. Frequently, these activists are bankrolled by public employee pensions and other institutions. But they are controversial, and some critics accuse them of being out for their own best interests rather than those of other shareholders. They are sometimes called corporate raiders in sheep's clothing.

Carl Icahn embodies the type. The Queens-born financier burst into public prominence during the 1980s as a corporate raider and greenmailer who extracted large amounts of cash from companies such as American Can and Owens-Illinois to stop his takeover attempts. As economic times have changed, Icahn has reinvented himself as a paragon of progressive governance, holding forth against golden parachutes, poison pills, outsized executive pay, empty-suit corporate boards, and compensation consultants. Icahn is in a small group because of the size of the companies he takes on: Time Warner, Motorola, and Yahoo, for instance. He seeks to change their strategy by influencing the CEO and board, and, failing that, he has the resources to launch a proxy battle to seat himself directly on the board.

Icahn has been called both "the best thing ever to happen to small shareholders" and "the new Gordon Gekko." Eliot Spitzer told us that, in comparison to investors who simply cash in their stock and walk away when they encounter bad corporate leadership, he sees Icahn as a good guy: "Sure he's doing it for purely mercenary reasons, but at least he'll take a position and try to shake up management." Icahn bluntly describes his motivation: "The board itself is not made accountable because corporate board elections are generally a joke." Icahn and his colleagues buy a significant equity position in a company and then try to force changes they believe will raise the stock price. These might include paying out cooped-up unproductive cash as dividends, buying back stock, exiting certain lines of business, reducing debt, firing the CEO, or putting the company up for sale. To some degree their deterrent power amplifies their direct influence; the very possibility of their waging a proxy battle and sitting at the board can be sufficient to change a company's behavior, for better or worse. But there are few investors with the means and skills of Carl Icahn—fewer than ten—and many of them are over seventy years old.

All of the impediments to shareholder rights have been crafted, and are defended and exploited, on behalf of management by a vast cast of lawyers, accountants, lobbyists, and others. This network is deeply entrenched in the governance system and afflicted with conflicts of interest. It not only stymies the influence of individual shareholders but also extracts an astonishing amount of money in what economists call "rents"—the fees for their services from the pool of money that shareholders invest in companies. If significant reform is to be brought about, it will have to overcome the best efforts of this interconnected and self-interested cadre to stop it.

7

Another Tangled Web

GREATLY EXACERBATING THE PROBLEM of flawed governance is the vast support system that has evolved to offer services—from expert analysis of account books, to the decipherment of legalese and various forms of cover—to CEOs and boards, for considerable costs. This almost diabolically complex and often interconnected network of hundreds of thousands includes: compensation consultants; proxy vote advisors; ratings agencies that evaluate companies' governance; agencies that rate company debt; directors' and officers' insurers; solicitors who work to garner votes in favor of proxies; acquisitions advisors; trade associations, such as the National Association of Corporate Directors and the powerful Business Roundtable; business and law school governance programs; media such as Directorship.com and *Corporate Board Member* magazine; mutual fund and pension fund managers; consultants for strategy, board self-assessment, and leadership development; a legion of lobbyists; and of course huge armies of lawyers, accountants, and investment bankers. Some of this vast cadre operate as priest-technicians, decoding the mind-numbing manual of the governance machine; others serve mainly to shield boards from accountability.

It's not hard to understand why their services are so popular. Any rational person would prefer to wait for a lightbulb to burn out in a padded cell than to understand how to price knock-in path-dependent equity derivatives, how auditors treat money-over-money and wrap-lease transactions involving nonrecourse debt subject to the provisions of FASB Technical Bulletin No. 88–1, or to fathom the "relative limitations of duty waivers for interested directors as disinterested for purposes of immunizing interested transactions from Delaware's fairness analysis in LLCs versus corporate forms," in the words of a recent Delaware Chancery decision.

The gatekeepers have become indispensable partners to part-time independent directors who often know little about the complexities of the rules governing the businesses they are meant to be overseeing and who are already overburdened with the increased demands on their time. Others provide analysis of the quality of governance, ostensibly in the interests of shareholders, while there are also those who play the part of custodians of shares—the managers of mutual funds and pension funds—and potentially exercise considerable influence over governance matters through their voting clout. Another group essentially provides outsourcing services. Some of them, such as insurers, simply provide indemnification. While many of these people do inspired work on investors' behalf, they do so at a staggering cost and within a system that is riddled with conflicts of interest to which too many of them succumb.

This Rube Goldberg governance machine siphons off vast amounts of wealth from shareholders in fees, commissions, inflated executive compensation, payments for legal settlements, and many other costs. Of course, our economic engine does throw off considerable profits for investors—when not afflicted by an economic meltdown. Every time the tooth of one gear engages the tooth of another gear of this governance machine, someone operating some part of the process pockets some investor money. Whether it's a lawsuit settled, an insurance claim paid on behalf of a CEO or board member, or a mutual fund asset churned, shareholders are paying the bill.

The exact amount of shareholder money extracted cannot be calculated. But to get some sense of how vast the sums are, consider the case of fees paid to investment funds—money skimmed off shareholder investments and pensions. Jack Bogle, the founder of the Vanguard Group of mutual funds, said that if you invested $100,000 in an exchange-traded fund that simply tracked the entire S&P 500 Index, starting in 1985, you would have had a $110,000 profit after twenty years. If you invested the same amount in the average stock mutual fund and carried all the risk, you would have had a $62,000 profit. The fund would have kept 43 percent of your profits. Bogle estimated that mutual funds, along with investment banks and other financial intermediaries, extracted fees of $2.225 *trillion* from 1997 to 2002.

Another cost is that for directors and officers insurance, which indemnifies firms and individuals from liabilities that arise from governance wrongdoing and from the payment of settlements of class-action suits. These suits can cost anywhere from millions to several billion dollars each. All of these costs are transferred to shareholders somewhere, and not to board members. Remarkably, it's almost impossible to find a director who has ever paid anything out of pocket for offenses other than in the handful of the most egregious cases like WorldCom and Enron. It just doesn't happen.

Most of the extraction of funds is less overt and is abetted by the intrinsic conflicts of interest that riddle the system. Consider the profits made by some of the ratings agencies. When the two companies that rate almost all debt securities, Moody's and Standard & Poor's, report operating margins that are close to 50 percent and several times that of Exxon-Mobil, it is reasonable to conclude that customers have been paying too much for their services. Moody's, in fact, had the highest profit ratio of any company in the S&P 500 for five years in a row. In 2007, Moody's earned pretax profit of $1.1 billion on revenue of $2.25 billion, a ratio that Cali cocaine dealers might envy.

Of course, there was a method to all that fee-paying. As we discovered in the wake of the financial implosion, the ratings agencies were racking up such considerable fees in large part for bonds that have now become toxic waste. The inherent conflicts are blatant. Since the agencies are paid by the bond issuers (who could essentially shop for the highest ratings) and the fees are higher based on the size and complexity of the transactions, the agencies have powerful financial incentives to produce those quality assurances. The issuers needed them because many of their institutional investor customers had high ratings-based requirements on what they could buy. The ratings agencies charged double or triple the fees for rating subprime mortgage-based debt than for plain vanilla corporate bonds. The Nobel Prize–winning economist Joseph Stiglitz, in discussing the 2008 financial crisis, argued "the ratings agencies . . . were the party that performed that alchemy that converted the securities from F-rated to A-rated. The banks could not have done what they did without the complicity of the ratings agencies." The ratings agencies' analytical models were based on assumptions that were fundamentally flawed and historical data that proved inapplicable. Very few financial services CEOs and directors had any real understanding of how these unimaginably complicated securities worked, but as profits skyrocketed from selling and trading them, these same leaders didn't ask questions. Many now say that they relied on the ratings to assess their risks. One CEO with experience in government and investment banking who has served on six boards told us, "Anybody with an ounce of sophistication knew the ratings were a joke. If they're claiming that as an excuse, they're either incompetent or they're lying—and shouldn't be on a board in either case."

Consider also the role of compensation consultants. To obtain advice about compensation—ostensibly at arm's length—corporations hire these experts, who are meant to provide boards with fair, impartial, current, and broadly informed opinions on pay for CEOs and other top executives. Sometimes they do just that, but too often they do their clients' bidding and tend to view the CEOs as being the clients.

In 2008, the congressional Committee on Oversight and Government Reform, chaired by Representative Henry Waxman of California, found "pervasive" conflicts of interest among compensation consultants. The committee's report said that from 2002 through 2006, "the median CEO salary increase of the twenty-five Fortune 250 companies that used compensation consultants with the largest conflicts of interest was 226 percent. In comparison, the median CEO salary increase without consulting was less than half as much (105 percent)." The report suggested but could not conclusively prove causality.

Warren Buffett commented on the problem in his 2005 annual letter: "A mediocre-or-worse CEO—aided by his handpicked VP of human relations and a consultant from the ever-accommodating firm of Ratchet, Ratchet and Bingo—all too often receives gobs of money from an ill-designed compensation arrangement."

A compensation consultant to high-tech companies on the West Coast explained the way the process works as follows:

> When you go in, you know what you have to do. You meet with the compensation committee and throw out some numbers. They go to the CEO and review the numbers and then come back to you. At this point it's all a process of finding out what they need and what they want. You say, "This set of comparables and companies puts you at the fiftieth percentile." They come back and say you have to be at the seventy-fifth. We have to find ways to rationalize it. They want the executive to be happy, and they need an outside firm to rationalize it. So, to get to the seventy-fifth they say, "But we are unique because of these factors, and so our man should have a twenty-five percent premium. And we don't want to lose him." So you do it.

The consequences of this siphoning off of investors' money are frightening. The United States faces a retirement-funding nightmare of staggering proportions just around the corner, with Social Security, Medicare, and most pensions in sad shape. We cannot afford to waste resources.

Yet the gatekeepers resist reforms that would increase disclosure and better regulate conflicts of interest. The mutual fund industry has vigorously fought regulation that would make hidden charges transparent and make performance and returns across funds more comparable; the CEOs' lobbying group fought increased disclosure of executive compensation. The accounting industry fought opening up its own books. Reform will also be difficult due to the sheer number of players with conflicts of interest. A number of the largest firms that assess companies' governance and recommend the way shareholders should vote on contentious proxy issues simultaneously act as consultants to the companies holding the votes. Headhunting firms that search for CEOs and new directors frequently also do consulting work for those same companies. Compensation consultants do lucrative business in a wide range of areas with the same companies they advise about pay. At Fortune 250 companies the pay advisors who also do consulting work earn eleven times more—an average of $2.3 million from the other consulting than they do from providing pay recommendations. For fear of jeopardizing all of that other business, few of these companies have proven willing to go out on a limb to recommend whacking a CEO's pay.

Those who get caught up in these conflicts of interest are by no means always conscious of doing so. There are those who purposefully exploit the plentiful opportunities to game the system, but a more pervasive problem is simply the way in which the conflicts of interest cloud people's judgment. The behavioral economist George Loewenstein has studied the psychological mechanisms whereby this process occurs. He writes:

> Serious accounting problems have long plagued corporate audits, routinely leading to substantial fines for accounting firms. Some of the errors, no doubt, are the result of fraud. But to attribute most errors to deliberate corruption would be to believe that the accounting profession is rife with crooks . . . The deeper, more pernicious problem with corporate accounting . . . is its vulnerability to unconscious bias. Because of the often subjective nature of accounting and the tight relationships between accounting firms and their clients, even the most honest and meticulous of auditors can unintentionally distort the numbers in ways that mask a company's true financial status. . . .

Institutions, not individuals, dominate American stock ownership. Institutions hold 70 percent of the votes. When John F. Kennedy took office in 1961, one in eight shares of stock was held by an institution. A half century later, at least seven of every ten shares rest in institutional hands. These institutional investors include public and private pension funds, mutual funds, insurance companies, banks, money managers, hedge funds, sovereign wealth funds, foundations, and the endowments of educational institutions. While they all have a fiduciary duty to act in the best interests of their beneficiaries, they differ greatly in what their beneficiaries' interests are, their investment horizons, the inherent conflicts in their roles, the management of their operations, and their willingness to use their voting power to improve corporate governance.

Mutual funds have enjoyed most of this phenomenal growth in the last decades as so many employers discontinued contributing to pension plans and replaced them with 401(k) programs. Today's mutual funds are the second-largest institutional investors—after pension funds—with more than $9 trillion in assets in the United States, including $5 trillion in equities. Investors now can shop at a gigantic bazaar of 9,500 mutual funds and 750 exchange-traded funds. Seven hundred companies offer such funds in the United States.

Large financial institutions like banks and insurance companies own many of these funds, amplifying the impacts of financial concentration. The problem of picking among the 8,000 traded stocks, which mutual funds were supposed to solve, has shifted to the problem of picking funds.

As a consequence of this explosive growth, fund managers can and do exert a powerful influence on cleaning up corporate governance. Unfortunately, however, their interests are often conflicted with those of the investors whose savings they manage. The crux of the conflict is that mutual funds sell themselves aggressively to corporations to be included as options in the employee 401(k) plans and pension plans. They may also offer billing, payroll, and other back office services. They are therefore in the position of both evaluating the investment-worthiness of companies and marketing their services to those same companies, while at the same time voting the shares they hold on behalf of their fund customers.

Of all the many conflicts of interest in the governance system, those involving mutual funds receive the least public scrutiny. Aided by its immensely powerful lobby, the Investment Company Institute, the industry has shown considerable influence in thwarting the promulgation of new SEC regulations. Funds often have no public annual meetings, and shareholders cannot effectively vote on any governance issues relating to the funds. Shareholders cannot nominate directors, who frequently serve for life. The chairman is usually the head of the group hired to invest the money. Many directors sit on the boards of scores of funds. The record belongs to Lee Ault, a busy seventy-three-year-old who, besides chairing the Venture fund of the Central Intelligence Agency and sitting on the board of Office Depot, sits on the boards of more than 350 mutual funds. Mutual fund boards have far fewer independent directors than do corporate boards, and the chairman need not be independent. The directors' biggest duty is to approve the contract by which the investment advisor team (that is, the people who select the funds, stocks, and bonds, formally known as "investment advisors") is paid, and this is generally done in a perfunctory fashion.

Fund managers cannot be sued by shareholders for anything short of outright theft. Until Eliot Spitzer, when he was New York's attorney general, pursued some funds for illegal market timing (favoring certain customers when trades are executed) and late trading (allowing the trading of shares after the close of business at that day's price instead of the next day's)—offenses that had been prevalent in the mutual fund industry—all the relevant regulators and authorities apparently had looked the other way. In

2003, only after a number of scandals, the SEC required funds and other investment advisors to disclose their policies for voting on proxy measures and any votes that are not consistent with the policies and how a shareholder or beneficiary could obtain information on how they voted. This has led to some improvement in their behavior, but major conflicts remain.

The Corporate Library and the American Federation of State, County and Municipal Employees conducted a study of proxy voting in 2007 and 2008 by twenty-nine of the largest mutual fund companies. The study showed that on average the funds supported 84 percent of management-sponsored compensation proposals. They separately singled out Barclay's, Ameriprise, and AllianceBernstein funds as the worst enablers of excessive corporate pay. Until investors can influence how mutual funds cast votes, this problem will persist.

How mutual funds make their money and how they cast their votes are frequently related. As major shareholders in companies, mutual funds often cast the deciding votes on issues such as executive pay plans, director elections, and a wide range of governance proposals.

Edward Siedle is a former SEC and mutual fund attorney who conducts forensic investigations into pension fraud. He has an especially refined view into mutual fund conflicts because pension fund trustees frequently hire mutual fund companies to handle their investments. "I can tell you from twenty-five years of experience that [mutual] fund companies clearly side with management—always have—for two reasons. One, they don't take their fiduciary responsibility to vote proxies seriously; and two, there's a conflict of interest. They are hoping to market to these very corporations they are involved with. It's one of the many conflicts of interest and compromises that results in mutual fund investors getting the shaft."

These voting decisions are implicit, Siedle says. They are "so ingrained in the nature of mutual fund management, it's rare that there would be any serious discussion about it at all. The companies would fully expect that the fund would just know how the proxies were to be voted—that is, with management."

Jack Bogle, who has been in mutual funds for sixty years and founded Vanguard in 1974, makes the point that funds *are*, for all practical purposes, part of management. He says, "Investment management has gone from a profession with elements of a business to a business with elements of a profession." He adds,

> Now the dominant form of management is the giant financial conglomerate. Companies, in effect, own themselves. Citibank, for example, holds 1 percent of Citigroup. They're all members of the Business Roundtable. Members of the Roundtable own one another; corporations own about 12 percent of corporate shares. Another 11 percent they arguably control by having moral suasion. That 12 percent is in their pension plans, the other 11 percent is in their 401(k) plans. They have enough power to be pretty confident that those 401(k) managers are not going to take them on over any issue . . .

The largest single bloc of votes in corporate America is controlled *by* corporate America itself. Jack Bogle notes a circularity in all of this:

> We're never quite sure who is paying the piper and calling the governance tune, and with what motivation. This is not merely asking the fox to mind the henhouse. It's more like asking the fox to mind the foxes in the henhouse.

In 2004, SEC staff studied the pension consulting industry, which provides advice to the trustees of the nation's massive pension funds on matters such as which money managers should be hired to invest the many trillions of dollars the funds control. The consultants thus influence who will receive billions of dollars in investment management fees and are supposed to judge in an unbiased, objective manner. The study examined a cross-section of twenty-four pension consultants who were registered with the SEC as investment advisors and found massive evidence of multiple conflicts of interest, under-the-table payouts, and undisclosed business relationships, especially with the consultants providing services to the very money managers they are helping to select. The SEC press release noted an especially shocking fact: "Although investment advisers owe their clients a fiduciary obligation—including to adequately disclose all material conflicts of interest—some pension consultants appear to have erroneously concluded that they are not fiduciaries to their clients." But when Christopher Cox took over the SEC four weeks after the report, this and numerous other lines of investigation abruptly stopped. The Government Accounting Office, though, pursued the issue on its own and found that these advisors reduced returns by 1.3 percent, a massive amount ($58 billion a year when imputed against all such managed returns) in real terms and also as a percentage of a plan's annual profit. Even so, the SEC did nothing.

Private pension funds control and vote upon more than $3.6 trillion in stock, and their votes are almost inevitably cast for the positions supported by management. These votes are cast by trustees who are almost always appointed by, and answerable to, corporate executives. "How can one expect corporate employees—with normal appetite for advancement—to be 'independent' of those who hire them?" Robert Monks, the shareholder activist, asks in his book *The Emperor's Nightingale*.

Those in charge of these funds may also be woefully unattentive to employees' interests, despite their legal duty to administer the assets "for the exclusive benefit of plan participants." An industry study showed that 36 percent of responding company sponsors—that is, the company employees overseeing the plan—either did not know the fees being charged to participants or mistakenly thought no fees were charged at all.

Pension trustees frequently take a hands-off attitude toward their responsibility. The trustee job offers little but trouble: it generally doesn't pay much, and it's got potential liability. Nonetheless, most companies that are saddled with providing a plan, pick trustees from within their own ranks. The trustees then farm out the management of plans to a mutual fund or investment manager, or they select an agent who picks money managers.

Even here, conflicts appear, because these intermediaries can turn over pension assets to vendors who provide kickbacks. A 2009 GAO report found outside plan managers who chose not to disclose such conflicts of interest had 29 percent lower returns than those who did disclose the conflicts. In the pension world, such a shortfall is huge.

The long-prevailing attitude in Washington toward this problem was best summarized by the words of Brad Belt, the Bush administration's head of the Pension Benefit Guarantee Corporation (PBGC). The PBGC is a government insurance program that steps in when pensions go bankrupt. According to Edward Siedle, in front of PBGC staff Belt asked, "What do we care if there are 'kickbacks' as long as they don't reduce returns?" According to Siedle and the industry's leading trade publication, *Pensions & Investments,* the PBGC, which has taken over 4,000-plus pension funds, has never audited a single one for fraud, nor has itself been audited. It is little wonder that, with such lax regulatory oversight and such close ties to the management of companies, the private pension funds have failed to represent the interests of their beneficiaries in reforming corporate governance. In fact, most have long served in a detrimental role.

Public pension funds, on the other hand, have been playing a more positive role as corporate governance watchdogs. Backed by $1.9 trillion in stocks (as of 2006), union pensions have been using their votes to spotlight issues such as excessive CEO pay, entrenched directors, underperforming executives, the lack of adequate disclosure, and a host of structural matters such as majority voting and proxy access for shareholders to nominate directors. And as union membership in for-profit corporations fell—state and local government employees' pension funds joined the battle. Government workers now own as much as 10 percent of all U.S. equity. The forces arrayed against the public pension fund managers representing these unions include executive lobbying groups with huge clout in Washington, as well as the managers of private pensions and mutual funds. The fight has sometimes come in the form of full frontal assaults. In its role as shareholder advocate through the years, the California Public Employees' Retirement System (CalPERS) has irritated and shamed executives with its highly influential "Focus List." Each year it shines a spotlight on a handful of specific companies it believes have the worst governance or most excessive executive pay practices. Shame has proven to be the best weapon, according to Michael Garland of Change to Win, a union advocacy group. Public shame costs far less than the typical $350,000 proxy fight, and seems to hit executives squarely in a vital organ: their self-esteem.

In 2006, the pay package of Pfizer CEO Hank McKinnell became a cause célèbre for union efforts. McKinnell, who was also a director of Moody's and ExxonMobil, served as chairman of the Business Roundtable (the lobby for CEOs) at the time, and the Roundtable's advocacy of Social Security privatization and other conservative agenda items put him in the crosshairs of the union pension funds. As *BusinessWeek* noted, "Labor and public pension funds are making McKinnell a poster boy for extravagant pay." The opposing armies collided at Pfizer's annual meeting in Nebraska, where McKinnell was attacked on the ground and in the air. Union members chanted, "Hank McKinnell rich and rude, we don't like your attitude." An airplane circled the meeting site, towing a banner that read, "Give it back, Hank." The "it" referred to McKinnell's pension, at the time calculated to be a lump sum of $83 million or as $6.5 million per year if he retired at sixty-five. His prior year's compensation totaled $18 million, of which $15 million was bonus or incentives, even though Pfizer's stock fell as much as 23 percent that year. During McKinnell's tenure as chairman and CEO to that point, $100 worth of Pfizer stock would have fallen to $56. The stock lagged the pharmaceutical industry index and Pfizer's fabled new drug pipeline had become sclerotic. A few years earlier, scandals at other companies grabbed headlines, and the board changed the future rules for executive pensions. But certain executives were grandfathered, including McKinnell. His pension calculation was based not only on salary and thirty-five years' service, but on his stock awards as well, which was highly unusual.

Leading up to the meeting, pension funds representing the AFL-CIO and state employee funds mounted a massive withhold-vote campaign against the compensation committee directors who had okayed McKinnell's package. They were joined by a coalition of irate investors led by Frederick "Shad" Rowe, an investment manager who at the time also chaired the Texas Pension Review Board. Rowe created Investors for Director Accountability with an all-star steering committee including Jack Bogle, Robert Monks, T. Boone Pickens, and Edward "Rusty" Rose. Rowe says they screened 1,000 large companies to find what he called "the most egregious disconnects" between pay and performance. They settled on McKinnell and Pfizer as "a first step on a long road to restore director accountability to owners." Pfizer had plenty of ammunition for the fight, though. Barclays bank was Pfizer's biggest shareholder, with 4.5 percent. Lynn Turner, the former chief accountant for the SEC, remembers how the battle was fought: "Two of my good friends, Peggy Foran [senior vice president, associate general counsel, and corporate secretary for Pfizer], and David Shedlarz [Pfizer's vice-chairman] got on a plane, met with the people at Barclays, and explained to them exactly how much they were getting in fees to manage those assets, and Barclays then totally voted for McKinnell." So did a host of other private institutional investors with Pfizer ties like Dodge & Cox, Fidelity, and Northern Trust.

At the annual meeting, McKinnell won 96-plus percent of the 6.2 billion votes cast. It is very rare for institutional investors to vote against a sitting chairman and CEO for any reason. However, two members of the compensation committee had about 30 percent of their votes withheld. In the director subculture, this is considered a major loss of face. As Pfizer's performance continued to spiral downward, the personally embarrassed board apparently grew tired of McKinnell's famously high-handed management style. By the end of the year, he had retired. The pension remained intact. As it turned out, the shareholders had approved not just the $83 million the pension funds had found objectionable, but $199 million, including $39 million in deferred compensation, bonuses, and vacation pay.

Within two more years, 14,000 Pfizer employees had been laid off, on much less lucrative parting terms.

One stock analyst eulogized the package as "a little over $2 million for every billion dollars in market cap lost during his tenure. Though this will receive some media attention, we view this as more annoying than material." Frequently, analysts trivialize pay packages from the perspective of a firm's total assets and expenses. In doing so they forget that the payout is huge to the executive, and the behavior it inspires has enormous ramifications for the stockholders—and these don't end when the executive departs. Were it not for union pension funds, some activist hedge funds, and gadflies, the relationship between pay and performance would be all but lost in the footnotes of SEC filings. In the end, McKinnell left, but only after most of the directors got 80 percent or more of the votes. He walked out with tens of millions of dollars in consolation money, but the pain of past and present employees, as well as shareholders, lived after him. Unfortunately there has been no swift or sure way to limit the damage, particularly with so many shares in apathetic or conflicted institutional hands.

Public pensions have been far from free of conflict and impropriety, however, and every embarrassment has provided ammunition to their opponents. There has been a series of scandals involving expenses, mismanagement, and the use of "finders." Finders are financial intermediaries who steer investment money from the pensions to specific money managers in return for paying political contributions to individuals involved with the state pensions. Plans in New York State, Maryland, Milwaukee, Massachusetts, New Mexico, Connecticut, Texas, Illinois, Alabama, and California have been implicated in scandals in recent years. While providing fodder to the enemies of public pension plans and governance reforms, these incidents shift the focus from investment and returns to corruption and incompetence. Here again, investors suffer from bad governance, originating not just from corporations, but from politicians and union officials.

Not every conflict is necessarily financial, a point frequently made by pro-management groups like the Business Roundtable and the U.S. Chamber of Commerce. Critics of union pension fund involvement fear the advance of partisan interests that bear no relation to the health of the company or the fortunes of other investors (or of management). Here the perennial conflict between management and labor is like a barroom brawl that spills out into the street, bringing a new kind of pressure to the aims of governance.

Public pension funds are run by trustees, and the trustees are either elected from membership, appointed by politicians, or given seats because they hold an office like state treasurer. This can lead to a wide range of political and financial agendas, not all of which have to do with increasing pension returns. The short and tumultuous reign of Sean Harrigan as head of CalPERS exemplifies the situation. Harrigan placed CalPERS on the battlement of the good governance movement from the moment he ascended to the top of the nation's largest pension fund in 2003. By the next year, the fund withheld votes from directors at 2,400 companies, mostly over the practice of permitting auditors to do certain consulting. CalPERS played a major role in unseating Disney's Michael Eisner and NYSE CEO and chairman Dick Grasso, while forcing policy changes at Royal Dutch Shell Group and other firms.

CEOs loathed Sean Harrigan as an unabashed union partisan who hit them too close to home, and they pounced on an opportunity to lash back at him. Harrigan had formerly headed the supermarket workers' union in the western United States. Once atop CalPERS he had led an unsuccessful attempt to unseat the chairman/CEO and two directors of the Safeway grocery chain. At that point, the corporate lobbies cried, "Conflict of interest!" and Harrigan by then had antagonized enough people—even going so far as to attack Warren Buffett's service on Coca-Cola's board—that under this pressure, he was sacked from the fund when a Schwarzenegger appointee cast a deciding vote against his reelection. Since then CalPERS has taken a comparatively more moderate path. Of late, CalPERS is mired in its own problems and tens of billions in market-related losses. Still, without public pension funds, there would be far fewer extragovernmental checks on the power of some CEOs and boards.

Investors depend on professionals who provide information, but in a larger sense, the professionals who advise us about the business and governance sell "trust" as their stock in trade.

Accountants along with attorneys and the analysts who rate equities or debt belong to a class of professionals known as "gatekeepers" in governance circles. They are supposed to keep companies and boards in line with regulations and the law, help with corporate leaders' management and oversight of the company, and provide analysis and disclosure of information that allow shareholders and others to assess a company's performance and sustainability. In the wake of the Enron and WorldCom scandals, then–Federal Reserve chairman Alan Greenspan told Congress that "shareholders and potential investors would have been protected from widespread misinformation if any one of the many bulwarks safeguarding appropriate corporate evaluation had held. In too many cases, none did." But the gatekeepers continued in their ways, with conflicts and negligence that certainly contributed to the 2008 financial crisis. How does this happen? Columbia Law School professor John Coffee, who is the foremost academic expert on the gatekeeping professions, summarized the situation succinctly: "Typically, the party paying the gatekeeper will be the party that the gatekeeper is expected to monitor."

Ever since it arrived in the United States from England in the late 1800s, the accounting and subsequently the auditing professions have struggled for a business model that steers them wide of the problems Coffee describes. So fraught with conflicts is the relationship between the Big Four accounting firms (Deloitte Touche

Tomatsu, PricewaterhouseCoopers, Ernst & Young, and KPMG are the only ones left standing after the accounting scandals of 2000) and their clients, that behavioral economist George Loewenstein, who has studied the failures of the profession, writes in a paper titled "The Impossibility of Auditor Independence," that "audit failures are the natural product of the auditor-client relationship. Under current institutional arrangements, it is psychologically impossible for auditors to maintain their objectivity." Another expert who has studied the problem, Charlie Munger of Berkshire Hathaway, describes the role accountants played in the 2008 crisis this way: "I would argue that a majority of the horrors we face would not have happened if the accounting profession developed and enforced better accounting." Munger concludes, "They are way too liberal in providing the kind of accounting the financial promoters want. They've sold out, and they do not even realize that they've sold out . . . Nobody is even bothered by the folly. It violates the most elemental principles of common sense. And the reasons they do it are: (1) there's a demand for it from the financial promoters, (2) fixing the system is hard work, and (3) they are afraid that a sensible fix might create new responsibilities that cause new litigation risks for accountants."

Accountants and auditors in America seem to have spent the last century dodging five major terrors: regulation, financial liability, legal liability, the imposition of uniform accounting practices, and offending current and future corporate customers by making audit rules and processes more rigorous and accurate. Corporations hire their auditors; they influence how deeply they are audited and, frequently, they have a hand in how the audit is presented. Throughout the years, the accounting industry, usually with the indulgence of the SEC, Congress, and other gatekeepers, has generally failed to keep its own act clean. Historically, the industry had largely been allowed to develop its own standards. So thoroughly was this abused that government has repeatedly stepped in with piecemeal reforms in the wake of repeated scandals, but some have argued that the problems may have only grown worse—and more expensive for shareholders and our economy.

The auditing profession has always had a great deal of clout in Washington. The Public Securities Litigation Reform Act (PSLRA) in 1995 made class-action law suits much harder to bring against accounting firms, and reduced liabilities and the size of penalties. The impetus for this act was the damage done to the profession from a wave of litigation that grew to monstrous proportions in the early 1990s. By 1992 auditing firms paid $785 million due to legal actions against them. This gobbled up 10 percent of revenue and most of the audit partners' profits. When Republicans took control of Congress in 1994, they rapidly moved to pass the act, and served to loosen constraints.

But the accounting industry had utterly failed to effectively police its policies or its members. The SEC, which has retained the right to oversee accounting firms since its inception in 1933, tried to let the accountants discipline themselves. This only led to a half dozen or more toothless internal agencies that the profession defunded or disbanded whenever they appeared to take the job seriously. In 1999, as the unseen audit crisis was peaking, the industry's peer review board failed to flunk a single accountant in the United States.

Professor Coffee suggests that there are a number of core reasons for the auditing gatekeepers' failures. First, he notes the rise of consulting services and their effect on the internal culture of accountancies. After each crisis—from the Great Depression to the Penn Central bankruptcy, the foreign bribery slush funds of the 1970s, the S&L scandals of the 1980s, and the Enrons and WorldComs—Congress, federal, and state regulators and the stock exchanges have mandated new requirements that have translated into vast amounts of new work, much of which can only be done by the major accounting firms that contributed to many of the problems in the first place. After Enron, the SEC attempted to rein in the consulting, but industry lobbyists beat back the ban, reducing its scope to an increase in disclosure requirements. It took yet another wave of scandals before Congress passed the Sarbanes-Oxley Act of 2002 (also known as the Public Company Accounting Reform and Investor Protection Act—or simply as SOX). So severe was the consulting abuse that SOX stripped the big accounting firms of their ability to consult for their audit clients on certain things such as information technology system implementation. Instead, the audit firms moved into other areas of consulting, particularly risk management and, ironically, the implementation of other SOX requirements.

Because consulting tends to be much more profitable than accounting and auditing, the latter began to get short shrift in staffing, time, and attention. In the 1990s the Big 5 (Coopers & Lybrand was then independent) stopped promoting the staid "bean counters" at the firms, and even tossed many out, in order to make room for rainmaker partners who sold more lucrative nonauditing services. Auditing, in effect, had become a loss leader for getting a foot in the door on expensive consulting projects, while the quality of auditing and accounting services suffered. Those who were supposed to be financial watchdogs for shareholders and others came to identify with the executives they were auditing. The pathetic result was demonstrated in a promotional video for Arthur Andersen that came to light after its negligent work for Enron contributed to that firm's collapse and a $60 billion loss for shareholders. The video featured two Arthur Andersen auditors proudly looking into the camera and saying: "[I'm] trying to kinda cross lines and . . . become more of just a business person here at

Enron. . . . Being here full time . . . day to day gives us a chance to chase the deals with them and participate in the deal-making process."

Another major factor cited by Coffee for lax oversight by gatekeepers is the decrease in competition between firms. The Final Four (as remaining accountancies came to be known) now perform 99 percent of large company audits, and the net effect of the industry's consolidation has been to enable auditors to specialize in specific industries, making customer turnover less likely. When the 2000 accounting crisis hit, *all* the firms (not just Arthur Andersen, which drew the most notoriety) were implicated in tens of thousands of instances of abuse. Auditors owned stock in the firms they audited. They got into joint business ventures with clients. They peddled highly dubious but highly profitable tax shelters to client firms and their executives. Even so, when SEC chairman Arthur Levitt tried to get auditors out of the consulting business, the audit industry and its congressional allies pursued Levitt and the SEC with a vengeance.

Congress did take decisive action, however, to clamp down on the rampant abuses exposed by the implosions of Enron and WorldCom, by passing Sarbanes-Oxley. But SOX had an ironic revenge affect on the accounting profession. It created new accounting requirements for companies that enriched the accountancies by providing them with a new full-employment act. Among its many other provisions, SOX mandated that a corporation's auditing committee comprise only independent directors. It nominally ejected the CEO and his staff out of the auditors' reporting chain. Audit committees had to have a qualified financial expert—and the workload became enormous. Of all the provisions in SOX's sixty pages of fine print, sections 404 and 302 have stoked the most tumult and anguish in the business community. Section 404 requires that companies set up, document, continually test, and perpetually report on a quarterly and annual basis a series of internal controls that will ensure accuracy in the firm's financial statements. Management must assess the controls, and external auditors must attest to the assessment. Section 302 stipulates stiff financial and criminal penalties for failure to do so.

These and other sections of SOX require executives to certify compliance on these requirements, as well as on the accuracy of financial statements—and impose stiff criminal and civil penalties for noncompliance. The procedures create mountains of documents and billable hours, and the lengths to which some auditing firms have taken this is extraordinary.

For accounting firms, SOX was manna from heaven. The Big Four are private partnerships and do not publish their own financial statements, so SOX revenues are impossible to calculate from that side. From the customer side, though, surveys show compliance is costing companies 100 times or more what the SEC estimated. The SOX phase-in in 2004 spiked audit fees by 67 percent. Between 2001 and 2006, audit bills increased 300 percent for S&P small-cap companies, grew 350 percent for mid-caps, and grew nearly 200 percent for S&P 500 firms. Firms with sales of more than $5 billion are spending $5 million or more a year on 404 compliance alone. Tyco, for example, which had one of the bigger problems to fix in this regard, estimates it initially spent about $100 million to meet the new requirements. Some firms are going private specifically to avoid these requirements. Several private equity executives told us SOX is the best silent partner they ever had because it makes public ownership so onerous.

One has to wonder about the benefits to shareholders of much of the services being provided in order to comply with SOX. Consider the case of National Instruments, a small high-tech company in Austin. The company paid PricewaterhouseCoopers $3 million to comply, and the billable activities performed included:

- Requiring an auditor to attend a meeting to prove it took place;
- Having the technical support "help desk" document every call it receives from employees;
- Proving that all of the physical keys to an office in Europe have been accounted for since it opened in 1995;
- Examining how the power supply to computer facilities is secured;
- Requiring people to respond to thousands of emails to prove they received them;
- Ensuring that every employee has a personnel performance evaluation;
- Checking the strength of the tempered-glass windows of the data center.

Meanwhile, even as their clients are prodded into greater transparency by SOX, the Big Four themselves are more or less opaque. They have no annual reports, and no requirement for outside directors. The PricewaterhouseCoopers website doesn't even disclose who its directors are.

Compared to accountants, lawyers have had an easy regulatory ride, which shouldn't be that surprising considering the vast number of attorneys in Congress and the agencies, as well as a revolving door between Washington and law firms that rivals that of corporate leaders. Lawyers as gatekeepers have generally avoided outside interference, and while they have been present at almost every corporate collapse, they've generally avoided liability as well. They work for the corporation, not the shareholders, although shareholders ultimately pay their fees and suffer from their silence. While major law firms were deeply involved in corporate wrongdoing ranging from the S&L scandals to Enron-era financial malfeasance, the Supreme Court nonetheless has severely limited shareholders' right to sue counsel for aiding and abetting fraud. After Enron, Congress had a chance to address this problem, but backed off due to ABA lobbying.

The single near-exception to this regulatory freedom is one provision of the Sarbanes-Oxley Act. Section 307 is commonly referred to as "Up the Ladder" and requires corporate attorneys (but not firms) who have "credible evidence . . . based upon which it would be unreasonable under the circumstances for a prudent and competent attorney not to conclude that it is reasonably likely that a material violation has occurred, is ongoing, or is about to occur" to report this evidence to the general counsel or CEO. If those two executives fail to "appropriately respond," then the lawyer must inform the audit committee or full board. But the provision is knotted with loopholes and has more escape hatches than a fleet of submarines. The ABA has picked this convoluted lawyer-speak apart. They ask, for example, what's an "appropriate response"? What is "credible evidence"? What are the "best interests of the organization"?

As much as the ABA doesn't like 307, it *really* doesn't like a measure currently being proposed by the SEC that would kick in if "Up the Ladder" does not work. It was proposed that whistle-blower attorneys go to the SEC if the board fails to act. "Considering the reality of the subordinate in-house counsel's experience, level of authority within the organization, general inability to effect change with the corporate entity, and fear of reprisals, many may seek to avoid making even the initial up-the-ladder report," Lisa Nicholson, an assistant professor at the University of Louisville Law School, writes. No one beneath the CEO's top inside lawyer is likely to rock the boat.

As for outside attorneys, one renowned governance law professor has pointed how wrongheaded it is to think that that the corporation is the client. In reality, it's the flesh-and-blood executives and the general counsel who determine whether to replace the outside firm of Dewey, Cheatham & Howe with Moore, Paine & Billings. Lawyers are unlikely to run the risk of losing the account to a competing firm. In a buyers' market for most types of legal talent, firms don't enhance their standing by turning in clients to the authorities.

Outside of a few mergers and acquisitions specialties, much of the practice of corporate law is mundane, routine, and commoditized. But it has grown rapidly and is increasingly concentrated. When Richard Nixon lost to JFK and went back into private practice at Adams, Duque & Hazeltine, only thirty-eight American law firms had more than 50 lawyers. By 2000, there were more than five hundred U.S. law firms with at least 100 attorneys each. Today, the ranks of the outside lawyers who provide expertise on corporate issues in the United States has grown to more than 100,000. Most work in huge firms with scores of offices around the world. These outside firms have become mega-conglomerates, with pyramidal organization charts and up-or-out promotion policies based in no small part on associates' abilities to "make rain" by making corporate clients happy.

Contributing to the problem of a lack of legal intervention in corporate wrongdoing is the remarkable imbalance in rewards for those who work for corporations versus those who work for the SEC. On top of the growth in sheer numbers, a meteoric rise in billings during the takeover craze of the 1980s led to breathtaking rates of price inflation by specialist firms. Star lawyers have come to behave like baseball free agents, and migrate from firm to firm, taking their clients along for the ride.

The best specialist outside counsels command staggering sums in fees. Wachtell, Lipton, Rosen & Katz frequently takes governance control of corporations that are caught in a storm, like the harbor pilot who takes over a supertanker's wheelhouse and brings the giant vessel to the pier as its own captain stands by. With the global economic collapse and all, the year 2008 was a bit off for Wachtell. Yet, its 217 attorneys still managed to generate $4.975 million in profit *per partner*.

Meanwhile, on the other side of the corporate battle lines, SEC lawyers make $102,000 to $160,000 after twenty years. In general, anyone who opposes corporate interests makes out much less well financially than those who work for the corporations. The head of CalPERS, which is the world's fourth-largest pension fund with more than $185 billion in assets under management, earned only about $300,000 in 2007, about 25 percent less than a midlevel Wachtell associate five years out of law school. But, then again, one might prefer to be behind the gatekeeper's gate—the head of CalPERS got less than one half of 1 percent of the of average compensation for the three men who served as CEOs and chairmen of Goldman Sachs, Morgan Stanley, and Merrill Lynch that year.

These CEOs themselves are at the very pinnacle of the gatekeeper food chain—the investment banks whose fees and compensation dwarf those of lesser corporate services professionals. The investment bank CEOs often find themselves clustered atop the lists of the nation's highest paid executives, as the three cited above did in 2007 with Merrill's John Thain ranking at number two, Goldman's Lloyd Blankfein at number six, and Morgan Stanley's John Mack at number nine. Their boards, in their own category, also do quite well. The ten Goldman Sachs independent directors, who had ten full board meetings in 2007, received an average of more than $640,000 each (a number that was somewhat depressed because Lord Browne of Madingley left the board in the middle of the fiscal year and was prorated at $346,032)—more than three times what their colleagues on Fortune 500 boards average.

The banks pay so well in a good year because they make tens

of billions creating, selling, and trading securities and taking calculated risks with shareholders' money in the financial markets. As gatekeepers, they develop and facilitate corporate transactions and often play a vital and creative role that is critically important in making our free enterprise system work smoothly. They can help to create a lot of value. At the same time, investment bankers can be incalculably destructive in pushing risky mergers and acquisitions, exotic debt securities, and questionable financial strategies on their corporate clients, as well as on themselves. This problem is compounded because they are typically paid more based on the size, the complexity, and the riskiness of the transactions, so there is a tremendous incentive to push ever closer to the edge, as well as a great deal of competitive pressure within and among the firms to do just that. As we have seen in the past few years, shareholders, taxpayers, and the entire global economic system can pay a heavy price when things go wrong.

Even with the scorched-earth aftermath for many investment banks after the financial meltdown, they will continue—though perhaps under some new rules—to make lots of money as gatekeepers. For one thing, the shakeout in the industry will drive up profits from the lack of competition. Like many of the other types of gatekeepers, the banks will also continue to operate with some blatant conflicts of interest and exorbitant fees. Just one example is the "fairness opinions" that are part of most M&As and certain other transactions. Boards require them to demonstrate they have met their fiduciary duties by getting a fair price for shareholders when they buy or sell businesses. These are among the most profitable and least risky services provided by investment banks. The conflict comes because they are often provided by banks that won't get paid for the M&A transaction itself unless the sale is completed or a bank that is looking for future business with the board. There is an obvious incentive to justify whatever the deal calls for and, in cases of insider-led transactions such as management buyouts, the conflicts can be especially extreme. In addition, the opinion typically includes disclaimer language like this: "We have not independently verified the accuracy and completeness of the information supplied to us with respect to [client name], and do not assume any responsibility with respect to it." It's not exactly a case of shareholders getting what they are paying for—the fees for these opinions can be millions of dollars for, at most, a few days' or sometimes mere hours' work. A survey of sixty-seven large deals done in 2007 showed fairness opinion fees climbing up to $7.5 million, with an average of $1.1 million. The SEC has recently strengthened disclosure requirements regarding conflicts and the justification for fairness opinions, but it remains an area that perfectly exemplifies how shareholders pay dearly for something that really just benefits the board by protecting it from liability.

THESE GATEKEEPERS HAVE a vested interest in preventing the boat from rocking, which will make the job of enacting more effective reforms more formidable. But as we will explore in the next and last chapter, there are reasons for hope.

8

Solutions

ARE BOARDS in danger of becoming vestigial organs?

In September 2008, in the biggest bank failure in our history, Washington Mutual's board was not even consulted as federal regulators arranged the emergency sale of the nearly insolvent company. Alan H. Fishman, the bank's newly appointed CEO—who received a $7.5 million signing bonus in a contract approved by the board for what turned out to be seventeen days on the job—was on a plane from New York to the company's headquarters in Seattle as the deal was struck and did not know about it until he landed. The board had recently forced the "retirement" of CEO Kerry Killinger, who served as chairman for seventeen years and pushed the strategy of subprime lending well after the housing bubble had already burst. Shareholders had been so angry at the April 2008 annual meeting that they booed Killinger's board-approved bonus structure, which excluded mortgage loan losses from the company's earnings calculation. The shareholders voted to split the chairman and CEO positions, and, in one of the few clear victories in the history of shareholder activists' efforts to withhold votes for a board nominee, gave Mary Pugh, the finance committee chair who oversaw risk management, slightly less than a 50 percent vote, thus requiring her to resign. Shareholders eventually lost more than $40 billion. It's little wonder that regulators treated the board as irrelevant during the bank's emergency sale.

Franklin A. Gevurtz, a law professor who wrote a comprehensive history of boards, initially concluded that "the corporate board of directors is a largely useless, if mostly harmless, institution carried on out of inertia." Upon further reflection, Gevurtz suggested that boards could be seen as useful, at least to managers, because they lend political legitimacy to the fiction that shareholders' interests are being taken into consideration.

Congressman Barney Frank, who chairs the House Financial Services Committee and was named by *Directorship* magazine in 2008 as the single most influential person on corporate governance, questions how directors could possibly fulfill their supposed duties. As keynote speaker at the magazine's annual conference, Frank told the several hundred prominent board members in attendance that boards' inability to control executives and manage risks had contributed to the financial meltdown. "Boards of directors, we were told, were one of the ways to prevent companies from taking too much risk," Frank said. "And it didn't work . . . I've never been a director and I would be reluctant to be one even after I retire—I wouldn't take it and no one would offer—but my own view is this: I get very nervous about being held responsible for things that I don't have complete control of. The notion that there would be very intelligent people doing very complicated things six and a half days a week and I would come in on a periodic basis and tell them how to do it better, I don't understand how you do that."

When asked what kind of people he'd consider putting on the board of a company his firm was preparing to go public, the head of a private equity company who has served on numerous boards, including as a director of one of the major stock exchanges, thought for a second and answered, "Curly, Larry, and Moe."

James McRitchie, who started one of the first websites devoted to improving corporate governance, CorpGov.Net, says that randomly selecting board members from among a company's stockholders would be an improvement over the current system, in which directors "select themselves and exist in a bubble where they and their CEOs are isolated from reality and actually seem to be regressing in their sense of a moral obligation to do the right thing." Robert Monks says, "Can we do without them? Hey, we are doing without them—and not very well. It's actually worse than nothing because it creates the illusion of something." Evidence of the low regard in which public company boards are held was embarrassingly obvious in the wiretap transcripts released in connection with former Illinois governor Rod Blagojevich's indictment for attempting to sell a U.S. Senate seat. Blagojevich was caught saying that if his wife could get on some corporate boards and "picks up another 150 grand a year or whatever," it would help him get through the next several years as governor.

Nevertheless, boards of directors are not going to disappear. Nor, despite their many flaws, should they. At the end of the day, the only practical way for shareholders to be represented *within* companies is through boards. No other entity can provide the monitoring, advice, and connections that boards, at their best, deliver. They serve a critical purpose in our economic system, and we all have an enormous stake in reforming them.

As Jeffrey Sonnenfeld of the Yale School of Management observed in a perceptive *Harvard Business Review* article in 2002, most of the boards of the failed companies in the Enron era were in fact not incompetent, corrupt, or negligent—and they had followed nearly all of the accepted structural and operating standards of good governance. Sonnenfeld suggested that the problems of boards are rooted in their social and cultural systems. "We'll be fighting the wrong war if we simply tighten procedural rules for boards and ignore their more pressing need—to be strong, high-functioning work groups whose members trust and challenge one another and engage directly with senior managers on critical issues facing corporations," Sonnenfeld wrote. CEOs and boards need to "understand the difference between dissent and disloyalty. . . . The highest-performing companies have extremely contentious boards that regard dissent as an obligation and treat no subject as undiscussable."

Fortunately, there are many directors and companies that provide models of cultural excellence and demonstrate how boards can and should work. Some of the best and most inspiring are what might be termed "phoenix companies"—those that suffered a near-death experience because of a major scandal or bankruptcy. A crisis like that sometimes gives a company an opportunity to fundamentally change its governance by bringing in new directors, rebuilding the board's culture, and ensuring that the board's relationships with the CEO and the shareholders are transformed. One of the most encouraging examples is the complete turnaround at Tyco International after the Kozlowski scandal.

Tyco's new CEO and chairman, Edward Breen, started work eight weeks after Kozlowski resigned. The company was reeling from the headlines about the scandal, a $25 billion load of debt from its acquisitions binge, and the loss of $90 billion for shareholders. Breen, a straightforward, modest, yet tough executive who, appropriately enough, lived in New Hope, Pennsylvania, and had been Motorola's president and chief operating officer during its turnaround, looked at the job as "the opportunity of a lifetime." On August 1, 2002, his fourth day at the company, Breen wrote a letter to Tyco's 250,000 employees. "We must have an absolute commitment to integrity and trustworthiness throughout the organization," he said. "That is a fundamental imperative. With that commitment, we will establish Tyco as a leader in creating and enforcing the best corporate governance practices." Breen hired Michael Useem, the director of Wharton's Center for Leadership and Change Management, as a consultant and convinced Jack Krol, the highly respected former chairman and CEO of DuPont, to serve as the board's lead director. Krol, who also headed the nominating and governance committee, was given significantly greater power than lead directors usually have. Breen also hired Eric Pillmore to fill the newly created position of senior vice president for corporate governance, reporting directly to Krol and charged with establishing an ethical culture within the company.

Krol describes the first few weeks as chaotic. "Investigators and lawyers were everywhere, customers were fleeing, suppliers insisted on being paid in cash, the employees were demoralized, there was a weak code of conduct that nobody paid attention to, and there weren't even rules on who could authorize spending. We were basically starting from scratch." Krol said that he and Breen got together immediately to put on paper how they would divide responsibilities. "Ed is very open, listens, and then actually does something about it," Krol said. He and Breen talked every day for the next six months. Krol, who had been a naval nuclear engineer, recalled that he "always thought about it in three phases. First, we had to *save* the company by restoring confidence, keeping it afloat during the investigation, and raising money to avoid bankruptcy. Then we had to *fix* the company by establishing a new culture and focusing on operations instead of acquisitions. And, finally, we had to *grow* the company by deciding on a strategy that would create value for shareholders. None of this was going to happen with the old board. They had not dug into things they needed to, meetings had been perfunctory, and they just weren't interested in change."

Breen determined early on that to restore credibility, Tyco had to do something no company its size had ever tried before: replace its entire board and almost all of the senior executives. As head of the nominating committee, Krol took on the task of convincing the old directors to leave and recruiting new ones. Eric Pillmore calls Krol the "visionary" and says Breen empowered them to create a truly independent board. In fact, none of the ten additional directors who eventually joined the board even knew Breen before joining Tyco. Krol and Pillmore created a matrix of highly specific backgrounds among the directors, engaged a top recruiting firm, and put the candidates through rigorous background checks, including screening for ethics, open-mindedness, and how they thought about governance. They also asked major investors for advice on candidates, which led to bringing in Jerry York, a notoriously tough questioner of management and a veteran of many boards, as head of the audit committee. Breen later told a Harvard Business School case writer, "It's not just the structure; it's the people. Everyone we selected felt that governance was a serious topic, and they knew it would be a high priority at Tyco. I say this because I know a fair number of people on boards, and they think of governance and they roll their eyes."

Breen, Krol, Pillmore, Useem, and the new directors implemented virtually every recognized best practice for governance, including a focus on open communications with shareholders and regulators and intensive annual evaluations of the CEO and directors. Krol is modest about these accomplishments (upon receiving an award for being a corporate governance model, he noted that the dictionary definition of model is "a small replica of the real thing"), but he and Breen succeeded far beyond shareholders' expectations. GovernanceMetrics International, a major governance rating agency, had once ranked Tyco at 1.5 out of 10—among the lowest of some four thousand companies. Within two years under the new leadership, Tyco achieved a perfect 10. It was one of only thirty-eight companies to do so. During that time, the stock price more than quintupled, and by 2007 the company was positioned to successfully reorganize into three separate entities that better reflected its lines of business.

CHARLES PERRIN is a new breed of director—a seasoned CEO at Duracell International and Avon Products who in midcareer made a switch to full-time board service. He currently is a director of the Campbell Soup Company and the nonexecutive chairman of Warnaco Group, the clothing company that had gone bankrupt in 2001 amid an SEC investigation of accounting problems and a traumatized culture that led to the firing of an imperial CEO whom the *New York Times* called "a hard-charging boss who spewed obscenities." After an exemplary turnaround process led by Perrin's boardroom mentor Harvey Golub, the former American Express CEO and chairman who headed Warnaco's restructuring committee, the company reemerged in 2003 as a well-governed enterprise that has since returned to financial success. Golub's philosophy as a director is summed up in a cover story he wrote for *Directors & Boards* magazine: "The Board is not the CEO's friend—it is the CEO's boss."

Warnaco's nine-member board includes three women and welcomes shareholder communication—the company's website even encourages direct emails to individual directors. Robert Bowman, the CEO of Major League Baseball Advanced Media (MLB.com) and a veteran of five public company boards, became a Warnaco director the day after Perrin's appointment as chairman in January 2004. Bowman says he and several other new directors were attracted to Warnaco because the cultural and financial turnaround was "an interesting learning experience for people who like to fix problems." He attributes the effectiveness of the board to Perrin's open leadership style. "Charlie does a great job of getting everyone on the board to participate and to ask tough questions without making it personal. He makes it okay for someone to simply say, 'I don't agree'—and that's pretty rare in a boardroom."

Another phoenix company is Tenet Healthcare, which had suffered a major scandal in 2002 when a Medicare reimbursement problem erupted that eventually cost $215 million to settle shareholder lawsuits and $900 million to settle with the federal government. In 2003, Ed Kangas, the former head of the Deloitte & Touche accounting firm who now is a full-time director and sits on several large company boards, was brought in to be the nonexecutive chairman of Tenet. The board recruited eight new directors, changed 80 percent of the executives, and tied pay to performance. Kangas is a big believer in financial literacy among directors and told us a number of his colleagues have asked him to conduct individual sessions to bring them up to speed. He says in the case of splitting the chairman and the CEO roles, it's critical for the chairman to understand the role is not to run the company, but to run the board and make sure it is doing all the proper oversight and advisory duties. "I always tell people I'm chairman of the board of Tenet, not the chairman of Tenet," he says. With his guidance, Tenet has recovered well.

SITTING IN HIS LIVING ROOM overlooking a lake in Wayzata, Minnesota, during the fall of 2008, ninety-year-old Bruce Dayton thought back thirty years and recalled meeting with his brother Ken for hours after each board meeting of their company to discuss how to create an ideal system of governance for what would, in time, become the Target Corporation, one of the ten largest retailers in the world. "We wanted to come up with something that would keep the business healthy long after we were gone," he said. Bruce Dayton served as board chairman from 1968 to 1976, then turned the chairmanship over to Ken and remained as a board member until 1983. Bruce was the financial expert and Ken the theorist; together they worked out what they thought would ensure the optimum relationship between the board and management. By 1986, Ken had developed these ideas into a speech he gave to a management forum, and by the next year into a booklet called *Governance Is Governance*. They had already implemented the concepts at the company, and it's remarkable how closely they parallel what today are considered the best practices for corporate governance.

They began with position descriptions for the CEO, the board, and the chair that the board would thoroughly debate, adopt, and change as necessary, with an annual review. The board's role, for example, was to serve as "representatives of the shareholders, to be the primary force pressing the corporation to the realization of its opportunities and the fulfillment of its obligations to its shareholders, customers, employees, and the communities in which it operates." Diversity was a primary goal, not with any set quotas, but an emphasis on providing a true mix of gender, backgrounds, experience, and perspectives on the board. The company was among the first to actively recruit women and minorities as board members, and these directors were never typecast or limited to serving as representatives. Most directors were to be outsiders; in the early 1980s, for example, when most boards were composed of insiders and a few professional services providers, the company's fifteen directors were to include twelve outsiders and no investment bankers, lawyers, or retirees. The average age of directors could not exceed fifty-five and all must retire by age sixty-five. A maximum term limit of twelve years was imposed. "It usually takes a year or two to really understand an enterprise," Ken wrote. "A board member then provides several years of ideas, input, and productivity. But after a certain period of time, the company is better off with fresh, new ideas."

They strongly agreed that the chairman of the board should not be the CEO, because it tends to result in a dictatorship that necessarily stifles a board. "It may be benign, even enlightened, but it is nonetheless a dictatorship," Ken wrote. "Any chair/CEO wears primarily the CEO hat and only occasionally takes on the more neutral and impartial role of the chair." They were clear that the board's role was not to manage, but to "support, encourage, challenge, stimulate, and help" the professional executives. The board was to receive information well in advance of when it must make a decision and allow time for thought and debate. They insisted on an intensive evaluation process, including self-review by the board and of the CEO: "Both must ask, 'How can we do a better job together?'" Finally, the board must see that the company's future is protected by "having backups, having successors, having people in training—the corporate capacity to carry on." The Dayton brothers' governance philosophy was summed up by Ken's conclusion: "Directors are ultimately responsible for an organization's welfare. CEOs come and go, but the corporation and the board go on and on."

The Target board has, indeed, gone on, and not just at the company. Because they are steeped in this empowering set of values, Target's directors are highly sought after by other companies, and their dedication to excellence in governance has seeded many other boards.

ONE DIRECTOR can change a board's culture, and that same director can spread those changes to multiple boards. Drawing from her early experience on Target's now legendary board beginning in the early 1990s, Michele Hooper, a financial expert with a University of Chicago MBA, has brought those lessons to Warner Music Group, PPG Industries, AstraZeneca, UnitedHealth Group, Seagram, and DaVita. Hooper learned from Target the value of having "a boardroom that allows for open and collegial discussion around the table without people getting upset or having a CEO who is going to put the kibosh on conversations." Today, she trains other directors through the National Association of Corporate Directors and also works as a managing partner of the Directors' Council, which finds candidates for boards. At UnitedHealth, Hooper is part of an unusual advisory committee that invites shareholders, including those from public pension funds, to add their voices to the nominating process for directors. Previously angry relationships have been repaired in this way.

THE FORCE FOR CHANGE can be an individual, like Michele Hooper, or an institution. Institutions, after all, control most of the corporate stock that has been issued, although for many years they were passive enablers of bad governance. The California Public Employees' Retirement System played a major role in changing that. The process began in 1984, when the Bass brothers of Texas inadvertently fired the governance shot heard around the world. After the Basses acquired 10 percent of Texaco, the company's board paid them a $137 million premium to sell their shares and drop any possible takeover bid. The holders of the other 90 percent of shares were not consulted. This so infuriated Jesse Unruh, who was then the treasurer of California, that he founded the Council of Institutional Investors, a group of pension funds expressly interested in promoting good governance, and helped propel CalPERS, the state's biggest pension fund, into governance advocacy. Their first targets in the late 1980s were firms with poison pills and staggered boards. Soon thereafter, CalPERS's charismatic CEO, Dale Hanson, hired researchers to meet with underperforming firms. CalPERS sought private meetings with corporations on their "focus list" to induce them to improve strategies and governance practices. If they cooperated, the effort remained private. If they refused, the fund and its allies emptied the PR arsenal: proxy resolutions, newspaper ads, and press releases. Enough companies refused meetings that CalPERS went public with the focus list beginning in the early 1990s. It has proved a powerful weapon in shaming corporations into doing the right thing.

The idea of engagement over governance has spawned similar efforts around the world. Hermes, the pension fund of British Telecom, and the Post Office created their own "focus funds," which take an activist approach to working with companies that underperform because of governance problems. Funds elsewhere have begun tackling governance issues and helping to create solutions that can be adopted in other countries.

The notion of say-on-pay, for example, originated in the United Kingdom in 2003. Six years later, the U.S. Congress began passing legislation to make such nonbinding resolutions on executive compensation much easier to put to a shareholder vote. Among institutional investors, international groups such as the International Corporate Governance Network, which comprises 450 members from forty-five countries with $9.5 trillion in assets, initiate higher governance standards through research and advocacy. With every sign that globalization will continue to advance, there's also reason to believe the international pressure for better governance will grow.

Embarrassing or shaming a board into reform can sometines work, along the lines of Bebchuk and Fried's concept of bad publicity creating an "outrage constraint" for excessive executive compensation. A classic case involving a slumbering board was when the shareholder activist Robert Monks took out a full-page ad in the *Wall Street Journal* prior to the 1992 Sears Roebuck shareholders meeting to publicize the board's opposition to five proposals that would make the company's leaders more accountable. Entrenched executives at Sears controlled the directors and resisted change; its stock had dropped significantly over the prior six years; and a Fortune survey rated Sears 487th out of 500 companies for the reputation of its management. Monk's ad featured silhouettes of the directors, each of their names, and a huge caption reading NON-PERFORMING ASSETS. Although the proposals failed to pass, the board was sufficiently embarrassed that it subsequently enacted a number of them and initiated a major restructuring. The market added $1 billion to Sears's market value in a single day when the changes were announced and its stock delivered a 37 percent excess return during the following year. A number of successful reform efforts in recent years have emulated the approach that Monks pioneered.

FREDERICK "SHAD" ROWE is an investment manager who has also served on the Texas Public Pension Board, including two terms as the Board's chairman. He founded a group called Investors for Director Accountability, which is unique among shareholder activists in that it is composed largely of wealthy and relatively conservative businesspeople, many of whom have been successful investors. Their statement of "Who We Are" says: "We emphasize that we are investors and capitalists. We prize the driven, egocentric, imperial Chief Executive Officer who builds shareholder value. But we want our representatives—corporate directors—to preserve that value for the shareholders for whom they are the direct, legal representatives." Rowe told us his concern is for the "people who aspire to retire" but who are seeing their investments disappear: "The question is who should get what's earned—the owners or everybody who gets in between?" He adds, "To get things changed, you just need a few people to be raked over the coals, some praised, and then demonstrate what the math is." The group initially focused on the ultimately successful battle to change the leadership at Pfizer, where CEO Hank McKinnell had severely underperformed. "When we got together to decide what company made the most sense to make an example of, we met and met and decided to take a rifle approach with Pfizer. They fit because they were a central holding of every deep value fund, the chairman and CEO was the head of the Business Roundtable, and had not done a good job creating a pipeline of new products, and especially because he'd done very well financially while the shareholders hadn't—the stock had dropped 40 percent over five years. They did a good job of talk over substance on good governance, and had papered it over pretty well, but talk is cheap. McKinnell was sort of the poster boy for overcompensation." Rowe and his group are now researching their next target and he says "I'm optimistic things can change for the better—I wouldn't be messing with this if I didn't think so."

A SINGLE TALENTED and committed director can turn entire companies on their axis and point them in the right direction. Ralph Whitworth runs the $7 billion Relational Investors fund from San Diego, California, and was called "The Lone Ranger of Boardroom Battles" by the *Financial Times*. A colleague in the governance world says that he's "one in a million. Everyone wants to hate him, but they can't." Whitworth designed the breakthrough "short slate" rule that the SEC adopted in 1994 to allow dissidents to propose a few directors rather than seek to replace all of a company's nominees. His fund works with up to twenty public companies at a time, holding them from two to three years. He provides both operating and extensive governance recommendations. If that fails, he and a partner (so they can get motions seconded), will try to gain board seats by negotiation or a proxy battle.

Whitworth took over distressed boards at Apria Healthcare and WasteManagement and helped revive both firms. He also played a major role in Bob Nardelli's departure as an underperforming CEO at Home Depot in 2007.

Whitworth's background includes working for Ronald Reagan, Paul Laxalt, and T. Boone Pickens. Paradoxically, his fund started up primarily with cash from a union pension fund, CalPERS. "People ask me what makes a good board member, an effective one," Whitworth says. "I could go through all the things on a spec sheet—integrity, smart, and so on—but thinking about that personality type, it's very clear that they are not there to be liked, but they are *likable*. We're not there the first day trying to make friends. We are trying to make sure people know we don't come with a social or political agenda; we come to do our jobs and pull up to the table as a representative of the shareholders." He says that changing one person in the boardroom can make a big difference. "People who were otherwise passive take the lead when you inject another element into board." For example, at Sovereign Bank, which in 2006 was the nation's third-largest S&L, Whitworth's addition to the board, under the most hostile circumstances conceivable, ultimately led to the firing of the entrenched CEO of seventeen years. This kind of strong and experienced corporate change agent would improve the performance of many boards.

So how do boards and shareholders find these ideal board members? Executive recruiters with expertise in director candidates are often the solution. Julie Daum, who heads the North American board services practice for Spencer Stuart is one of the best. She told us that about a third of the directors nominated in the past few years are new to board service and that she sees many nominating committees beginning to "be far more open and casting a wider net for people not necessarily known by the CEO and other directors." The key characteristics she looks for are an ability to stay out of the weeds and think strategically, to exercise good judgment even with incomplete information, to ask tough questions especially regarding risks, to listen well, to invest both time and one's own wealth in the company, to have or acquire strong financial knowledge, and to maintain a long-term view.

"I ALWAYS SAY adapt before Congress adopts. Boards have to get back to the proper oversight of management, engagement with corporate strategy and corporate performance . . . and away from the check-the-box stuff with the lawyers sitting there and the bills running up." That's the type of advice Ann McLaughlin Korologos brings to the boardroom, based on her experience as Ronald Reagan's secretary of labor, as the chair of major nonprofits and research institutions such as the Aspen Institute and the RAND Corporation, and as a director of companies ranging from American Airlines and Microsoft to Kellogg's and Host Hotels & Resorts, Inc. As presiding director at Fannie Mae, she guided the organization through its 2004 accounting crisis, delivering congressional testimony, overseeing the internal investigation, and eventually accepting the CEO's resignation. She blames the problem on "institutional arrogance." "There was nothing illegal, but there were a lot of wrong things." She says she learned a valuable lesson from the experience that she has passed on to directors at other companies: "The moral of the story for me as a board member is 'listening with different ears'—picking up the signs early when you're told 'Oh, well, that's the way we do it' or 'Yeah, we know that' or 'We tried that already.' You've got to listen with different ears inside and outside the boardroom—and particularly to employees and customers." Korologos does this by keeping informed. "How much time should you spend on a board? It should be every day; not a day goes by that there's not something important that comes out about the industry or that particular company or a competitor."

ALMOST EVERY SIGNIFICANT movement begins with a dreamer who will not be deterred. Glyn Holton's passion, which he says consumes 95 percent of his time, is the investor suffrage movement, developed to amplify the voice of shareholders in the oxymoronic process called "shareholder democracy." Holton, who develops complex mathematical models to help sophisticated investors evaluate risk, compares the investor suffrage movement to the campaign for women's voting rights that began in a chapel in Seneca Falls, New York, in 1848. "How many saw how they were going to get from that little church house to a point where women would have the right to vote?" he asked. "Only one person at the conference in Seneca Falls actually lived to see women get the right to vote. I hope it doesn't take me seventy-two years."

Holton has created a network of volunteer field agents around the country. They appear at annual meetings to make motions and ask tough questions. He also envisions an electronic proxy exchange by which trusted online intermediaries would collect and concentrate votes associated with shares held by mutual funds and brokerage accounts. These intermediaries would concentrate shareholder power on initiatives consistent with the owners' values and interests. Holton believes that votes could be aggregated into superblocks. He hasn't worked out all the details but is undeterred. "People have a hard time envisioning what capitalism will look like when people other than gadflies are involved."

WHEN SHAREHOLDERS try to change a company's direction, sometimes commitment matters more than wealth. In 2000, Los Angeles attorney Les Greenberg grew disenchanted as an investor in the Luby's cafeteria chain when he and his wife noticed a deterioration in the quality of Luby's services. His research suggested that the CEO and board were running the company into the ground. When he created a Luby's-related message board on Yahoo, he became the first person to organize shareholders for a proxy fight through the internet. Greenberg spent less than $15,000 to mount a campaign to elect a new slate of directors and says management outspent him 17 to 1. Nevertheless, his candidates ultimately won 24 percent of the vote, other shareholder-friendly proposals his group supported gained a majority vote, and Luby's CEO resigned later that year. "I spent maybe a thousand hours on it and hope pension funds with more resources learn from what we did," Greenberg says. "Fear is a great motivator—and challenging entrenched directors is the best way to improve boards." Today he runs a shareholder-oriented website at www.concernedshareholders.com, which he maintains from a home office where the computer screen is propped on stacks of Yellow Pages phone books.

Jim McRitchie, a retired state worker now living in Elk Grove, California, is the editor of CorpGov.net, which he says attracts more than half its vistors from China and India. McRitchie is a big advocate of investor education, which he feels would "deal with some of the short-termism and get people to act like owners rather than bettors at a racetrack." McRitchie collaborated with Greenberg on a 2002 petition to the SEC to greatly liberalize proxy access. Although the effort failed at that time, both men kept up the pressure through their respective websites, and the current proxy access measures are direct descendants of their efforts. Their examples show that informed, persistent individuals can have an outsized effect on governance.

"I'M HERE ON BEHALF of capitalism. . . . Nothing makes us happier than when CEOs earn hundreds of millions of dollars, because they earn it by creating wealth for shareholders." That's Nell Minow speaking before the House Committee on Oversight and Government Reform, which is the sort of thing she does frequently. Minow is the editor and chairman of the Corporate Library, a governance rating and research firm, and she's being both ironic and disarming. All companies aspire to higher profits, but on the journey they sometimes lose sight of their ethical duties. Minow provides the moral compass they can use to chart their course. She and her mentor, Robert Monks, founded Institutional Shareholder Services (ISS), a proxy advisory service, and then Lens, Inc., an investment fund based on firms with good governance. In 1995 they wrote *Corporate Governance*, the definitive textbook on the subject.

In a typical Minow performance, she adroitly navigates the troubled waters of polarized committees without compromising her principles or effectiveness. Her wisdom and wisecracks both engage and flummox critics ready to typecast her, perhaps as some sort of Nader Raider or a do-gooder unfamiliar with the rough and tumble of corporate politics. At the House Oversight Committee hearing, in the spring of 2008, the subject was the pay of CEOs at the big banks implicated in the recent financial catastrophe. Minow invoked the name of her law school, the University of Chicago, which is associated with Milton Friedman, a man most of the bankers under scrutiny, who were going to testify after she did, would idolize. Then she made clear what she thought of them: "These guys that are going to be on the next panel, these are not scapegoats, and they're certainly not virgins. Yeah, there's a lot of blame to go around. There are a lot of people involved in this mess, and you heard about all the different parts of it. It takes a village to create this kind of disaster. But certainly these people are a part of it. And certainly the pay created perverse incentives that poured gasoline on the fire and, if I can switch metaphors in the middle of a sentence, put a lot of economic crack into our system." In a world where CEOs, attorneys, politicians, and regulators routinely hedge their words to obfuscate their points, Minow's directness is refreshing. Here's a brief sample from a recent interview:

> I think of myself really as an anthropologist, looking at how these creatures behave. Boards of directors are like subatomic particles—they behave differently when they are observed.
>
> A real litmus test for governance is the CEO ego index—in particular buying stadium-naming rights, building a new corporate headquarters, being on the cover of business magazines, having chairs at universities endowed in

their name, or moving the corporate headquarters to Boca Raton. When Lucent bought a golf course, that was an automatic *F*. I mean, that's like driving off the curb during a driving test.

LAWYERS ARE LEAD PLAYERS in corporate governance. Management is usually the client, and the desire to condone its positions on governance issues can be overwhelming. One attorney, Ira Millstein, frequently bucks the conventional wisdom. Compared to Martin Lipton, who is the partisan street fighter among high-powered corporate New York lawyers, Millstein is a statesman. A star at Weil, Gotshal & Manges since 1951, he has seen corporate governance evolve since before many of today's lawyers were born. Remarkably, for someone in his early eighties, his thinking is flexible. To this day prestigious legal publications continue to name him Corporate Lawyer of the Year. While Lipton seems to oppose any changes that would tilt the power balance in the direction of shareholders, Millstein is more open. For example, he acknowledges that majority voting and "say-on-pay" lead to better communication between boards and shareholders. "One way to make it work is for the governance committee of the board to talk to major shareholders about different issues," he says. "That's how 'say-on-pay' really works in England, and it's a model that can work here in the United States. But we've still got a long way to go before we get to that stage, because U.S. boards and their lawyers are wary about talking to shareholders."

Few corporate lawyers would embrace reforms that might discomfort their clients. Ira Millstein, together with his law partner and fellow thought leader Holly Gregory, can and does, while also helping them to understand.

OUR ECONOMY—and the world's—recently stood at the brink of a total collapse. Individuals and groups are working to improve the culture of boards, elevate the quality of gatekeepers, and increase the participation of shareholders. But if capitalism's incessant flirtation with catastrophe is to be stopped, we must acknowledge that regulatory and legislative structural changes alone will be insufficient. Many of the underlying cultural problems continue to fester, and unintended consequences from purely regulatory solutions will continue to surprise and disappoint us.

Shareholders must shed their apathy and their ignorance. They must demand higher standards of performance and profound changes from the CEOs, boards, gatekeepers, and the financial institutions they pay to grow their investments. Transitory public rage over scandals or excessive executive compensation focuses on only a small part of the deeper problems and must be channeled to demand a transformation in how our companies are governed.

Real progress demands fundamental changes in the culture of boardrooms. The changes must begin internally, in ways that may be influenced, but cannot be controlled, by Congress, the SEC, the stock exchanges, or even corporate bylaws. Moral exhortations will get us only so far. One cannot legislate morality any more than one can demand strong leadership or good character. But one or two talented board members can make a huge difference in awakening the dormant leadership of their colleagues. And it *is* possible to transform boardrooms into places where collegial skepticism, organizational integrity, and a sustainable balance of power become a behavioral norm rather than a rarity.

Here are our suggestions for reforming our dysfunctional system of corporate governance.

CHANGING BOARDROOM CULTURE

Create a new class of public directors: Federally mandated reforms that open the board nominating process will necessarily create a demand for new director candidates. Who will they be? Narrow special-interest nominees likely won't get enough institutional support to win. Nor would they be ideal directors. Candidates drawn from the traditional inner-circle pools promise no meaningful change. We need a new kind of full-time director—"super directors," if you will. When he was the head of the SEC in the 1930s, William O. Douglas, the future Supreme Court justice, said that American business would benefit from a cadre of designated "public directors," who would comprise a minority on boards. In 1991, professors Ronald Gilson and Reinier Kraakman of Stanford and Harvard law schools respectively, suggested that "institutional investors should establish a nonprofit organization that would identify individuals who could become professional directors and who would serve on up to six boards at a time." In 2003, James Fanto, a Brooklyn Law School professor, picked up this thread when he called for a government entity that would identify a pool of highly qualified independent directors from diverse backgrounds who might counter the problem of boards being almost exclusively drawn from an inner circle of elites who think alike and share biases.

Some form of public or professional directorships would certainly be a key reform for corporate governance and an important way to improve boardroom culture. Corporations might, for example, be required to put three candidates (or a third of their board, whichever was greater) from the pool on the ballot for plurality election, dropping an equivalent number of incumbents. One or more also would serve on each of the major committees. They would undergo thorough background checks and be required to comply with strict conflict of interest and disclosure rules. This new class of super directors would undergo extensive training to cover the deficits current directors show in industry knowledge, financial and accounting skills, and the dynamics of group processes. They would be "professional" in the sense that they would be extensively trained in all the requisite skills. Companies might even be required over time to add a majority of directors with such training. They might serve on at most two or three boards at once and receive a higher rate of pay than other directors because of their training and the higher level of contribution they would bring. They could make a good, though not extravagant, living, while working full-time. To ensure objectivity, such directors might even be paid independently, perhaps through a very small assessment on large companies or even publicly. Covering the current annual compensation of one-third of the directors of all the Fortune 500 companies today would amount to less than $400 million. The U.S. taxpayers' bailout costs resulting from AIG's disastrously bad corporate governance would pay that amount for more than four hundred years.

Experience shows that the addition of even a small number of such directors to boards could function like a trim tab on an aircraft rudder: a small change in one component can fundamentally alter the direction of the entire enterprise. This does not mean that the chairman would not continue to be the leader of the board. Super directors, however, could work with the chairman as sort of group-process consultants. James Fanto's idea that a government agency would be the originator of the pool of super directors is probably not the optimal approach, although an organization of some kind would be needed to select and educate candidates, drawing from experienced executives, investors, and professionals who might be interested in new career challenges or have recently retired.

Create a director training consortium: Formal certification of all directors is an unworkable idea that has frequently come up and never gone anywhere, but because the boardroom environment is more challenging than ever, the learning needs of directors have grown. There currently exists a hodgepodge of optional director training programs at universities, associations, and for-profits, but they are not consistent and most are insufficiently rigorous. All directors would benefit from better initial and ongoing training. At present, board work is a part-time job, but directors report devoting twice as much time each month to board duties—twenty hours—as they did a decade ago. Audit committee members spend even more. During a corporate crisis, the job can become a full-time responsibility.

Good governance of corporations is impossible as long as the myths prevail that (1) a good businessperson, by definition wise about deals and operations, automatically makes for a good director; and (2) directors are too bright and important ever to benefit from training. Shareholders deserve no less than a best-faith effort from directors, and education is a great place to start.

A consortium of the major business schools should create a formal and permanent directors' institute with East Coast and West Coast campuses. Its purpose would be to assure that directors are intensively trained for initial board service and then remain current on business, strategic, legal, financial, regulatory, and accounting developments, as well as techniques for improving group process. Such an institute could be funded easily by a tiny unit surcharge on large stock and bond trades, as well as upon derivative and option activity.

A fee of one one-hundredth of one cent per share on the current volume of the U.S. stock exchanges would yield over $50 million annually—more than enough to fund such directors' training, as well as objective research on improving boards and perhaps even an organization that could implement the "public director" concept. Alternatively, one billion dollars—perhaps donated by wealthy individuals like Warren Buffet, George Soros, or Carl Icahn who have been especially perceptive and outspoken about the flaws of our current system of corporate governance—could create an endowment that would fund such efforts in perpetuity.

Insist on greater gender, ethnic, experiential, and, most important, perceptual diversity: There have been demands for more board candidates of diverse gender and ethnic origin for years. In 2003, Norway gave its public companies three years to make sure that 40 percent of their directors were women. They complied. Meanwhile, many companies look for directors with specific expertise, like "Asia" or "packaged goods development." These criteria are important, but there is a far more important type of diversity: diversity of perspective. Groups of any type frequently tend to select similar members to promote collegiality. Boards are no different, and this tendency leads to blind spots, poor processes, and errors in judgment.

The tools required to improve perceptual diversity already exist. For example, the Korn/Ferry recruiting firm prides itself on its extensive proprietary behavioral and psychological assessment process for executive candidates. But when it comes to recruiting board members, the assessment process is never used. Some variation of "You're not going to test Jack Welch" is the justification commonly invoked. Shareholders should say, "Yes, you are." Absence of diversity can be fatal to a board's work. Boards and potential director nominees should be tested to assure they can bring a full spectrum of thought processes and approaches to every decision. Even if the board cannot be balanced in this way, awareness of the imbalance has value.

Impose term limits on independent directors: The post-Enron reforms attempted to change boardroom culture by increasing the number and power of so-called independent directors, but CEOs have continued to influence the nomination process, and directors have continued to identify with the CEOs with whom they spend so much time. One solution to this problem is to force turnover on the board. The United Kingdom has nine-year term limits after which directors can no longer be considered independent. That's a policy that should be adopted in the United States. It should be strengthened by making it, at most, a seven-year limit. The loss of experience would be outweighed by reducing cronyism. New boards would be allowed to phase in the requirement with staggered limits but would still have annual elections for all directors. If an individual director were truly indispensable, he or she could remain on the board but would no longer be considered independent and thus would be ineligible to serve on key committees. Alternatively, such directors might be retained as nonvoting advisors to the board.

Limit directors to serving on three or fewer boards: The "overboarding" that has been prevalent among directors at some of the companies that have collapsed recently suggests that a limit of at most three public company directorships should be imposed. Given the increased complexity and time requirements of the role, directors need to focus.

Directors need to put skin in the game: Shareholders deserve directors who think like owners and not like reflexive defenders of management. Exchange rules should set up minimum requirements for true ownership by directors and bylaws should require them. The "play money" distributed in the form of stock options and gifts of restricted stock should not be included. Directors should have a meaningful percentage of their net worth invested in companies they serve, something along the lines of 3 percent to 6 percent, depending on the number of directorships they hold—and they should have holding period requirements that go beyond their tenure on the board.

Initiate more communication between directors and shareholders: Other than through the typically unread annual proxy statements and the notoriously useless annual meetings, shareholders currently have little or no communication with the directors they supposedly elect. There is a vast gulf into which accountability and responsibility vanish. Those two qualities are precisely what is lacking in many boards, on both the individual and the collective levels. Unfortunately, to trigger real disclosure and communication from a board there has to be a scandal, severe financial difficulties, or the shaming effects resulting from whistleblowers, journalists, congressional hearings, court cases, or corporate filings. An executive's divorce proceedings will also sometimes do it.

Every three months, the CEO and CFO of most large public companies hold a conference call with securities analysts to discuss the company's status. Although they rarely do, shareholders can listen in. To create better accountability, board members should participate and field questions during these calls or similar ones held especially for shareholders. Directors would be put in the hot seat and would have to have done their homework to avoid embarrassment. In addition, boards should be encouraged to make greater use of the internet and other ways of maintaining closer contact with shareholders, consistent with SEC requirements that all investors have access to disclosures.

STRENGTHENING ACCOUNTABILITY AND SHAREHOLDER RIGHTS

Although Congress and other regulatory groups continue to tinker with structural changes, the changes could be significantly broader than has thus far been contemplated. Incremental changes that enhance shareholder rights and ensure greater accountability by corporate leaders certainly will help, but most are too timid and too easy to circumvent. We need a stronger set of laws, regulations, exchange listing requirements, and corporate bylaws.

Split the chairman/CEO role: No one can reasonably expect a person to oversee himself or herself. The CEO works for the board, not the other way around; the continuation of combined roles inhibits the boards in exercising its responsibilities because it creates an insurmountable imbalance of power. Lead directors have served as a half-step toward a solution, but often the lead director appointment, the board agendas, and the flow of information are still controlled by the CEO. Proposals for the separation to be implemented when a new CEO takes office have not worked because if other CEOs remain chairmen, there is the appearance of a demotion and loss of face. The change should be mandated by law.

Allow shareholders to call an Extraordinary General Meeting: In the UK and many other developed countries, a group of shareholders (usually 10 percent or more) can call for an Extraordinary General Meeting, in which a majority of those voting may remove directors. Some form of this right, with appropriate restrictions, should be the norm in the United States.

Add some clout to say-on-pay: This measure allowing shareholders to vote on executive compensation is nonbinding. If executive pay programs fail these votes over three consecutive years, executive pay should be reduced by a meaningful percentage set in advance in corporate bylaws.

Ban staggered boards: Boards are staggered to thwart takeover attempts, but in reality this simply serves to entrench directors. All directors should stand for election on an annual basis.

Require majority votes in noncontested elections: Currently, corporations can choose to retain a director who has failed to win a majority vote. This is bad policy that sends the wrong signal and defeats the purpose of elections. Fifty-percent-plus-one votes should be a requirement.

Provide easier access to put rival director slates on the proxy: When combined with minimum ownership requirements by those making board nominations, this is a long-overdue reform. However, there should be holding requirements for stock *after* the election, as well as before, and there must be better regulation of manipulation by hedge funds and others who can control votes without having actual ownership.

Require boards to establish risk committees: The existence of a risk committee does not ensure that risks will be properly monitored, but it at least forces their consideration. In the wake of the recent financial meltdown, the need for better monitoring of risk is clear. Boards should advise on what constitutes sensible risks and should make executive compensation sensitive to risk (on the upside *and* the downside), a task that must be closely coordinated with compensation committees.

Reform executive compensation: We must end the practices that allow high pay for low performance. Executives (and directors) must truly cast their lot with long-term investors. Short-termism has tremendously damaging societal and financial impacts. Executives must be required to hold shares and options for longer periods; equity rewards should be indexed to screen out some of the effects of overall rising markets and relate to the company's cost of capital; tax gross ups, options reloading, and excessive perks and retirement benefits should be restricted; bonuses should be structured to reward multiyear performance; and clawbacks should recoup money paid out for illusory earnings. A forthcoming book by Michael Jensen, Kevin Murphy, and Eric Wruck entitled *CEO Pay—and What to Do About It* includes over forty specific and practical measures that would provide sorely needed, comprehensive reforms. (A preliminary version is available at http:ssrn.com/abstract=561305.)

Require shareholder approval for golden parachutes: Massive compensation when a CEO is fired without cause, retires, or leaves after a sale or merger is often unnecessary as part of employment agreements, but it has become the norm because of weak boards. A board's failure to dismiss a CEO for cause if it is clearly warranted should be considered a breach of fiduciary duties.

Open the nominating process to daylight: Following their own governance problems, companies such as Pfizer and UnitedHealth have established advisory nominating committees comprising representatives of large shareholders, including union pension funds. These groups provide input about desired board member qualifications, offer nonbinding direction to the nominating process, and propose and evaluate candidates for vacant director seats.

Create a real board evaluation process. The post-Enron reforms mandate an annual evaluation process for boards. It is usually perfunctory and a waste of time. The corporate secretary distributes one- or two-page questionnaires and checks a box: "Done." In boards that take this process seriously, a thorough review of a board member's contributions and behavior is extremely valuable. Outside of boards, research clearly shows that prompt behavioral feedback can have tremendous positive effects on performance. These sorts of sessions, possibly facilitated by an outside consultant every six months, would significantly upgrade the quality of discussion and decision making in the boardroom while helping to keep CEOs' feet firmly on the ground.

Empower and encourage boards to gather independent information: Too many CEOs discourage board members from "walking the shop floor" to talk to employees, customers, and others to develop their own sense of the companies. Such CEOs want to control all information. Board meetings become occasions for what one former General Motors director we spoke to called "only good news and happy talk." Another director said he had discovered a chart used by management to predict sales and cash flow; the whole enterprise relied on it, yet this had been kept from the board. When the information was shared with directors, it vastly improved their understanding of the business and its performance. While this reform cannot be legislated, it should be encouraged and written into all board charters.

Explore lessons from foreign, nonprofit, and private company boards: Corporate boards in the United States could learn many lessons from exploring what has worked well in other countries and in the best-run private and nonprofit companies. A comprehensive study of corporate governance in five major countries concluded that Germany has especially inclusive and comprehensive boards—with requirements both for labor representation and for two separate governing entities, including one that focuses on operations and one that oversees management and broader strategy. American nonprofit boards generally put more personal resources into the organization, focus on a public purpose, and are restricted from lobbying and self-dealing in order to maintain their tax-exempt status. Moreover, their operations and decision making are typically more transparent, and they place a greater emphasis on their communities and other stakeholders than do their for-profit counterparts. Privately held companies often have been run by founder-entrepreneurs or their heirs, but more recently, many are owned by private equity firms and the company's executives. Far more directly than at public companies, the boards of private firms are composed of and reflect the views of the people who own most of the stock. They can take a longer-term perspective because they are less dependent on public quarterly reports or daily stock fluctuations. As a result, their boards are better able to think strategically, and they are composed of people who ask tough questions and bring a wide range of relevant experiences to the boardroom.

End the conflict of interest in mutual fund voting: Mutual funds should be out of the voting business, because the potential for conflicts is too great when the funds are also seeking investment business from corporations' 401(k) and pension plans. Fund shareholders should control the votes of shares the funds buy with their money and be able to designate a third party to decide how to vote their shares. The internet and computer programs should make this reform technologically feasible. Glyn Holton's concept at isuffrage.org deserves further development and implementation. A number of corporate governance critics have advocated formally separating control of voting rights from financial intermediaries, just as has been recently done with stockbrokers who until January 2010 could vote their customers' shares on uncontested director elections and "routine" proxy proposals. (In 2008, such discretionary broker votes accounted for an estimated 16.5 percent of all votes and determined the outcome of a number of elections.)

Require more disclosure in director elections: Board candidates should be required to provide personal background and disclose any relationship, including social, with corporate executives. Once elected, they should be present at annual meetings and required to answer questions.

Reform voting processes to end manipulation by management: Close shareholder elections are almost always won by the position favored by management because managers know in advance how many of the votes are being cast and can strong-arm conflicted institutional investors. Similarly, there are many instances of shares being double-counted through margin lending, short sales, and derivatives—or being skipped because of bad record keeping. In some cases, shareholders are being cheated out of their rights. There should be a thorough study of how and why voting abuses occur in our current system, and reforms should be enacted.

REDUCE GATEKEEPER CONFLICTS AND IMPROVE THEIR CONTRIBUTIONS

Entire classes of gatekeepers suffer from conflicts, flawed business models, and other problems that lead to shareholders paying exorbitant fees for services that are often contrary to their interests.

Even well-meaning people and companies don't always do the right things. It is unreasonable to expect reform from within, and past attempts to require it have failed. Outside intervention must resolve the contradictions that afflict gatekeepers.

Reform the auditors' business model: Professor John Coffee noted that auditors have perennially suffered from an unsustainable business model that causes them to do unethical things, such as being complicit in earnings management and neglecting their responsibility to detect fraud. Though frequently asked to do so, the profession never has been able to regulate itself adequately. To solve the inherent conflict in how auditors are paid, corporations and stock exchanges should remit a small transaction fee to a new tripartite (management, accounting industry, and investor) quasi-public agency that would assign auditors to firms, oversee their work, and pay them. This would take corporations out of the loop. Since the industry has proven itself incapable of creating consistent and effective accounting rules on its own, another tripartite group should wade into this mess and fix it, with the idea of removing discretion over the choice of accounting principles from the client and giving investors more meaningful financial information. The Public Company Accounting Oversight Board created by the Sarbanes-Oxley Act of 2002 has broad powers, but needs to greatly increase its standard-setting and enforcement role.

Fix "Up the Ladder": This provision of Sarbanes-Oxley had a noble intent. When corporate attorney's saw a crime, they had to report it up through the ranks to the executives and board. But the law is now so riddled with loopholes that it is almost worthless. Corporations and CEOs are not the clients of corporate attorneys; shareholders are the clients. Congress and the SEC should revisit the issue and create a workable solution that balances attorney-client privilege with the legal profession's need to better serve the public interest.

Reform the ratings agency model: It is a blatant conflict for issuers to be paying for ratings. As with auditors, sell-side analysts and ratings agencies should be independent of the firms that purchase their services and should be paid by an independent group funded by shareholder transaction fees and assessments levied on securities issuers and the rated firms. The government should allow greater competition, regulate pricing, and create a specialized standard-setting and enforcement body.

Disclose lobbyist expenses: SEC filings (preferably annual reports) should fully disclose the expenditure of shareholder money both for business lobbying and for the organizations funded by companies. These expenditures have almost as pernicious an influence on corporate governance as they have on politics. Shareholders frequently must pay for lobbying that is blatantly against their interests. All this must be disclosed. If it cannot be stopped or limited, at least investors will know how their money is used and can vote accordingly at the next corporate election.

More funding for SEC enforcement. The SEC and other federal regulatory entities have, in general, failed to adequately enforce existing securities laws because the enforcement function has lacked adequate funding and staff. The SEC's enforcement staff received no raises for five consecutive years, and its lawyers and accountants voted to unionize. According to a 2009 GAO report, "Enforcement management and investigative attorneys agreed that resource challenges have affected their ability to bring enforcement actions effectively and efficiently." The SEC needs to be funded to keep up with the growing demands placed upon it. If that requires a tax or additional fees on certain exchange activities, it's money well raised and well spent.

Federalize more corporate law: The race to the bottom is real. Defenders of Delaware law believe, despite overwhelming evidence to the contrary, that a robust and open takeover market, along with the wisdom contained in stock prices, has created a race to the top. The takeover market has been thoroughly gummed up by courts and gatekeepers, and the events of 2008 should put the canard of omniscient market wisdom to rest. At a minimum, the Congress should look at how to better ensure shareholders' rights to remedy the effects of negligent boards and to help decide in which state their company incorporates.

SHAREHOLDERS MUST AWAKEN AND PARTICIPATE

Some fixes don't come from legislatures, courts, governing bodies, or the industries themselves. The governance machine too often works to reduce the potential power of individual shareholders by obfuscating the issues with jargon, bureaucracy, and red tape while making it all but impossible to challenge poor management. This is no model for effective engagement or even for reliable, understandable, and accessible sources of information. Shareholders must exercise responsibility by educating themselves and getting involved. The financial media should assist by increasing the resources devoted to covering boards and shining a stronger light on governance issues. The vast powers of the internet must be developed to increase the quantity and quality of information and participation in corporate governance in both directions—by improving disclosure and by allowing shareholders to demand accountability from those entrusted with their investments.

Ignorance by many enables abuse by a few. A shocking number of Americans do not understand how basic finance, the stock markets, and corporate governance works. There is a staggering societal cost when so many Americans drown in credit card and other debt, don't understand basic investment concepts, and remain ignorant about economics. Financial education at the high school level ought to be mandatory, and students should learn early what they have a right to demand from boards and the companies they own. At the undergraduate and graduate business school levels, there must a greater emphasis on ethics, organizational behavior, and the fiduciary duties of corporate leaders. Once better educated, the public needs to understand *how* to engage with the governance system, and actually to *do so.*

As long as investors remain "supine," as Louis Brandeis described them in 1912, abuses will continue, investments will be lost, and lives will be ruined. Our recent collective national experience underscores how essential corporate governance is to preventing devastating losses and ensuring our economic security. Boards can play the single most effective role in advancing the future opportunities and prosperity of our families, our communities, and our country. If we expect and demand more of them, they will rise to the challenge and answer that call.

Acknowledgments

WE'VE BENEFITED FROM the experience, wisdom, and advice of many people in the course of researching and writing this book. We particularly want to thank Lucian Bebchuk, Kim Bishop, Carolyn Kay Brancato, Bob Bowman, Ed Breen, Rinaldo Brutoco, Drew Buckley, Doug Chia, William Cohan, H. Rodgin Cohen, Kathleen Connell, Ken Daly, Julie Daum, Bruce Dayton, William Domhoff, Bill Donaldson, James Donnelly, Charles Elson, Armando Falcon, Jesse Fried, Michael Garland, Les Greenberg, Holly Gregory, Joe Griesedieck, Gordon Grieve, Bob Harlan, Warren Hellman, John Helyar, Hazel Henderson, Ellen Hexter, Glyn Holton, Michele Hooper, Eric Jackson, Dennis Jaffe, Michael Jensen, Phil Johnston, Edward Kangas, Roland King, Ann McLaughlin Korologos, Dennis Kozlowski, Jack Krol, Kevin LaCroix, Joe Mayol, Patrick McGurn, Douglas McIntyre, Roger McNamee, Jim McRitchie, Nell Minow, Robert A. B. Monks, Teresa Dixon Murray, Charles Perrin, Eric Pillmore, Michael Ray, Peter Ressler, Rusty Rose, James Segel, Hersh Shefrin, Howard Sherman, Ed Siedle, Jeffrey Sonnenfeld, Jack Stuppin, Kerry Sulkowicz, David Swinford, Bob Thomas, Lynn Turner, James Westphal, Ralph Whitworth, David Young, Shirley Young, and Michael West. We also thank the many other people we interviewed who asked that their names not be used. Of course, the opinions and conclusions in this book and any errors of commission or omission are those of the authors and should not be attributed to any of those who have assisted us.

We especially thank Pres and Helen Blake for their personal example and their continuing support of corporate governance reform. Also Frederick E. "Shad" Rowe of Investors for Director Accountability for his unstinting efforts to promote the cause of better corporate governance.

A number of organizations have been extraordinarily helpful as well. Not all of them necessarily agree with our ideas, but they do share a desire for a healthy debate on corporate governance issues. They include the Millstein Center for Corporate Governance and Performance at Yale Graduate School of Management, the Stanford University Law School Directors' College, the Aspen Institute, the Conference Board, and the National Association of Corporate Directors. We would especially like to thank Nell Minow for her enthusiastic help in understanding many current issues relating to corporate boards and for providing access to the excellent resources and staff of the Corporate Library. The appendix to this book lists dozens of books, websites, and other resources that we used for our research and that we recommend for readers seeking additional information. We would also like to thank the staff at the Harvard Business School's Baker Library for their assistance in finding research publications.

This book would never have come to fruition without the exquisite editorial judgment and skill, as well as the inexhaustible enthusiasm, of Emily Loose, our editor at Simon & Schuster's Free Press. Richard Pine of Inkwell Management is a tremendously gifted literary agent who made the business process of this book pleasant for everyone. Sharon Delano provided invaluable help in making the manuscript more readable. Barry Harbaugh checked the facts on every page. Maura O'Brien at Free Press did a wonderful job in coordinating the book's production.

We are also grateful for the encouragement and support of friends and relatives: Miriam Altshuler and Tom Mansfield; Kurt Andersen and Anne Kreamer; Paul Ayoub; Andy Borowitz and Olivia Gentile; Mark Bryant; Dan Buck; Jeff Conti; Bob Foran; Bill, Inez, Cheree, Mark, Penny, and Christina Gillespie; David Gross; Walter Isaacson; Rick and Valerie Lyon; Santiago Lyon and Emma Daly; Jenny Martinez; Patricia Marx; Henry and Celia McGee; George Meyer and Maria Semple; Juice Nelson; Edith, David, Debra, and Steffie Orlean; Foster and Tricia Reed; Leona Rosenberg; Sally Sampson; Ellis Seidman; Ruth Shannon; Catherine Stern; Kathleen Suryan and Richard Benton; Mike Sturm; John Tabor; Doug and Janet Tashjian; Greg Torres and Betsy Pattullo; Robert Weil; David and Charlotte Winton; Penny Winton; Kelly Wise; and Patricia Woodworth.

Finally, we would like to thank our families for their endless patience and sustenance: Susan Orlean; Jay and Austin Gillespie; and Ben Zweig.

Appendix

Recommended Resources

THANKS TO THE INTERNET, the dedication of many people and organizations involved in corporate governance, and the slow but steady progress from legislation and companies that are setting new standards for communication, investors have more opportunities to get informed and become involved. This means casting proxy votes that normally wind up in the trash, but also much more. The following is a partial list of resources that can help further inform and help us all to become more active shareholders.

A number of authors, journalists, website founders, and organizations are providing a wealth of excellent information on the failures and successes of individual boards and companies, as well as developments affecting the reform of corporate governance. We are highly indebted to them for many of the stories and issues discussed in this book. A few in particular that we recommend are listed below.

Authors whose books on corporate governance are especially enlightening: Robert Monks and Nell Minow's *Corporate Governance*; Steven Davis, Jon Lukomnik, and David Pitt-Watson's *The New Capitalists;* John Coffee's *Gatekeepers*; Lucian Bebchuk and Jesse Fried's *Pay Without Performance*; Paul W. MacAvoy and Ira Millstein's *The Recurrent Crisis in Corporate Governance*; Colin B.

Carter and Jay Lorsch's *Back to the Drawing Board*; Michael Jensen's *A Theory of the Firm*; and Margaret Blair's *Ownership and Control*. Journalists and writers who have provided especially insightful reporting and commentary with a focus on boards: Gretchen Morgenson, Louise Story, Joe Nocera, and Stephen Labaton of the *New York Times*; Joann Lublin and Alan Murray of the *Wall Street Journal*; John Helyar of Bloomberg; James Surowiecki of the *New Yorker*; Carol Loomis of *Fortune*; Michelle Leder of Footnoted.org; Daniel Gross of Yahoo Finance; Bethany McLean; James Stewart; Judith Dobrzynski; Allan Sloan; Steven Davidoff; Felix Salmon; Paul Krugman; the staff of American Public Media's *Marketplace;* and those two primary news sources of many in the younger generation, Jon Stewart of *The Daily Show* and Stephen Colbert of *The Colbert Report,* have done much to hold corporate leaders' (as well as the financial media's) feet to the fire in the wake of the recent financial meltdown.

Publications and organizations that have contributed much to the understanding of corporate governance include the National Association of Corporate Directors, the International Corporate Governance Network, the Conference Board, Catalyst, the Council of Institutional Investors, the Aspen Institute's Corporate Governance and Accountability Project, *Corporate Board Member* magazine and its website BoardMember.com, *Directorship* magazine and its website Directorship.com, *Directors & Boards* magazine, FindlayOnGovernance.com, IcahnReport.com, 247WallSt.com, RiskMetrics Group's Risk and Governance Blog, Governance Metrics International, TheRacetotheBottom.org, and the annual surveys on corporate governance issues by Spencer Stuart and Korn/Ferry International. Internet sites that have invaluable information:

Organization	URL	Description
Americans for Financial Reform	http://ourfinancialsecurity.org/about/our-coalition/	A coalition of 200 organizations pressing for financial reform.
Transparent Democracy.org	http://transparentdemocracy.org	Assistance in political and proxy voting.
Harvard Law School Forum on Corporate Governance and Financial Regulation	http://blogs.law.harvard.edu/corpgov/	Highly sophisticated discussion of major governance issues.
The Corporate Library	www.thecorporatelibrary.com and http://the corporatelibrary.typepad.com/blog/	One of the best sources of governance news.
D & O Diary	www.dandodiary.com	A fine blog about governance issues, with a frequent emphasis on D&O insurance.
CorpGov News	http://corpgov.net/news/news.html	Well-written and timely updates on governance developments.
iSuffrage	http:///isuffrage.org	Grassroots initiative on proxy rights transfer.

Organization	URL	Description
ProxyDemocracy	www.proxy democracy.org	Mutual fund voting records and more.
Concernedshareholders .com	www.concernedshare holders.com	A seemingly inexhaustible catalogue to various governance outrages.
Footnoted.org	www.footnoted.org	Daily look at things companies try to hide in their SEC filings.
The Conference Board	http://tcbblogs.org/ governance/	Excellent survey of current governance issues.
RiskMetrics Group	http://blog.risk metrics.com/index .html	Comprehensive research and analysis on key issues.
Shareowners.org	www.shareowners.org	New organization to educate and activate individual investors.

Notes

CHAPTER ONE: Out of Control

2 *Between 1980 and 2006:* Bernard S. Black, Brian R. Cheffins, and Michael D. Klausner, "Outside Director Liability," *Stanford Law Review,* Vol. 58, pp. 1055–1159, 2006.

6 *Executives who worked closely:* authors' interview with Merrill Lynch executives, 2009.

6 *For a while, the arrangement:* Merrill Lynch Annual Report, February 22, 2007, pp. 1–4.

7 *They also caught:* Landon Thomas and Jenny Anderson, "Merrill Lynch Weighs Ouster of Top Officer," *New York Times,* October 27, 2007.

7 *During August:* SeekingAlpha.com, October 25, 2008.

7 *the board then began:* Bradley Keoun and Jesse Westbrook, Bloomberg.com, "Tully Says O'Neal Ruined Merrill's Hit-by-Bus Succession Plan," November 1, 2007.

8 *At the Merrill Lynch:* Bloomberg.com, April 24, 2008.

8 *even though he had: Wall Street Journal,* January 18, 2008, p. C-1.

8 *Lynn Turner:* interview with authors, June 29, 2009.

9 *Finance committee chair:* Bloomberg.com, December 5, 2008.

9 *When Merrill Lynch first:* ml.com, "History: The Early Years."

10 *The Merrill Lynch shareholders:* losses for Merrill shareholders and subsequent company examples are calculated from the market capitalization high during the period under discussion to the final level at sale, government takeover, bankruptcy, or CEO resignation.

10 *He once told:* Claudia H. Deutsch, "Chief Says Kodak Is Pointed in the Right Direction," *New York Times,* December 25, 1999, p. B7.

10 *Upon GM's announcement:* Bill Vlasic, "GM's Directors Stand Behind Wagoner," *New York Times,* August 7, 2008.

11 *Wagoner relished his:* Daniel Howes, "GM: Strike at Delphi University," *Detroit News,* November 25, 2005, P. 1-A.

11 *As GM vice chairman:* Danny Hakim, "G.M. to Seek Cuts in Union Health Benefits," *New York Times,* March 24, 2005.

12 BusinessWeek *hailed:* Judith H. Dobrzynski, "At GM, a Magna Carta for Directors," *BusinessWeek,* April 4, 1994, p. 37.

12 *In November 2005:* Ric Marshall quoted in *The Corporate Library Blog,* June 1, 2009.

12 *some directors:* Bloomberg.com, June 1, 2009.

12 *One prominent director:* interview with author, July 2009.

13 *Another former board member:* "CEO Finally Ran Out of Options," *Wall Street Journal,* March 29, 2009.

14 *Yet the only one:* Lehman Brothers Holdings Inc. Definitive Proxy, March 5, 2008.

14 *In an April 2008:* Aline van Duyn, "View from the Markets," FT.com, video interview with Henry Kaufman, April 26, 2008, author's transcript.

15 *Without a trace of irony:* "Intelligent Investing" Forbes.com, transcript of interview with Steve Forbes, July 20, 2009.

15 *Kaufman neglects to mention:* Henry Kaufman, *The Road to Financial Reformation* (New York: Wiley, 2009), p. 39.

15 *Lehman securities filings:* Peter Robinson, Bloomberg.com, September 18, 2008.

16 *The supine Board:* New Jersey Complaint, p. 111.

16 *John Helyar:* interview with author, February 2009.

17 *In a conference call:* SeekingAlpha.com, "Lehman Brothers Preliminary F3Q08 Earnings Call Transcript" September 11, 2008.

18 *As they have grown:* Thomas R. Dye, *Who's Running America* (New Jersey: Prentice Hall, 1995) pp. 15, 19, cited in Dennis Gilbert, *The American Class Structure in an Age of Growing Inequality,* 7th edition (California: Pine Forge Press, 2008) p. 161.

19 *A 2004 study:* Stewart J. Schwab and Randall S. Thomas, "An Empirical Analysis of CEO Employment Contracts: What Do Top Executives Bargain For?" (April 9, 2004) *Washington and Lee Law Review,* Vol. 63, 2005, p. 231.

19 *Michael Jensen, a former: Q2: A Publication of the Yale School of Management,* Fall 2007, interview transcript from website.

21 *As one historian:* Franklin A. Gevurtz, "The Historical and Political Origins of the Corporate Board of Directors" (March 30, 2004), p. 24. Available at SSRN: http://ssrn.com/abstract=546296.

22 *In 1776:* Adam Smith, *The Wealth of Nations,* 1776, Cannan Edition (New York: Modern Library, 1937) p. 700.

22 *A separate problem:* Alexis de Tocqueville, *Democracy in America,* translated by George Lawrence (New York: Harper and Row, 1966), p. 558.

22 *The largest such enterprise by far:* Francis Bazley, *New Jersey as a Colony and as a State,* (The Publishing Society of New Jersey, 1903), p. 250.

22 *It is remarkable how closely:* Ron Chernow, *Alexander Hamilton* (New York: Penguin Press, 2004) pp. 372–388; *Calendar of the S.U.M. Collection of Manuscripts,* "Introduction", pp. 1–5 at www.pattersongreatfalls.org.

23 *Its deputy governor:* letter dated April 30, 1792, Alexander Hamilton and Harold C. Syrett, *The Papers of Alexander Hamilton* (New York: Columbia University Press, 1979) pp. 348–49.

24 *The lesson Hamilton drew:* Letter from Hamilton to Philip Livingston, April 2, 1792, *The Papers of Alexander Hamilton,* ibid., p. 272.

26 *A recent survey:* Korn/Ferry Institute, *34th Annual Board of Directors Study,* December 18, 2008.

26 *For each of the past seven:* TK Kerstetter, "Lead, Contribute, or Get Off the Board!," The Board Blog, Boardmember.com, July 17, 2009.

26 *William George, the highly regarded:* "Boards in the Bull's-eye," Directorship.com, October 1, 2008.

27 *In the meantime: Financial Times,* July 9, 2007.

27 *AIG's former CEOs:* Politico.com, October 7, 2008.

28 *H. Rodgin Cohen:* presentation at Harvard Law School, December 2008; interview with author, January 2009.

31 *As corporate governance expert:* interview with authors, June 17, 2008.

32 *Despite recent improvements: New York Times,* "S.E.C. Member Says Agency Has Bowed to Executives," October 9, 2004.

32 *Only a third of individual shareholders:* "The Smart Way to Tell Firms How to Operate," *Wall Street Journal,* March 17, 2007, p. B1, citing information from Georgeson Inc.

32 *In mid-2007, a national:* Pepperdine University, Graziadio School of Business and Management, "Corporate Board Investor Survey," 2007, at http://bschool.pepperdine.edu/research/investorsurvey/.

33 *In mid-2009:* U.S. Chamber of Commerce, press release, June 10, 2009.

33–34 *A Chamber executive's op-ed:* Thomas Quaadman, *The Metropolitan Corporate Council,* July 2009, pp. 1–2.

34 *As Columbia Law School:* John Coffee, *Gatekeepers: The Professions and Corporate Governance* (Oxford University Press: 2006).

35 BusinessWeek *called the law: Business Week,* "How Bill Clinton Helped Boost CEO Pay," November 27, 2006.

35 *Data from the Economic: The State of Working America 2008/2009,* Economic Policy Institute, 2009, pp. 220–223.

36 *At a 2009 House hearing:* Representative Jackie Speier (D-CA), June 11, 2009, www.house.gov/apps/list/hearing/financialsvcs_dem/hrfc_061109.shtml at approximately three hours and fifty minutes into the webcast. Citation from Douglas Chia.

36 *As Eliot Spitzer commented:* author's interview, September 20, 2009.

37 *and finally, the fail-safe device:* House Oversight Committee hearing, October 7, 2008, Lynn Turner's testimony.

37 *Robert Monks:* interview with authors, June 2009.

CHAPTER TWO: Ripple Effects

41 *The report says that: Report of Investigation by the Special Committee of the Board of Directors of Hollinger International, Inc.,* August 31, 2004, pp. 33, 373, 386, 493, 505–506.

42 *At Black's criminal trial:* Chicagoreader.com, July 16, 2007.

42 *As of late 2007:* Theresa Tedesco, "Hollinger Shareholders Left Out to Dry," *Financial Post,* December 10, 2007.

43 *"There was some:* ibid. Quote from Richard Powers, assistant dean and executive director, Joseph L. Rotman School of Management, University of Toronto.

43 *By mid-2009, the company:* "Bankrupt 'Chicago Sun Times' Parent Skips Pension Payments," *Editor & Publisher,* July 20, 2009.

44 *The mind boggles:* "The Stock Slump of 2008: Wrecking Ball to Wealth," *Washington Post,* January 11, 2009, p. F5; Raphael Minder and Alan Beattie, "Plunging Assets Cost $50,000bn," FT.com, March 8, 2009.

44 *It further warned:* IMF "Global Financial Stability Report," April 2009; *The Guardian,* April 22, 2009, "Global bank losses likely to reach $4.1 trillion, says IMF" in www.guardian.co.uk.

44 *According to the stock market commentator:* author's interview with Douglas A. McIntyre, February 2, 2009.

45 *Cayne was later named: Portfolio,* April 22, 2009, www.portfolio.com/executives/2009/04/22/20-Worst-CEOs.

46 *Cayne himself:* Paul Tharp and Zachery Kouwe, "Bear May Have Lived," *The New York Post,* March 23, 2008, in nypost.com.

48 *As William Cohan:* interview with authors, October 2008.

48 *Cohan had interviewed:* William Cohan, *House of Cards* (New York: Doubleday, 2009), p. 60.

48 *House of Cards:* ibid., pp. 58–60.

49 *In fact, it would be: Financial Week,* March 28, 2008, in FinancialWeek.com.

49 *J. Richard Finlay, a governance:* FinlayonGovernance.com, "Did Bear Stearns Really Have a Board? Part 1," March 25, 2008.

50 *When the board:* Stephen Davidoff, "Euthanizing Bear," *New York Times Dealbook,* May 9, 2008.

51 *"Cayne's closest friend:* William Cohan, "The Rise and Fall of Jimmy Cayne," *Fortune,* August 4, 2008.

52 *But "Jimmy stayed on:* author's discussion with Bear Stearns senior managing director, May 29, 2008.

55 *Mozilo often referred:* Connie Bruck, "Angelo's Ashes," *New Yorker,* June 27, 2009, pp. 46–55.

55 *His low regard for employees:* Jeff Bailey, "The Mortgage Maker vs. the World," *New York Times,* October 16, 2005.

56 *A 2006 internal email:* SEC Complaint, June 4, 2009, p. 20.

56 *Mozilo's email:* "A Real Countrywide Email from the Office of Angelo Mozilo," loansafe.org, May 20, 2008.

56 *Mark Zachary, who had been:* "Countrywide Whistleblower Reports 'Liar Loans,'" NBC News, July 1, 2008.

57 *A lawsuit by:* California Attorney General's Office news releases, June 25, 2008, and October 6, 2008.

57 *Countrywide paid each of its:* Countrywide Proxy Statement, April 27, 2007.

57 *Two union-affiliated:* Kathy M. Kristoff and E. Scott Reckard, "Countrywide Critics Slam Board's Pay," *Los Angeles Times,* November 9, 2007 in LATimes.com; Jonathan Stempel, "Countrywide Lead Director Should Quit, Groups Say." Reuters.com, November 8, 2007; William Patterson letter to Harley Snyder, November 7, 2007, at ctwinvestmentgroup.com.

58 *In mid-2008:* author's discussion with Martin Melone, June 2008.

58 *Later, another former:* author's e-mail exchange with Countrywide director, September 2008.

59 *KB's CEO and chairman:* "KB Homes ex-CEO Bruce Karatz Accused of Stock Option Fraud," *Los Angeles Times,* March 6, 2009.

59 *In 2008:* "Twice Bitten: One Town's Foreclosure Nightmare," MSN Real Estate, http://realestate.msn.com/article.aspx?cp-documentid=13107784&page=0.

60 *An aerial survey:* David Streitfeld, "Blight Moves in After Foreclosures," *Los Angeles Times,* August 28, 2007.

62 *"The managers and boards:* interview with authors, February 2009.

62 *While two-thirds of the estimated:* International Monetary Fund, "Global Financial Stability Report," April 2009.

63 *Lehman's Asia chief executive:* Michael Smith, "Lehman Buys Australia's Grange," Reuters.com, January 18, 2007.

63 *Lehman sales representatives:* Clancy Yeates, "Toxic Assets Leave Black Hole in Highlands Shires Coffers," www.smh.com.au, April 20, 2009.

63 *A report in* Euromoney: Eric Ellis, "Australia: Out of Pocket in the Outback," *Euromoney Magazine,* October 31, 2008.

64 *In the meantime:* Mark Whitehouse and Serena Ng, "Synthetic CDOs Hit Local Councils on Other Side of World," www.theaustralian.news.com.au, December 26, 2008.

64 *"The whole process:* author's interview with Michael West, March 2008.

CHAPTER THREE: Networks of Power

66 *"whether it be the Inner Circle:* Michael Useem, *The Inner Circle: Large Corporations and the Rise of Business Political Activity in the U.S. and U.K.* (New York: Oxford University Press, 1986).

67 *A classic example is Vernon:* Brett D. Fromson, "Jordan's 10 Board Positions Worth $1.1 Million," *Washington Post,* February 6, 1998, p. G1.

67 *Gramm attended:* from sworn statement by Gramm, August 20, 2003, cited in Kurt Eichenwald, *Conspiracy of Fools: A True Story* (New York: Broadway Books, 2004), pp. 248–49.

68 *While serving as an Enron:* "Blind Faith: How Deregulation and Enron's Influence in Government Looted Billions from Americans," *Public Citizen,* December 2001, p. 10.

68 *Gramm wrote an op-ed:* quoted in Frank Partnoy, *Infectious Greed: How Deceit and Risk Corrupted the Financial Markets* (New York: Holt, 2003) p. 183.

68 *Boards who consistently:* quoted in Salon.com. Gary LaMoshi, "Wendy Gramm Has No Regrets," January 28, 2004, http://dir.salon.com/story/tech/feature/2004/01/28/wendy_gramm/index.html.

70 *reportedly with one:* author interview with Douglas Brinkley, July 2009.

70 *"Americans as a group:* Domhoff quoted in press release, "Renowned Scholar Discusses His Research on Dreams and the 'Power Elite' during Public Lecture April 27," UC Santa Cruz, April 4, 1994.

71 *This is the third-worst:* Marco Cagetti and Mariacristina De Nardi, *Wealth inequality: data and models, WP-2005-10,* Federal Reserve Bank of Chicago, 2005.

72 *As the means of information:* C. Wright Mills, *The Power Elite* (Oxford, UK: Oxford University Press, 1959), pp. 8–9.

72 *"In the post–World War II era:* authors' interview with G. William Domhoff, January 23, 2009.

73 *America's top five defense:* "Defense News Top 100 for 2008," *Defense News,* www.defensenews.com/static/features/top100/charts/rank_2008.php.

74 *The ratio of contractors to:* R. J. Hillhouse, "Who Runs the CIA? Outsiders for Hire," *Washington Post,* July 8, 2007.

74 *The Bush administration brought:* Dror Etzion and Gerald F. Davis, "Revolving Doors: A Network Analysis of Corporate Officers and U.S. Government Officials," *Journal of Management Inquiry* 17:3 (September 2008): p. 157.

74 *The number of:* Jeffrey H. Birnbaum, "The Road to Riches is Called K Street," *Washington Post,* June 22, 2005.

74 *The* Washington Post *reported:* Jeffrey H. Birnbaum, "Washington's Once and Future Lobby," *Washington Post,* September 10, 2006.

75 *"The guidance from:* "Meet NAFTA 2.0, Maclean's, Luiza Savage, September 13, 2006.

77 *Several McCain:* www.RichardAboulafia.com, June 2008 newsletter, www.richardaboulafia.com/shownote.asp?id=272.

78 *An air force officer:* "US Air Force General Urges Quick Action on Tanker," Reuters, September 3, 2008.

79 *the degree of connectedness:* Gerald F. Davis, Min Yoo, and Gerald E. Baker, "The Small World of the American Corporate Elite: 1982–2001," *Strategic Organization,* 1 (2003), p. 301.

79 *A 2002:* Gwen Moore, "Elite Interlocks in Three U.S. Sectors: Non-profit, Corporate, and government," *Social Science Quarterly,* 83:3 (September 2002), p. 740.

80 *You're damn right:* Useem, *The Inner Circle,* pp. 47–48.

80 *David Yermack:* David Yermack, "Deductio ad absurdum: CEOs donating their own stock to their own family foundations." NYU Working Paper. No. FIN-08-014. Electronic copy available at: http://ssrn.com/abstract=1096257.

81 *Today, 82 percent:* Spencer Stuart, 2008 Spencer Stuart Board Index.

81 *"My sense is that:* authors' interview with James Westphal, January 29, 2009.

82 *A 2006 study:* Vicki Kramer, Alison Konrad, and Samru Erkut, "Critical Mass on Corporate Boards: Why Three or More Women Enhance Governance," Wellesley Centers for Publications, 2006.

84 *MIT Professor Peter:* Peter M. Senge, *The Fifth Discipline: The Art & Practice of the Learning Organization, 2nd edition* (New York: Doubleday, 2006), p. 163.

86 *Between 1997 and 2007:* Kevin Gray, "The Banana War," *Condé Nast Portfolio,* October 2007, p. 162.

87 *"It was our clear understanding:* Roderick Hills, speech at Stanford Directors College, June 23, 2008.

88 *"They left there:* Gray, supra.

90 *Leon is also:* James B. Stewart, *Den of Thieves* (New York: Simon & Schuster, 1992), pp. 138[25].

91 *The Chiquita case:* Sue Reisinger, "Hard Choices," *Corporate Counsel,* December 1, 2007.

93 *"Is it ever appropriate:* Hills speech.

CHAPTER FOUR: Hand in Glove

97 *In the publicly held:* Joel M. Podolny, interviewer, "Do Markets Need Integrity?" *Q2: A Publication of the Yale School of Management,* fall 2007, interview transcript from website http://qn.som.yale.edu.

97–98 *Eisner was in office:* "The Louse in the Mouse House," Slate, August 6, 2002.

98 *Largely because of the glaring:* "Best and Worst Corporate Boards," BusinessWeek .com, January 24, 2000, and December 2, 2003.

98 *William B. Chandler III:* In re The Walt Disney Company Derivative Litigation, judge's opinion, August 9, 2005, pp. 86, 14.

99 *"By virtue of his:* ibid., pp. 135–36.

99 *The judge was equally:* ibid., p. 96.

99 *In mid-2009, some four:* author's discussion with Michael Eisner, July 3, 2009.

100 *Gary Wilson, who:* Gary Wilson, "How to Rein In the Imperial CEO," *Wall Street Journal,* July 9, 2008, p. A-15.

102 *During the emergency:* Jonathan A. Knee, *The Accidental Investment Banker* (New York: Oxford University Press, 2006) pp. 43–44; Brett Messing and Stephen Sugarman, *Forewarned Investor,* Career Press), p. 78.

102 *According to a shareholder:* Barry Burr, "Non-Compete After Death? Shareholders Mortified by Shaw's 'golden coffins,'" FinancialWeek.com, January 28, 2009.

102 *A comprehensive study:* Gilbert Probst and Sebastian Raisch, "Organizational Crisis: The Logic of Failure," *Academy of Management Executive,* 2005, Vol. 19, No. 1, p. 94.

103 *The good news:* ibid., p. 97.

104 *A 2007 Booz Allen study:* Booz Allen news release, www.boozallen.com, May 22, 2007.

104 *"Why have intelligent:* Berkshire Hathaway 2002 Annual Report, pp. 16–17.

106 *The story further noted:* David Enrich, "Michael Klein Takes Leave of Citi, Pandit," *Wall Street Journal,* July 22, 2008.

106 *Surveys in 2007:* PricewaterhouseCoopers and *Corporate Board Member Magazine,* Annual What Do Directors Think? survey, 2007 and 2008.

107 *"It's all pretty boring:* authors' interview with Roland King, October 16, 2008.

108 *According to two consultants:* Keith B. Meyer and Robert S. Rollo of Heidrick & Struggles, "Boards *Think* They're Doing a Good Job . . . but CEOs Disagree," from second quarter 2008 edition of *Directors & Boards,* accessed through www.board member.com, August 4, 2008.

108 *A separate survey:* Colin B. Carter and Jay W. Lorsch, *Back to the Drawing Board,* Harvard Business School Press, 2004, pp. 207, 208, 211.

109 *A highly respected business:* author interview, January 2009.

109–110 *The dilemma these ideal:* Albert O. Hirschman, *Exit, Voice, and Loyalty,* Harvard University Press, 1970.

110 *Target's cofounder:* author's interview with Bruce Dayton, October 2, 2008.

110 *Over tea in her:* authors' interview with Shirley Young, September 9, 2008.

112 *Look, for example, at:* "Lifestyle," boardmember.com, www.boardmember.com/lifestyles.aspx, October 20, 2009.

114 *In fact, according to calculations:* Graef Crystal, "A $75 Million Consolation Prize?" GraefCrystal.com, May 4, 2009.

114 *Aubrey McClendon:* "The 400 Richest Americans," September 17, 2008, www.Forbes.com.

115 *As a result:* "The Highest Paid CEOs of 2008," Associated Press, May 1, 2009.

115 *According to the proxy:* Chesapeake Energy Definitive Proxy Statement, May 13, 2009, pp 50, 51, 63–65.

116 *The basketball sponsorship:* Letter from General Counsel Henry J. Hood, SEC filing, schedule 14A, April 30, 2009.

116 *The three-member compensation committee:* Randy Ellis, "Chesapeake Responds to Lawsuit," *The Oklahoman,* April 30, 2009.

118 *it would be unseemly:* Chesapeake Energy Definitive Proxy Statement, May 13, 2009, p. 39.

119 *A presentation by:* "Wall Street's Perspective on North America and Unconventional Resources?" Morgan Stanley, October 17, 2005, p. 19.

119 *Two public pension funds:* Ben Casselman, "Chesapeake Holders Denounce CEO Pay," *Wall Street Journal,* April 28, 2009, p B-1; Christopher Palmeri, "Chesapeake Energy Battles CEO Compensation Furor," *BusinessWeek,* April 29, 2009.

120 *Jan Fersing, a shareholder:* SEC Filing, Form 8-K/A, Chesapeake Energy Corporation, Exhibit No. 99–1, June 22, 2009, "2009 Annual Meeting of Shareholders Transcript, pp. 12–13.

121 *Eliot Spitzer told us he:* author's interview with Eliot Spitzer, September 20, 2009,

122 *By now every: Report of the Special Examination of Fannie Mae,* Office of Federal Housing Enterprise Oversight, May 2006, p. 42.

123 *She is described by:* authors' interview with Nell Minow, June 17, 2008.

123 *Korologos said that:* author's interview with Ann Korologos, July 3, 2009.

123 *Stephen Ashley, who:* lecture to Cornell University graduate students, http://cornelleclips.blogspot.com/2006/06/update-on-stephen-ashley.html, June 20, 2006.

124 *"Fannie Mae was a good:* author's interview with Armando Falcon, March 13, 2009.

124 *According to the Center:* Bruce Feirstein, "The 100 to Blame," VanityFair.com, September 25, 2009.

126 *The company's compensation committee:* Countrywide Financial 2007 Proxy Statement, p. 24.

127 *When a shareholder:* E. Scott Reckhard and Kathy M. Kristof, *Los Angeles Times,* "Mortgage Firm CEO Defends His Pay," June 15, 2006, pg. C-1; *New Yorker,* ibid., p. 53.

127 *As a U.S. House:* U.S. House of Representatives Committee on Oversight and Government Reform, Committee Staff Analysis, quoted in Russell Mokhiber and Robert Weissman, "Neither Honest Nor Trustworthy: The 10 Worst Corporations of 2007," *Multinational Monitor,* November-December, Vol. 29, No. 5 at www.multinationalmonitor.org.

128 *As one example:* Kathy M. Kristof, "One Last Joyride for Countrywide's President?" *Los Angeles Times,* August 1, 2008.

129 *A 2005 study:* David Yermack, "Flights of Fancy: Corporate Jets, Corporate Perquisites and Inferior Shareholder Returns," March 2005. Available at http://ssrn.com/abstract=529822, cited by Michelle Leder of footnoted.org in Twitter discussion September 23, 2009.

129 *In 2007, the Corporate:* Paul Hodgson, "Up, Up and Away," The Corporate Library, September 4, 2007.

130 *By far the best:* Lucian A. Bebchuk and Jesse M. Fried, *Pay Without Performance: The Unfulfilled Promise of Executive Compensation* (Boston: Harvard University Press, 2004).

130 *Bebchuk, in a separate:* Lucian A. Bebchuk and Robert J. Jackson, "Executive Pensions," *Journal of Corporation Law,* Vol. 30, No. 4, 2005, abstract, p. 1.

130 *When asked what:* authors' interview with Jesse Fried, January 27, 2009.

131 *A case in point:* Phred Dvorak and Serena Ng, "Check Please—Companies Discover It's Hard to Reclaim Pay from Executives," *Wall Street Journal,* November 20, 2006, pp. A1 and A12.

132 *The year before:* Louis Lavelle, "CEO Pay: The More Things Change . . . ," *Business Week,* October 16, 2000, in www.businessweek.com.

133 *included voluminous perks, such as access: Marketwatch* May 13, 2009, www.marketwatch.com/m/story/271d63d8-10e0-449b-ad7b-268344b91181/0.

133 *He wrote in an explanatory:* Jack Welch, "My Dilemma—and How I Resolved It," *Wall Street Journal,* September 17, 2002, p. A-14.

134 *Not long before:* L. Dennis Kozlowski, "The Vitals of Accountability," *Directors & Boards,* fall 1995.

135 *Abraham Zaleznik, a:* edited interview with Abraham Zaleznik, "Online Extra: The CEO as Thief: A Psychological Profile," www.businessweek.com, December 23, 2002.

136 *He resigned in 1994:* Memo from Robert A. G. Monks to L. Dennis Kozlowski, January 3, 1994, quoted in Robert A. G. Monks and Nell Minow, *Corporate Governance,* 4th ed. (Chichester, England: Wiley-Blackwell: 2008), p. 575.

136 *"Kozlowski wouldn't have:* author's interview with Robert A. G. Monks, April 24, 2009.

138 *When Wendy Lane,* Engen, John "Tyco Director Says, " 'I've Fallen Off the Cliff,' " *Corporate Board Member Magazine,* Special Legal Issue, 2003.

CHAPTER FIVE: Extraordinary Delusions

145 *prominence in the:* Arijit Chatterjee and Donald C. Hambrick, "It's All About Me: Narcissistic CEOs and Their Effects on Company Strategy and Performance," *Administrative Science Quarterly,* 52:3 (September 2007), pp. 351–86.

146 *Although some firms:* Richard Roll, "The Hubris Hypothesis of Corporate Takeovers," *Journal of Business,* 59:2 part 1 (1986): 197.

146 *CEO hubris:* Mathew Hayward and Donald Hambrick, "Evidence of CEO Hubris," *Administrative Science Quarterly,* 42:1 (March 1997):120.

148 *"Previous literature:* "CEO Overconfidence and the Urge to Merge," Knowledge @ Wharton, February 25, 2004.

149 *McClelland found:* David C. McClelland and David H. Burnham, "Power Is the Great Motivator," *Harvard Business Review,* 81:1 (2003): 117.

150 *"Affiliation" includes:* David C. McClelland, "Toward a Theory of Motive Acquisition," *The American Psychologist,* 20:5 (1965):321.

151 *Jack Stuppin, who:* authors' interview with Jack Stuppin, February 2, 2009.

153 *"Rats given the choice:* Randy Shore, "Gambling Affects Brain, Research Finds," *Vancouver Sun,* February 29, 2008.

155 *"Emotions become perceptual:* Madeline Drexler, "The Science of Decisions," *Kennedy School Bulletin* (Winter 2009):18.

156 *Researchers from:* John Coates and Joe Herbert, "Endogenous steroids and financial risk taking on a London trading floor," *Proceedings of the National Academy of Science* 105:16 (2008), 6167–72.

161 *What's been happening:* Greg Ip, "Snow Defends President's Handling of Economy," *Wall Street Journal,* March 20, 2006.

162 *Yet thirty months later:* John Snow, "Statement to the Committee on Oversight and Government Reform, United States House of Representatives," October 23, 2008.

164 *"a deterioration of mental:* Irving Janis, *Groupthink: Psychological Studies of Policy Decisions and Fiascoes* (New York: Houghton Mifflin, 1982), p. 9.

166 *"One key question:* Hersh Shefrin, *Behavioral Corporate Finance* (New York: McGraw-Hill/Irwin Series in Finance, Insurance, and Real Estate, 2005), p. 10.

166 *gave honest feedback:* "Governance 101: Flattery Will Get You Everywhere," www.soxfirst.com, January 14, 2008.

166 *"The two critical factors:* author interview with James Westphal, February 13, 2009.

167 *After some negotiation:* Ralph Whitworth, Remarks to the Weinberg Center for Corporate Governance, University of Delaware, 2004.

168 *"When corporate directors:* James Westphal and Poonam Khanna, "Keeping Directors in Line: Social Distancing as a Control Mechanism in the Corporate Elite," *Administrative Science Quarterly,* 48:3 (2003): 361–98.

169 *"The primary qualification:* authors' interview with Nell Minow, June 2008.

170 *Useem's research:* Michael Useem, *The Inner Circle* (New York: Oxford University Press, 1984), p. 38.

171 *"The other guy:* author's interview with Warren Hellman, March 1, 2009.

171 *Relying on:* Westphal, p. 369.

172 *In the face of ambiguity:* Donald C. Langevoort, "Resetting the Corporate Thermostat: Lessons from the Recent Financial Scandals About Self-Deception, Deceiving Others and the Design of Internal Controls," *Georgetown Law Journal,* 93 (2004): 95.

173 *As Professor Hersh:* author's interview with Professor Hersh Shefrin, February 17, 2009.

CHAPTER SIX: The Myth of Shareholders' Rights

179 *"When Pres first:* author interview with James Donnelly, April 14, 2009.

180 *I don't spend:* John Hechinger, "Sundae punch: Allegations swirl at ice cream shop," *Wall Street Journal,* June 9, 2006.

180 *I believe in:* Trudy Tynan, "Founder Seeking to Spark Turnaround at Age 86," Associated Press, December 21, 2000.

181 *The company looked: Blake v. Friendly Ice Cream Corp.,* 21 Mass Legal Reporter 131,

2006 Mass. Superior. Lexis 241 2006 WL, 1579596 (Mass. Superior Ct. May 24, 2006).

183 *As governance experts:* Nell Minow and Robert Monks, *Corporate Governance* (Chichester, UK: Wiley-Blackwell, 2008), p. 234.

185 "*Empirical research:* Jonathan Macey, *Corporate Governance* (New Jersey: Princeton University Press, 2008), p. 135.

185 *We started:* author's interview with James Donnelly.

186 *The CFO said: Blake v. Friendly Ice Cream Corp.*, p. 8.

189 *Today Blake proudly points:* Fabrizio Ferri, V. G. Narayan, and James Weber, *Shareholder Activists at Friendly Ice Cream* (Allston: Harvard Business Publishing: 2008), Case 108024-PDF-ENG.

190 "*Everyone knows where:* authors' interview with Lynn E. Turner, June 29, 2009.

190 "*The Delaware Chancery court:* authors' interview with Prof. Jesse Fried, January 27, 2009.

193 *Japan is not:* Japan Society, "Ichigo's Scott Callon Leads Japan's First Successful Shareholder Revolt," May 3, 2007, www.japansociety.org/ichigos_scott_callon_leads_japans_first_successful_shareholder_r.

193 *While notions of:* Stephen Bainbridge, *The New Corporate Governance in Theory and Practice* (New York: Oxford University Press), p. 143.

193 *His attitude:* Martin Lipton and William Savitt, "The Many Myths of Lucian Bebchuk," *University of Virginia Law Review,* 93:3 (2007): 754.

194 *UCLA Law Professor Lynn A. Stout:* "Shareholder Control and Corporate Boards," *Washington Post,* March 2, 2007.

194 "*The votes and:* Henry Manne, "The 'Corporate Democracy' Oxymoron," *The Wall Street Journal,* January 2, 2007.

197 *Sister Pat Daly:* "God Vs. GE," *Harper's Magazine*, August 1998.

201 *In commenting:* James McRitchie and Les Greenberg, Letter to Request for Rulemaking To Amend Rule 14a-8(i) To Allow Shareholder Proposals To Elect Directors, addressed to Jonathan G. Katz, Secretary, U.S. Securities and Exchange Commission, August 1, 2002.

203 "*from the relatively:* "Management Always Wins the Close Ones," Yair Listokin, Yale Law & Economics Research Paper No. 348, 2nd Annual Conference on Empirical Legal Studies Paper, *American Law and Economics Review*, April 2007.

203 *A University of:* David K. Musto, "The Market for Record-Date Ownership," Wharton School of Business, July 4, 2002. EFA Berlin Meetings Presentation Paper.

203 *Borrowers generally:* Henry T. C. Hu and Bernard Black, "Empty Voting and Hidden (Morphable) Ownership: Taxonomy, Implications, and Reforms," *The Business Lawyer,* American Bar Association, 61:3 (2006): 1028.

204 "*This decoupling . . . is:* ibid., 1011.

204 "*bring Deutsche over the:* Jon Swartz, "Fiorina voice mail surfaces in H-P-Hewlett fight," *USA Today,* April 10, 2002.

206 *Eliot Spitzer told us:* author's interview with Eliot Spitzer, September 2009.

206 "*The board itself:* The Icahn Report, "Corporate Democracy Is a Myth," www.icahnreport.com/report/2008/06/corporate-democ.html, June 18, 2008.

CHAPTER SEVEN: Another Tangled Web

209 *Jack Bogle, the:* John Bogle, *The Battle for the Soul of Capitalism* (New Haven: Yale Press, 2005), p. 163.

210 *the ratings agencies charged:* Elliot Blair Smith, "Bringing Down Wall Street as Ratings Let Loose Subprime Scourge (Part I)," Bloomberg.com, September 24, 2008.

211 *"pervasive" conflicts of:* "Executive Pay: Conflicts of Interest Among Compensation Consultants," U.S. House of Representatives, Committee on Oversight and Government Reform, Majority Staff Report, December 2007.

211 *"A mediocre-or-worse:* Berkshire Hathaway Annual Letter, 2005.

213 *Serious accounting:* Max Bazerman, George Loewenstein, and Don A. Moore, "Why Good Accountants Do Bad Audits," *Harvard Business Review* 80 (2002): 97.

216 *"I can tell you:* authors' interview with Edward Siedle, May 18, 2009.

217 *"Investment management has gone*: John Bogle interview with Lisa Scherzer, "Bogle: American Capitalism Is Doomed," *SmartMoney,* October 13, 2005.

217 *We're never quite:* Bogle, *Battle for the Soul of Capitalism,* p. 81.

218 *In 2004, SEC staff:* Securities Exchange Commission Staff Report Concerning Examinations of Select Pension Consultants, May 16, 2005.

218 *The SEC press release:* The SEC Securities and Exchange Commission, *Press Release on Staff Report Concerning Examinations of Select Pension Consultants,* May 16, 2005.

218 *The Government Accounting Office, though:* John Wasik, "Four-year SEC probe of pension consultants barely yields slap on wrist, *Boston Globe,* October 2, 2007.

218 *"How can one expect:* Robert Monks, *The Emperor's Nightingale* (Reading, MA: Addison-Wesley, 1998), p. 147.

219 *A 2009 GAO report:* Charles Jeszek, 2009 GAO Testimony Before the Subcommittee on Health, Employment, Labor and Pensions, Education and Labor Committee, House of Representatives, March 24, 2009.

219 *According to Edward Siedle:* Siedle interview, supra, and "Regulation & Legislation," *Pensions & Investments,* June 1, 2009.

222 *Lynn Turner:* authors' interview with Lynn Turner, July 10, 2009.

222 *One stock analyst:* Les Funtleyder quoted in Mike Huckman, "Pfizer's McKinnell—The $200 Million Dollar Man," CNBC, December 22, 2006.

225 *"shareholders and:* Alan Greenspan, testimony to the Federal Reserve Board's Semiannual Monetary Policy Report to Congress, Before the Committee on Banking, Housing, and Urban Affairs, U.S. Senate, July 16, 2002.

225 *"Typically, the party:* John Coffee, *Gatekeepers: The Role of Professions and Corporate Governance* (New York: Oxford University Press, 2006) p. 3.

226 *"audit failures are:* Max Bazerman, Kimberly Morgan, and George Loewenstein, "The Impossibility of Auditor Independence," *Sloan Management Review,* 38:4 (1997): 90.

226 *"I would argue:* "Q&A With Charlie Munger," Legal Matters, *Stanford Lawyer,* Spring 2009.

228 *The pathetic result:* Arthur Andersen from video quoted in *Pump and Dump: The Rancid Rules of the New Economy,* Robert H. Tillman and Michael L. Indergaard (New Jersey: Rutgers University Press, 2005), p. 203.

231 • *Requiring an auditor:* Bullets directly quoted from *Sarbanes-Oxley 404: The Section of Unintended Consequences and Its Impact on Small Business,* American Electronics Association, February 2005.

232 *"Considering the reality:* Lisa H. Nicholson, "Sarbox 307's Impact on Subordinate In-House Counsel: Between a Rock and Hard Place," *Michigan State Law Review,* 2004: 559 (2004): 612.

233 *The best specialist:* "Who wants to be a millionaire? Meet Wachtell's new partners." Above the Law Blog, November 8, 2008, drawn from "The Am Law 100," *American Lawyer,* 2008.

234 *Meanwhile, on the:* Debra Cassens Weiss, "Associates Happiest with Wachtell Pay, Which Is on the Hefty Side," *ABA Journal,* August 6, 2008.

234 *Their boards, in their own:* Goldman Sachs Definitive Proxy, March 7, 2008, pp. 11, 34.

236 *A survey of:* Jeffrey Marshall, "Are Fairness Opinions a Good Thing?" *Financial Executive,* December 1, 2007.

CHAPTER EIGHT: Solutions

238 *Franklin A. Gevurtz:* "The Historical and Political Origins of the Corporate Board of Directors," *Hofstra Legal Review,* 33:89 (2004) 72. March 30, 2004, p. 66.

238 *Congressman Barney Frank:* Barney Frank, "Exclusive: Congressman Barney Frank on Regulation and the Role of the Director," edited transcript of keynote speech at *Directorship* conference, Directorship.com, December 12, 2008.

238 *the head of a private:* authors' interview with private equity executive, September 2008.

239 *James McRitchie, who:* authors' interview with James McRitchie, June 2009.

239 *Robert Monks says:* authors' interview with Robert Monks, June 2009.

239 *As Jeffrey Sonnenfeld:* Jeffrey Sonnenfeld, "What Makes Great Boards Great," *Harvard Business Review,* September 2002, pp. 106, 111.

240 *Tyco's new CEO and chairman:* author's interviews with Jack Krol and Eric Pillmore, August 2009; Tyco press release, August 1, 2002; Rakesh Khurana and James Weber, "Tyco International: Corporate Governance," Harvard Business School Case 9-408-059, revised March 9, 2008, pp. 5–12.

241 *Krol describes the first:* author's interview with Jack Krol, August 2009.

242 *Krol and Pillmore created a matrix:* Harvard Business School Case, ibid. p. 10.

243 *"a hard-charging boss:* Leslie Kaufman, "After 15 Years, Executive's Short Goodbye," *New York Times,* November 17, 2001.

243 *Golub's philosophy as:* Harvey Golub, "A CEO Looks at the Director's Role," *Directors & Boards,* Winter 2004.

243 *Bowman says he:* interview with author, February 2, 2009.

244 *Sitting in his living room:* authors' interview with Bruce Dayton, October 2, 2008; *The Birth of Target,* Bruce Dayton with Ellen B. Green, privately published, 2008, pp. 101–17.

247 *Hooper learned from Target:* authors' interview with Michele Hooper, June 30, 2009.

249 *A classic case involving:* Robert A. G. Monks and Nell Minow, *Corporate Governance,* ibid., pp. 478–85; authors' interview with Robert A. G. Monks, June 2009.

250 *Rowe told us:* authors' interview with Frederick "Shad" Rowe, June 8, 2009.

250 *Ralph Whitworth runs:* Francesco Guerrera and James Politi, "The Lone Ranger of Boardroom Battles," FT.com, February 25, 2008; and authors' interview with Ralph Whitworth, April 24, 2009.

252 *Julie Daum:* author's interview with Julie Daum, August 18, 2008.

252 *"I ALWAYS SAY adapt:* authors' interview with Ann Korologos, July 3, 2009.

253 *"How many saw how:* authors' interview with Glyn Holton, April 24, 2009.

254 *"I spent maybe:* authors' interview with Les Greenberg, December 2008.

255 *Jim McRitchie, a retired:* authors' interview with Jim McRitchie, May 22, 2009.

256 *At the House Oversight:* testimony of Nell Minow, CEO Pay and the Mortgage Crisis, U.S. House Committee on Oversight and Government Reform, March 7, 2008, p. 106.

256 *Here's a brief sample:* authors' interview with Nell Minow, June 17, 2008.

257 *One attorney, Ira: Directorship,* "Ira Millstein on Governance," October 1, 2007, in Directorship.com.

259 *"institutional investors should:* as quoted from Fanto, below, from Ronald J. Gilson & Reinier Kraakman, "Reinventing the Outside Director: An Agenda for Institutional Investors," *Stanford Law Review,* 43:4 (1991), 883–992.

259 *In 2003, James Fanto:* James Fanto, "Whistleblowing and the Public Director: Countering Corporate Inner Circles," November 2003, Social Science Research. Network Paper Collection at http://ssrn.com/abstract=471261.

272 *a 2009 GAO:* GAO Report on SEC Enforcement, released May 6, 2009.

Index

About the Authors

John Gillespie worked in Massachusetts state government, including as a speechwriter. He then served as an investment banker for eighteen years with Lehman Brothers, Morgan Stanley, and Bear Stearns and was the executive vice president and CFO for The Mentor Network, a nationwide human services company with twenty-four thousand employees. He graduated from Harvard College, where he studied American history and literature, and has an MBA from the Harvard Business School. He is married to *New Yorker* writer Susan Orlean.

David Zweig has worked at Time Inc. and Dow Jones and cofounded Salon.com. He was most recently senior editor of the World Business Academy, an international research and education institute dedicated to promoting responsibility in business and pioneering best practices to solve problems in business ethics. He currently consults on improving the performance of executive groups. He graduated from Yale College, where he was the editor of the *Yale Daily News,* and has an MBA from the Harvard Business School.

Questions for Discussion

1. Is there an irresolvable conflict between directors' roles as "monitors" and "strategic advisors" with respect to the CEO?

2. Given how nominees for a board of directors are selected, how can directors avoid capture by the CEO of their company and how might the selection process be improved?

3. How could boards better align compensation with performance for top executives?

4. How do Directors and Officers Liability insurance and the business judgment rule affect how boards operate? How might these protections be modified to avoid excusing negligence?

5. Should we require that the roles of chairman of the board and the CEO always be separate?

6. Is there an inherent conflict between a director's independence and his or her having sufficient knowledge and experience relevant to the company's business? What can be done to make the definition of director independence more meaningful?

7. How should evaluations of board members be conducted to avoid their being a perfunctory exercise?

8. How could boards get information that is not biased by the executives' point of view? Should boards have their own budgets and staff members?

9. Some have argued that because directorships are a part-time job, it is not possible for boards to provide meaningful strategic guidance to a company. Do you agree—and how might this issue be addressed?

10. What is the single most important duty of the board?

    Risk management

    CEO succession planning

    Strategic advice

    Maximizing shareholder value

Sustainability of the enterprise

Other?

11. Do you think that gender and ethnic diversity on boards generally adds value, or that it is irrelevant?

12. If you were asked to become a director, what would you want to know before accepting the job?

13. How should directors be compensated?

14. The United States has extremely diffuse ownership of equity compared to Europe. How does that affect the accountability of CEOs and directors?

15. What can be done to reduce shareholder apathy?

16. Why have U.S. companies allowed a significantly lower shareholder ability to nominate and replace directors than in other developed countries? Would boards become victims of special interests if the American system were more democratic?

17. Should boards be accountable only to shareholders—or to other stakeholders, such as employees, customers, suppliers, taxpayers, and communities, as well?

18. Why do institutional investors, who control the vast majority of shareholder votes, so often routinely approve the positions recommended by management in corporate elections?

19. Should directors be subject to term limits?

20. How can a board effectively oversee the management of risk?

21. Should some sort of accreditation or continuing training be required for directors?

22. Does good governance generally improve share price?

23. Are professional services providers such as auditors, rating agencies, compensation consultants, and lawyers compromised by how they are hired and paid? How might the system be improved on behalf of investors?

24. The term *shareholders* covers constituencies with widely varying interests and goals. How can boards and managers deal with this issue?

25. Should corporations' spending on political campaigns and lobbying be limited, better disclosed, or approved by shareholders?

26. On balance, have corporate governance reforms such as Sarbanes-Oxley been worth the trouble and expense?

27. Some have argued that the market corrects corporate governance problems as share prices drop and control changes to other hands. Others suggest the issue should be addressed by regulation and greater power for shareholders. What do you believe is the best approach?

28. There is a move afoot to federalize some aspects of corporate law, taking power away from the states. What are the pros and cons of this?

29. Should directors be required to invest a significant amount of their own wealth in the company?

30. The investor Warren Buffett blamed the failure of corporate governance on "boardroom atmosphere" and the majority of directors lacking at least one of the three traits he valued (being "business-savvy, interested, and shareholder-oriented"). How would you change the culture and composition of boards to address these shortcomings?